A Lady of Cotton

A Lady of Cotton

HANNAH GREG,
Mistress of Quarry Bank Mill

DAVID SEKERS

in association with

The National Trust needs your help to bring Quarry Bank back to life. As Britain's last unaltered factory community, Quarry Bank provides a unique experience of life during the Industrial Revolution. Help us to complete Quarry Bank for future generations.

★ Worker's Cottage & village shop – £263,435 is needed to open up the last un-renovated worker's cottage, capturing what living conditions were like for the mill workers

★ Quarry Bank House – £147,648 is needed to open the Greg's family house and showcase the rich archive, which includes the culturally unique workers' library

★ Upper Gardens – To restore the stunning curvilinear glasshouses to their former beauty, we need £539,803 to train apprentices in the skills needed to restore them and to once again produce food for the estate

★ Northern Woods – £70,000 is needed to recreate the grandeur of the Greg's woodland Pleasure Gardens, and to restore the bridges and stunning viewpoints for everyone to enjoy again

Visit www.nationaltrust.org.uk/quarrybankappeal to find out more or donate.

Front cover images: Miniature of Hannah Lightbody, probably before her marriage in 1789. *National Trust/Quarry Bank Mill Archive*; Quarry Bank Mill, Styal. *National Trust*

First published 2013
in association with National Trust

The History Press
The Mill, Brimscombe Port
Stroud, Gloucestershire, GL5 2QG
www.thehistorypress.co.uk

Reprinted 2015

British Library Cataloguing in Publication Data.
A catalogue record for this book is available from the British Library.

ISBN 978 0 7524 9008 3

Typesetting and origination by The History Press
Printed in Malta by Melita Press

Contents

Preface and Acknowledgements

Family papers unseen for generations, preserving their voices unheard and their stories unread: these are treasures dreamt of by historians. Faced with such a prize, they first have the task of forging the pieces together to form a narrative, and then they have the delicate responsibility of interpreting it. The universe of Hannah Greg as she saw it, emerges here from just such a collection of manuscripts, largely in her own words, including a vivid diary she wrote in the years before and just after her marriage.[1]

However, family papers rarely tell the whole story. Inevitably, personal papers, especially those constructed to inform later generations, tend to omit anything scandalous or scurrilous. Passions and family rows seem to be hidden from us, and although we hear about some of the major incidents in characters' lives, we rarely hear their daily laughter. It is also a limitation that inevitably, here, we see the picture from Hannah's viewpoint. Records to illustrate the lives and thoughts of Hannah's less literate contemporaries – the mill workers and apprentices, for example – hardly survive. Where I think it could be helpful I therefore provide information to describe some of the context and background of issues, personalities and places that Hannah encountered.

Some important questions remain, however. Might the Gregs' paternalism have been seen as condescension by some of Gregs' workforce? How can we, in our godless age, fully appreciate the role of religious faith in the Gregs' time? Attitudes in society have always evolved, and I have tried to show how public opinion altered during the Greg's lifetime, so that the Gregs' views (on the employment of children, for example) that might have seemed advanced when they were young, seemed outmoded a generation later.

The one-sidedness of the existing evidence might tempt an imaginative writer to amplify the narrative by conjuring up some fictitious personalities, or by attributing imaginary thoughts and emotions to historical figures. Historical fiction is a temptation that I have resisted, but readers may want to use their imaginations to look beyond the surviving written record, and peer creatively into the hearts and minds of the subjects of this book. Those who are interested in exploring more of the historical context of the period and of Hannah's life and activities are invited to look at my website, which presents additional information in the form of essays and notes.[2]

I have been lucky to have lived and worked close to the history of the Greg family, and met several descendants while living in the village of Styal in the 1980s, when it still retained much of the character of an Industrial Revolution factory community. There were many residents who could trace back their descent through generations of workers at Quarry Bank Mill and even through mill apprentices. Although the National Trust had long been the landlord, a direct descendant of the Gregs who still lived nearby was a leading figure in the village. This was Mrs Kate Jacks, a senior member in the Unitarian Norcliffe Chapel, who was also a wise and supporting voice for many of the elderly tenants. Often dressed informally, her appearance – with her small stature, stout shoes, quiet voice and her cigarettes – hardly conveyed her personal authority in village matters. But she commanded respect, and was able to speak up for the tenants, to keep an eye on their well-being, and to see that the familiar standards in the village were being maintained by the landlord. No one resisted her suggestions. We have only one description of Hannah's appearance: 'Her small active figure was to be seen everywhere and her energy was as widely directed as it was untiring': a description that might have been written for Kate Jacks, even in her old age.[3]

Kate Jacks had great pride and interest in her family's history, and it was she who suggested to me that Hannah Greg's pioneering work in this factory community deserved fuller recognition. From the outset she supported the project to convert the mill into a working museum, and made available many family papers. Her descendants, Diana Edward, Kitty Gore and Kath Walker, also generously lent or gave family papers to the National Trust, and I am grateful to them, and to Emily Janes and Michael Janes and other members of the Greg family for permission to quote from them. I also owe particular thanks to Nick Lightbody, Dr Tim Paine and Jenny Smith for generously providing access to their collections of family papers. It is thanks to their foresight and generosity that so many of these papers survive to convey the voices of their antecedents.

The archive at Quarry Bank Mill also houses papers left by the Trust's original benefactor, the late Alec Greg, who gave the whole property to the National Trust in 1939 and who generously supported the museum project at its inception. Dr Mary Rose was the first to write a comprehensive history of the Mill, and this has been an invaluable point of reference. I am also grateful to Jonathan Hudleston, the historian of the Hodgson family, for agreeing to let me quote from his work, and to Sheila Ormerod and Esther Galbraith, other historians of the Greg and Lightbody families.

Some of the family papers in the hands of Kate Jacks, which were subsequently lost, were the basis of short articles on Hannah and Samuel Greg, written by Peter Spencer, and I am grateful to his widow Rosemary Spencer for permission to quote from his work. Lt Col T.H. Pares has kindly provided information on John Pares and his family, as well as permission to quote from his family papers on loan to the Derby Record Office.

I am grateful to generations of staff at Quarry Bank Mill for their continuing support and advice: Eleanor Underhill, Amanda Lunt and Alkestis Tsilika of the present generation; Josselin Hill, Caroline Hill, Adam Damer and Eric Wilkin among former employees. The brunt of many of my requests and enquiries has been helpfully borne by the volunteers, Bridget Franklin and Ann Rundle in particular.

I would also like to thank James Rothwell, the former curator of the National Trust north-west region, Grant Berry, National Trust Publications Manager, and my editor at The History Press Lindsey Smith.

The editors of the *Journal of Enlightenment and Dissent*, who published an essay on Hannah Greg and my edition of the *Diary of Hannah Lightbody*, have kindly given their permission for me to quote from these publications. I have continued to receive valuable advice and illuminating suggestions from Dr Martin Fitzgerald, Dr David Wykes, Ruth Watts and Gina Luria Walker in the field of Dissenting History. David Howman has kindly provided information on the Liverpool abolitionists, and Alex Kidson and Mrs F. Spiegl on images of Liverpool and its leading citizens. I am indebted to Lionel Burman for his wide-ranging information and guidance on aspects of cultural history in Liverpool and beyond, and for his steady encouragement since this biography was conceived.

I am grateful likewise to the staff of the following institutions and libraries: London Library, Liverpool University (Special Collections), Liverpool Maritime Museum, Liverpool Record Office, Greater Manchester County Record Office, British Library, Dr Williams's Library, London Borough of Hackney Archives, Derbyshire Record Office.

Finally, my thanks to Judith Mirzoeff and to my long-suffering wife, Simone, who have been constructive critics of several versions of this text.

Introduction

Manchester was already an established centre for the textile trade when, towards the end of the eighteenth century, a number of enterprising merchants built large water-powered mills in some of the surrounding river valleys. They equipped them with the newly invented spinning machinery, and in very little time became large employers, making significant profits from the fibre of fashion: cotton.

These mill masters had little choice but to recruit, train and house workers from far afield. While some masters treated their workers shamefully, it was not uncommon for others to care for them, believing this could be a form of enlightened self-interest. Many of the leading masters and merchants were Dissenters, members of a marginalised religious sect noted for business acumen and networks of commercial connections.

Within decades, steam power enabled these cotton entrepreneurs to locate their mills in towns. Employment grew and cotton manufacturing became a cornerstone of Britain's Industrial Revolution; but working and living conditions deteriorated sharply, especially during trading slumps. Poverty, starvation, epidemics and misery reached unprecedented levels and drew public attention to industrialisation and its inhuman consequences.

Hannah Greg's lifetime (1766–1828) corresponded with this Industrial Revolution, and with a sequence of equally massive social and political upheavals. It was on the eve of her marriage that the French Revolution reached its first climax with the storming of the Bastille. The rejoicing of radicals and reformers in Hannah's circle was soon replaced with concern, and then dejection, as the government went to war with France and attacked groups such as the Dissenters who were slow to swear loyalty to the Church and the State. Their freedom of expression and talk of reform were supressed; for three decades Hannah and her circle felt ostracised and marginalised.

Brought up in a climate of Enlightenment, learning and a sense of progress, Hannah was by birth and by inclination a positive believer in society changing for the better. Her Dissenting faith supported this; but what part was she to play now that the climate had changed? And what scope was there for a woman to make the most of her intellectual gifts and education? Would marriage be a constraint, and if so, what sorts of compromise would it entail? Would the political climate inhibit or even expunge Hannah's convictions about making society fairer and politics less corrupt? What chance was there for her to assist the community of mill workers and apprentices on her doorstep at Quarry Bank, or the masses of the poor and starving in the textile districts?

The Gregs emerged from three difficult decades with their convictions intact. Hannah's marriage had become companionable, although at a price, as convention still inhibited the expression of her views if they were at variance with those of her husband. Hannah had to manage a large family and household before devoting her remaining energies to her writing or to helping the poor in her community. But in overcoming these challenges, she matured and left her mark as a pivotal figure both in the factory community and at the *salon* that she created at her home.

Would she live to see the outcome of the long-term ideals that she and Samuel shared, and would the reformers whom they had covertly supported achieve social and political change? In the end, the large industrial towns did win the battle for fair political representation; municipal government was modernised; corruption at elections all but eliminated. Dissenters were permitted to hold office, Unitarianism was officially tolerated, and many Dissenters were elected to Parliament and on to reformed local councils. Then the long battle for free trade was won, and Manchester soon became internationally famous for its liberal economic philosophy.

Hannah's children and many of her friends' children contributed to or shared in these triumphs, but Hannah did not live to see them. Before her death she had very deliberately imbued her children with her beliefs, and indeed throughout her life she saw education as the wisest investment to make the world a better place. When young she thought that intellectual learning would be sufficient, but it was a sequence of unexpected setbacks that provided her most memorable lessons in life. Overcoming them helped her acquire a degree of wisdom.

List of Illustrations

Tylston, Lightbody and Greg Families

(Note: names in **bold** are referred to in the text)

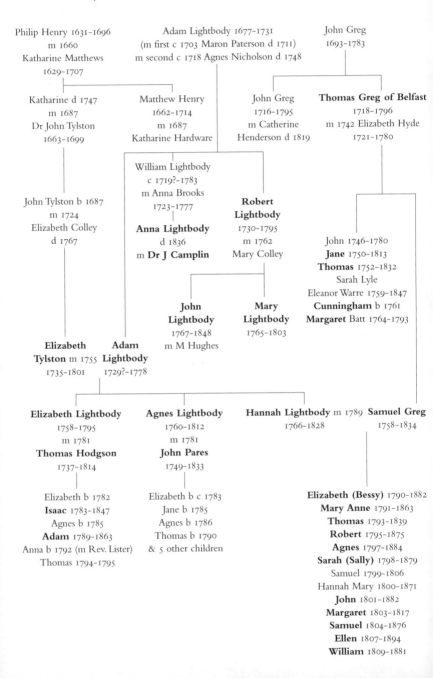

Philip Henry 1631–1696
m 1660
Katharine Matthews
1629–1707

Adam Lightbody 1677–1731
(m first c 1703 Maron Paterson d 1711)
m second c 1718 Agnes Nicholson d 1748

John Greg
1693–1783

Katharine d 1747
m 1687
Dr John Tylston
1663–1699

Matthew Henry
1662–1714
m 1687
Katharine Hardware

John Greg
1716–1795
m Catherine
Henderson d 1819

Thomas Greg of Belfast
1718–1796
m 1742 Elizabeth Hyde
1721–1780

William Lightbody
c 1719?–1783
m Anna Brooks
1723–1777

**Robert
Lightbody**
1730–1795
m 1762
Mary Colley

John Tylston b 1687
m 1724
Elizabeth Colley
d 1767

Anna Lightbody
d 1836
m **Dr J Camplin**

John 1746–1780
Jane 1750–1813
Thomas 1752–1832
Sarah Lyle
Eleanor Warre 1759–1847
Cunningham b 1761
Margaret Batt 1764–1793

**John
Lightbody**
1767–1848
m M Hughes

**Mary
Lightbody**
1765–1803

**Elizabeth
Tylston** m 1755
1735–1801

**Adam
Lightbody**
1729?–1778

Elizabeth Lightbody
1758–1795
m 1781
Thomas Hodgson
1737–1814

Agnes Lightbody
1760–1812
m 1781
John Pares
1749–1833

Hannah Lightbody m 1789 **Samuel Greg**
1766–1828   1758–1834

Elizabeth b 1782
Isaac 1783–1847
Agnes b 1785
Adam 1789–1863
Anna b 1792 (m Rev. Lister)
Thomas 1794–1795

Elizabeth b c 1783
Jane b 1785
Agnes b 1786
Thomas b 1790
& 5 other children

Elizabeth (Bessy) 1790–1882
Mary Anne 1791–1863
Thomas 1793–1839
Robert 1795–1875
Agnes 1797–1884
Sarah (Sally) 1798–1879
Samuel 1799–1806
Hannah Mary 1800–1871
John 1801–1882
Margaret 1803–1817
Samuel 1804–1876
Ellen 1807–1894
William 1809–1881

One

The formation of her mind:
Hannah's family background and upbringing

Fatherless

Even though she had been aware of her father's frail health, nothing can have prepared Hannah Lightbody for his death. While only 11 years old and at boarding school, she was cut off from her family and deprived of their affection and solace. She witnessed neither his death nor his funeral, so she had to find her own way, over time, to come to terms with this loss. It was the first of several trials that would mould Hannah's character.

Adam Lightbody died in Bath on 30 March 1778 at the age of 52 and was buried at Weston. Earlier in the month he had travelled there from his Liverpool home with his wife and elder daughters and had been 'taking the waters' when his condition deteriorated. He had been suffering, they understood, from gout. Bathing was recommended to alleviate the symptoms, but it is possible that Adam was actually suffering from respiratory or heart problems, which at that time were sometimes diagnosed as a form of gout.

It was a consolation, as the elder daughter explained, that her father had died peacefully, without pain and expressing his faith in eternal salvation. Two days before he died, she recorded, he was 'pretty certain he should not recover, gave us some directions relating to affairs at Liverpool, and discovered not the least regret at the thought of never returning thither.'[1]

His youngest daughter Hannah was at her boarding school in Ormskirk some 10 miles north of the family home in Liverpool when her headmaster, the Rev. Henry Holland, gave her the devastating news. She was told that she may not attend the funeral in Bath; her mother said that she must stay at school until the family returned home to Liverpool in early April. As a result she was not allowed out to accompany the family's minister, Dr Yates of Kaye Street Chapel, when he hurried down from Liverpool to Bath to preach the funeral sermon. Hannah had to bear her grief, unconsoled by any relations, for almost a fortnight.

Meanwhile, the rest of the family were joined at the funeral by cousins and acquaintances and then returned slowly from Bath, retracing their steps and recalling their mood of optimism and happiness not long before as they had travelled south hoping for a cure.

Then in early April Mr Holland took Hannah home to Liverpool to join in the family's rituals of grief and mourning, participating in the formal receptions for friends and relations, who had each been sent the black gloves and ribbons that convention required. They included her father's numerous cousins and nephews, some prominent merchants, several physicians and a bevy of ministers from the various Dissenters' chapels where Adam had worshipped. The relatives living in Scotland were not expected to attend, but the occasion demonstrated how firmly the Lightbody family was integrated into the mercantile and social life of this flourishing town.

The elder sisters provided what comfort they could for their mother. All three sisters inherited an equal share of the Lightbody inheritance, to be held in trust until their 21st birthdays. This may have been a benefit for the elder two, whose marriage prospects were perhaps enhanced, but becoming an heiress cannot have been of any great comfort to Hannah, who was then returned to school.

It is hard to imagine a lonelier prospect than that facing Hannah back at boarding school. Even though some of her older cousins, the Nicholson boys, had been at the same school a few years before her, it was an environment deprived of family affection. Of the friends that she made there, the girl she liked most contracted a fever a few years later and died. She was cut off from her sisters, who were six and eight years older and had each other for company. Hannah probably admired and envied them, but hardly considered them as her close companions.

The Rev. Henry Holland's school may have been spartan, but it had high academic standards. As Hannah grew up she became studious and observant, but also withdrawn and undemonstrative. She had a tendency to draw attention to herself by worrying about her health. While it would be misleading to make claims or allowances for Hannah based on the early loss of her father – family tragedies and personal setbacks were familiar occurrences among all levels of society – this event may nevertheless help to explain her introspection and her faith, if not her determination. Determination and indeed ambition were characteristic traits of her father's family.

Hannah's family background

In the seventeenth century the Lightbodys were prominent textile merchants in the Presbyterian community of Dumfries. By the middle of the eighteenth century, Adam Lightbody and his brothers had built on Scottish family connections in Liverpool to establish a successful business partnership there. They soon achieved respectability and status in their Liverpool community as a result of steady ambition and perseverance. By the time Hannah was growing up, they were well established and financially secure and, as a mark of their status, Adam signed his will as Adam Lightbody *Esquire*. He remains a shadowy figure, but his daughter Hannah was conscious of his standing as a merchant and as a reputable citizen.[2]

Hannah's mother, Elizabeth Lightbody, may well have been the more gifted and caring member of the family. She was born Elizabeth Tylston on 17 July 1735, the great-granddaughter of Philip Henry. This Dissenting minister and preacher based in Chester was among the 2,000 ejected from their ministry in 1662 for refusing to conform to the prescribed Anglican liturgy. He was particularly noted for his integrity and courage, and quickly became a figurehead among Dissenters, who were now excluded from official posts and prevented from taking university degrees. His descendants were proud of his example and seem to have been considered as one of the aristocratic families of Dissent.[3] As John Tylston put it in a letter to his betrothed, Katharine Henry, Hannah's grandmother:

> I prize you more for the sake of your virtuous education than if both of the Indies were your portion … and you are more dear to me upon the account of your excellent and religious parentage than if all your veins were filled with Royal blood.[4]

Elizabeth inherited from her forebears a strong current of religious belief and Dissenting faith. Among them were women of strong character and conviction, several of whom wrote diaries that were handed down, read and discussed, providing moral and ethical as well as religious reflections. So it is perhaps not surprising that Elizabeth was devout, as well as cultivated, articulate, modest and quietly benevolent. She belonged to a family tradition that saw women as powerful partners in a marriage, who were encouraged to have minds of their own, and to perform roles in society independently of their husband's work (see plate 1).

Experiencing two stillborn sons and one surviving only a few weeks, Elizabeth had her own bereavements and disappointments to endure, but her positive view of religion was a comfort, contrasting with the bleaker tenets of non-conformity such as Calvinism. She was well versed in the Bible, and was fond of aphorisms, a practice soon adopted by her daughter Hannah.

Elizabeth had a lively and enquiring mind, was widely read and well travelled. She was befriended by many leaders of Dissent in London and north-west England, and on friendly terms with its intellectual elite, especially at the time of the heyday of the Warrington Academy[5], when its intellectual vigour spilled over into Liverpool, giving Elizabeth and her Nicholson cousins the chance to participate in some of the boisterous social life of the younger tutors and students. Among these friends was Mrs Anna Barbauld, an acquaintance possibly dating from the 1760s when, as a young poet, Anna was growing up in the academy.[6]

The Lightbodys and their eldest daughter went on a tour to Scotland in about 1768, calling in on Adam's relatives, and possibly also their businesses. Elizabeth's journal reveals some of the wide curiosity and culture that her daughter Hannah was to inherit. On hearing a preacher whose theological position did not match her own, she noted: 'cd not help wish his doctrine tend'd more to make them happy & give a more worthy idea of the Goodness of the Deity.' At the Duke of Argyle's she sees 'the manufacture of Cambric which they bring to great no. people & have the yarn from France'. The great masterpieces of art were also admired: in Edinburgh they 'went to see a great number of fine paintings – of Raphael's & many of Rubens & other great masters', and she made an extensive list of the great pictures seen at Hamilton Palace.[7]

Further evidence that Elizabeth had an enquiring mind is provided by her membership of the Liverpool Library (there were few female subscribers at that time), and by her presence among the Octonian Society, a select group who met to discuss literature and philosophical issues in each other's homes. She was a caring and compassionate person, and perhaps her most remarkable legacy is the record of her benevolence to the poor. Her will demonstrates her devotion and concern for many good causes, and in her lifetime her subscriptions to the poor house and the dispensary (which provided medical help for the poor) were no doubt frequent and generous (though anonymous).

In the mid-1790s, when living on her own in Duke Street, partially blind and infirm, Elizabeth employed a Mrs Seaward of Denison Street to be her housekeeper. She brought with her a young daughter Catharine – also known as Kitty – to help her to attend to the needs of some of the poorest people in the town. Elizabeth taught Kitty to read, and Kitty recalled many years later how this inspired her:

> The old Lady would say to me: 'Catharine, I am going out' and then she would be carried out in her Sedan. She was too lame to walk, & could not very easily get into her carriage. I used to take a little basket & walk by her side. We would stop at a cellar, into which she sent me to see how the poor woman was & when I had come out again, she would say: 'how does she look? Is there any fire in the grate? Is there any coal in the house?' Then she would send me for anything that was wanted.[8]

Kitty recalled that her mistress believed in discipline, neatness and order. She also believed that even the poorest had innate potential that they could develop. Learning to read would give them access to the riches of the Bible, and this would be a source of guidance and comfort to them. She brought up her daughter Hannah with these convictions, and took her, too, on similar visits to the poor in Liverpool.

Elizabeth Lightbody's surviving letters confirm her caring, maternal cast of mind. Having lost several children in childbirth, suffered illness and feared the epidemics that carried off children indiscriminately among her family and friends, she became all the more attached to her three daughters and the growing numbers of grandchildren.

Her daughters were Elizabeth (born 1758), Agnes (born 1760) and Hannah (born 1766). We know nothing about the education of the two elder girls. Both seem to have been affectionate daughters, good wives and mothers as well as competent housekeepers for their respective husbands. After Adam's death, his widow had the sole responsibility for Hannah's education and for ensuring that, in time, the three co-heiresses (as they were called) found suitable husbands. (See p. 14 for a family tree.)

The first two did well, both marrying in 1781. Elizabeth married Thomas Hodgson in November – when he was 44 years old, twenty-one years her senior. He was a self-made merchant, born and brought up at Caton near Lancaster.[9] She died suddenly in a diphtheria epidemic in 1795 at the age of 37, followed a few weeks later by the death of her infant son. Elizabeth Lightbody's younger daughter Agnes married John Pares on 15 March 1781.[10] The second son of Thomas Pares, John Pares (born 1749) like his father was a leading hosiery manufacturer and merchant, living in The Newarke, a large medieval house and warehouse in the historic centre of Leicester.

Hannah's school and circle in London

With her two elder daughters married, Elizabeth Lightbody's thoughts turned to the next phase of the upbringing of her youngest daughter, Hannah. By the end of 1782 she was 16, a serious child with an appetite for reading and learning, and ready to leave her school at Ormskirk. In some Dissenting circles at that time it was a fresh but important aim to educate daughters as well as sons. Many agreed with the liberal thinker John Locke, who was in favour of giving daughters 'an education almost as rigorous as their brothers', so as to develop their potential, while recognising the limited opportunities for women to apply their learning. This view was in contrast to most of the rest of society, where it was the convention that a girl's education would end at

the age of 15 or 16. A minority might then be sent to a boarding school in or near London where many had been established
since the seventeenth century to cater mainly for the daughters
of ambitious parents in the provinces.

The popular curriculum for girls in these schools appeared
to focus on social accomplishments such as deportment, music,
dancing, needlework and drawing. The expectation would
be that such skills would be more refined and no doubt more
fashionable if they were attained in the metropolis. Even this syl-
labus was apparently regarded as a form of over-education, since
once married a woman would have little time or opportunity to
demonstrate her prowess in the diverse artistic talents recently
acquired. And were she to undertake anything more stretching,
then questions might be raised about her marriageability.

By the 1780s the wife's role within marriage was widely recognised as one of companionship. An over-educated or bookish
female mind was regarded with suspicion and even hostility, and
seen as an impediment to mastering the disciplines of household
management, and thus was a deterrent to prospective husbands.
It was the frequent subject of mockery in novels, cartoons and
plays (for example in Sheridan's *The Rivals*).

As for bluestockings – women who were learned in classical
languages, philosophy or science – they were regarded by many
men as an aberration, a betrayal of their gender, and by most
other women as unbecoming. Real intellectual distinction in a
woman was regarded as odd and disadvantageous.

It was evident that by the age of 16 Hannah was studious
and had a good mind that she wanted to cultivate, but there
were no suitable schools for her in or near Liverpool. It was
also clear that she was unlikely to develop her potential by staying at home with her widowed mother. The solution to these
quandaries came in advice that Elizabeth received from her
cousins in London. Thomas Rogers was a wealthy banker living
at Newington Green, bringing up his six children after his wife
had died in 1776. Several of his daughters had been educated at

the nearby school at Fleetwood House in Stoke Newington, and it seems that he recommended it and offered Hannah hospitality in his home nearby, with cousins of a similar age as a surrogate family.[11] She was duly sent off to London, probably returning home rarely over the following three years. A portrait of Hannah may date from this period: it shows a serious, observant face, pale brown eyes, a mouth that betrays a sense of humour and auburn hair in ringlets falling around her neck (see plate 2).

Miss Elizabeth Crisp and her sister Sarah had started the boarding school at Fleetwood House in 1772, using a part of the large old building standing in its own grounds just off Stoke Newington High Street. In the new year of 1783 when Hannah started as a pupil there at the age of 16, her first impressions would have been of the scale and age of the building. This imposing mansion built in Queen Elizabeth's time had sixty or seventy rooms, with a large garden and 98 acres of land. In the upper part of the house there was said to be a little room used for hiding persecuted non-conformists during the reign of Charles II. There is a record of seats being arranged in the Newington Chapel for the pupils of Miss Crisp's school, in 1792, which suggests that the school provided education specifically or solely for the daughters of Dissenters.

Stoke Newington at this time was little more than a single street, bordered by parkland, leading down to the New River. Rambles in the ancient landscape and lush countryside were not discouraged and it is likely that Hannah first discovered her love of walking, nature and the open air in this north London village. A party of schoolgirls, which could perhaps have included Hannah, were glimpsed enjoying the romantic environment on the edge of the village on a summer's evening in 1785 by the youthful poet Samuel Rogers. He recorded the magic of the moment in some rather wistful lines inscribed: 'To a Party of Young Ladies who were sitting on a bench in Queen Elizabeth's Walk at Eight o' clock last Thursday Night,' composed on Saturday, 14 May 1785:[12]

> Evening had flushed the clear blue sky
> The birds had sung themselves to sleep,
> When I presumed, I don't know why,
> In Old Queen Bess's walk to peep.
>
> And there was she; her belles and beaux
> In ruffs and high crowned hats were there!
> But soon as you may well suppose,
> the vision melted in the air.
>
> When hark! Soft voices, thro' the shade,
> Announced a little fairy train.
> And once, methought, sweet music played,
> I wished to see, but wished in vain.

The school provided the girls with the usual accomplishments such as deportment and dancing as well as sewing and music. Hannah played the piano and could compose. But the curriculum went much further: it seems to have included French, some mathematics, history, religion, literature, the classics (including classical philosophy, morals and ethics), the history of art, geography, as well as English and foreign literature. Hannah was probably also taught debating, which was becoming an accomplishment acceptable among women. By the time she left in 1786 at the age of 20, she had blossomed into a star pupil, to judge by the warm welcome given her on her return visit in the winter of 1787/88. At first, however, she was homesick, as she recalled almost forty years later when writing to her granddaughter who, it was reported, had 'returned to school in distress'. Hannah wrote: 'I remember well that, when I used to go to school, a letter was most valuable to me soon after I arrived.'[13]

Hannah's first letter home, dated Sunday 16 February, was addressed to her mother who was staying with her married daughter Agnes in Leicester. It is all the more poignant for being formal:

Dear Mama, You will be surprised perhaps at the date of this but you shall hear how I got here; yesterday Miss Mitchell and Miss

Rogers came for me before dinner; and desired I might stay till Monday; my Governess gave me leave, and I made no objection: 'tis only a pleasant walk from Stoke Newington. I long very much to hear how you got home, and how you found all our dear friends there … I stood in the stocks yesterday and doubt not that by the means of those and dancing I shall in time hold up my head. Doctor Price called here last night, he was not well enough to preach today. The compliments of this family attend you … Do not forget what pleasure your Letters give me always. I remain

> Your affectionate & grateful
> H Lightbody[14]

It seems that Hannah was not happy learning deportment, a ritual accomplishment that she found pointless. But as she was of less than average height, a sedentary reader of books and (as far as we can tell) self-deprecatory by nature, it is likely that lessons in deportment taught her to hold her head high, to appear confident and to make the most of her looks.

Hannah's upbringing was largely in the hands of her able teachers, but she also owed much to the Rogers family who provided a second home for her, with the companionship of cousins, a father figure in Thomas Rogers, and another cousin, Miss Mitchell, who looked after them all as well as taking care of the household.

For several decades the villages of Stoke Newington and Newington Green in north London had been a centre for writers, academics and especially for Dissenters, a reputation well known to Hannah's mother. Dissenters had first arrived in the mid-seventeenth century and established various 'academies' on the Green, where Daniel Defoe and Samuel Wesley (the composer) were among the students. Isaac Watts (1674–1748), the hymn writer, lived at Fleetwood House and then at the Green. Their chapel was built on the Green in 1708 and still stands.

In the 1780s Thomas Rogers was a leading light among the Rational Dissenters in London[15] and a major figure in the formation of the new Dissenting academy, Hackney New College.[16] His house at Newington Green was next door to Dr Price's, the polemical writer who has been called the 'first and original left-wing intellectual in British history',[17] a man of great energy and vision who seems to have combined actuarial brilliance, erudition and industry with personal charm. They met for weekly discussions at dinner, and their houses would have been full of progressive debates about the education of men and women, of freedom of worship, and modern ideas about education, politics and society. Hannah's arrival in this milieu coincided with unprecedented intellectual and political vitality. It was probably there that Hannah got to know of Price's protégée, Mary Wollstonecraft, who was then starting up a school of her own nearby. Hannah also seems to have met many of the leading educators, radicals and reformers who wanted the wrongs in society righted.[18]

How much of this climate of intellectual and political ferment rubbed off on Hannah? It is impossible to say with any certainty, but she knew Price and many of his circle well enough to call on them when visiting London a year after leaving school. Spending weekends and vacations with the Rogers family exposed her to many lively discussions with such intellectuals, and to debates with her cousins, the Rogers children, too. It is also clear that by the time she returned to Liverpool at the age of 20, she had formed firm ideas of the value of a woman's mind. She had no doubt that she was entitled to develop it by study. And she believed, in accordance with the teaching of Price and Dr Joseph Priestley, that mankind was capable of attaining perfection. Though not won over, it seems, by their revolutionary ardour, her sense of social injustice nevertheless had been awakened. She may not have been a true bluestocking, but there is no indication that she preferred frivolous pursuits to the life of the mind. Yet one question remained: was her

The formation of her mind

education going to be an advantage, as she returned to life at home with her mother in Liverpool? She had developed poise and self-confidence in the company of adults, and remained an avid reader, at times withdrawn and contemplative, at other times enthusiastic and voluble. But how would these attributes be met with in Liverpool society?

Returning home at a propitious time

Back in Liverpool, Hannah's mother was alone, but occupied with supporting her two elder daughters as the first grandchildren were born. Both Thomas Hodgson and John Pares were aware of the exceptional climate for business investment following the end of the American War of Independence. Far-sighted entrepreneurs wanted to grasp this opportunity. It would later be seen as the start of a new Industrial Revolution.

John Pares was in an advantageous situation, as since 1778 at Calver Mill in Derbyshire he had gained practical experience of the demand for cotton yarn and of the profitability of cotton spinning using Arkwright water frames. He was now prepared to challenge Arkwright's patents (which were punitively costly) and prepared to invest with a team of experienced businessmen in another spinning mill.

Since 1773 Thomas Hodgson had also been thinking of diversifying his business investments away from the Africa trade. He and his brother-in-law John Pares agreed to invest in a new cotton-spinning mill in his home village of Caton in 1784. His partners included Isaac Capstick, Hodgson's sister's husband.

Unknown to Hannah and her family, a young Irish textile merchant called Samuel Greg, who was based in Manchester, was pursuing a similar goal. He spent part of 1783 riding around the countryside in the environs of Manchester in search of a suitable site to erect a cotton-spinning mill of his own. He had a sound knowledge of the markets, having worked for several years for his uncles who were prominent merchants, arranging the weaving and distribution and export of linen, wool and cotton mixtures. He had become a partner in the firm when one uncle had retired, and had benefited from the rise in value of stocks that he had acquired, following the end of the American War of Independence.

The site he chose was at Quarry Bank in the valley of the River Bollin near Wilmslow, 9 miles south of Manchester. He arranged to lease it from the Earl of Stamford, and began building a modest-sized spinning mill. He engaged a mainly local workforce, some expertise to train them, leased some local farm-workers' cottages to house them and started the operation in 1784. By the time it was making its first profits a few years later, Greg had become a highly successful and thriving businessman. He was still an eligible bachelor.

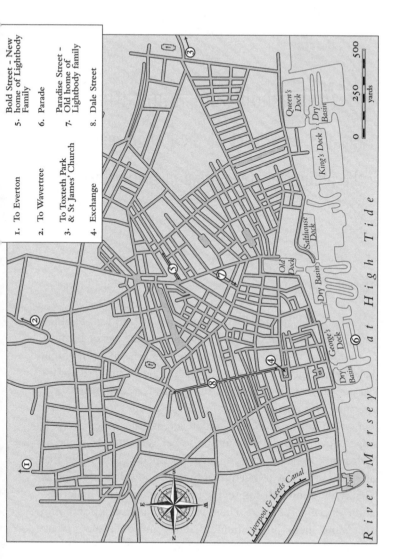

1. To Everton
2. To Wavertree
3. To Toxteth Park & St James' Church
4. Exchange
5. Bold Street - New home of Lightbody Family
6. Parade
7. Paradise Street - Old home of Lightbody family
8. Dale Street

River Mersey at High Tide

Liverpool & Leeds Canal

King's Dock
Queen's Dock
Dry Basin
Salthouse Dock
Old Dock
Dry Basin
George's Dock
Dry Basin
Fort

0   250   500
yards

1 Map of Liverpool in the late 1790s, from William Moss's *Liverpool Guide.*

Two

'Melancholy and admiration': Hannah's experience of the Enlightenment and the Industrial Revolution in the north-west

Hannah's Liverpool

In 1786, after several formative years in London, Hannah returned to her family home in Liverpool at the age of 20, more confident and better informed than when she left. She might have been expected to view the town of her birth with a critical perspective, sharpened by the sophisticated culture of the metropolis, but this was not the case. Hannah looked back on her youth in Liverpool as a golden age, and she long acknowledged how much the town meant to her. What did she see in it?

It is not in fact hard to discern the aspects of the town that appealed so greatly to her at that time. She loved its commercial vitality, the constantly improving urban scene, its rural hinterland and especially its culture. There was then a climate of optimism as advancements in medicine, science and technology were matched by progress in commerce and faith in the improvement of the fabric of society.

Hannah loved striding round the town and out into the surrounding countryside, her favourite walks often taking her past familiar landmarks and inspiring views. Stepping out of her front door in Paradise Street, she stood in the commercial centre of the town between Church Street and Lord Street, surrounded by the large family homes of the merchants, which at that time still stood adjacent to their counting houses and warehouses. Perhaps this quarter was no longer quite as elegant as it had been; the flotsam and jetsam of a busy seaport had always been perceptible, but now the surrounding streets had become an area peopled with small traders as well as merchants. The old Town Dock was only 100 yards away, and beyond it on either side east and west stood the complex of warehouses, timber yards and the building site where the large Kings Dock and Queens Dock were under construction (see map p. 29).

> The whole complexion of the place was nautical. The docks, however, were stupendously grand, the inner one – Town Dock – lying in the centre was filled with a forest of masts; besides this were three very large docks linked via flood gates, intermixed with dry docks for repairing; the lower dock had a fine, wide quay on its outer side, which made for an agreeable walk, being lined with trees on either side.

This was the Parade, a favourite promenade with fine views across the River Mersey to the shore of Wales.

Turning north, along Castle Street towards the elegant Exchange building, Hannah would enter the town centre, still medieval in scale, cramped and overcrowded. The great majority of houses were:

> in middling and lower style, few rising above that mark; the streets were long, narrow, crooked and dirty. You scarcely saw a well-dressed person, nor half a dozen gentlemen's carriages; few of the shops appear so well as in other great towns. [1]

The congestion was exacerbated by the street-widening schemes under way in the old heart of the town. At the focal point of this commotion stood the Exchange, the hub for brokers, some senior merchants, insurers, just a few banks, and the Common Council. To reach the site of the Lightbody linen warehouse, Hannah would turn right, inland, to wander up Dale Street, a fashionable area with fine shops.

Heading uphill and out of town, Hannah would pass sail-makers, blacksmiths, coopers and crate-makers, all businesses connected with the port. Behind the prosperous facades, immigrants clustered in side streets and overcrowded courts, many of them families drawn in from the hinterland as well as from Scotland and Ireland, looking for employment as the town's trade expanded. They would find homes wherever they could, often in unsanitary cellars. As the density of housing and traffic diminished, from a brow looking back over the town Hannah could see ropewalks spread out from the town centre, while terraces of new housing invaded the surrounding fields. The plumes of smoke from the distant sea shore came from the factories making salt, sugar, glass and pottery.

Leaving the charming hillside village of Everton to her left, it would take Hannah barely half an hour along the country lane to reach Wavertree, the straggling village where William Lightbody bought a number of houses and parcels of land following the enclosure of the common. Hannah's mother liked her small house there; Hannah too appreciated the country air and rural surroundings. Returning towards the town, she often took the route through Toxteth Park, Lord Sefton's great estate. Its meadows and hedges were an oasis for wildlife and there were extensive views over the Mersey estuary and Otterspool. The country lane westwards back to Paradise Street passed Park Chapel, the original chapel for the Dissenting community, and then St James's church standing on the edge of the built-up area, before dropping down to the old Town Dock.

There were parts of the town that Hannah deliberately avoided: for example, the rough character around the dock area, an aspect common to seaports since time immemorial, where sailors frequented the liquor houses and brothels. The former were reckoned to number one in seven of all trading establishments in the town (there is no statistical record of the density of the latter).

The town became more cosmopolitan than its growing rival and neighbour, Manchester. It was teeming with foreign faces, fashions and languages; it imported tobacco, sugar, rum and exotic materials such as mahogany, plants destined for the apothecaries or for collectors among the local gentry, and foods such as turtle (the favourite treat in the Greg household). Stories of foreign places, religions and customs were handed on. There was a risk of foreign diseases as well as the usual local epidemics, and the provision of hospitals for the sick and workhouses for the poor, though ever growing, failed to keep pace with demand. As Hannah remarked soon after her return home, as the town centre was constantly being improved and refashioned: 'Walked up town with my Mother and felt a mingled sensation of Melancholy and Admiration at the appearance of present devastation and the prospect of future grandeur it exhibited.'[2]

Hannah observed and commented on the resulting juxtaposition of squalor and splendour, but she was impressed by the commercial vigour that brought the town its exceptional prosperity. As the old town centre became more commercial, a number of merchant families moved out to the more salubrious and fashionable villages on its fringe, such as Everton or Toxteth Park.

Liverpool's Dissenting community

As their commercial achievements and status grew, whether as merchants, professionals or artisans, the town's leading Dissenters continued to feel marginalised. They had their chapels and ministers, and many were cultured and charitable, but they were outside the charmed circle who ran the town and its trade.[3] Civic power lay in the hands of the Tory, Anglican Common Council, a self-perpetuating oligarchy of great power and a track record of commercial success.

Hannah's family was prominent among these outsiders. The Lightbodys and their minister, John Yates, and the bulk of his congregation at Kaye Street Chapel, probably felt that their Dissenting faith was tolerated, though regarded with wariness. The same was true of the other Dissenting congregations, at Gateacre Chapel and at Benn's Garden Chapel. Many of the leading Dissenters in the town were Whig supporters. In the 1790s, at the time of the French Revolution, groups such as these were soon branded by the Common Council as Jacobins and regarded with suspicion and even, at times, hostility.

Wherever Hannah went she was welcomed among Dissenters. She was an articulate adherent to this faith, and was looked on as a scion of one of its founding fathers. This sect and network was a distinctive and significant aspect of her world and a strong influence on her character.

Dissenters had in common a belief in doing good or acting well, using reason, but discarding religious dogma, as well as miracles; nor did they accept the doctrines of atonement, predestination or the notion of original sin. Adverse to the straightjacket of a set liturgy, congregations tended to develop individual and distinct nuances of belief. Science and reason, these Dissenters believed, helped them to understand God's creation.

The attraction of this faith to Hannah's generation is not explained simply by saying that entrepreneurs needed a liberal and tolerant environment in which to succeed. It appealed to people who were capable of thinking for themselves, and to those who opposed the conservative establishment in Church and State. This faith also appealed to artisans, but their greatest strength lay in a strong network of successful merchants and manufacturers. Commercial success was not the end of their ambitions, for leading Dissenters emerged among the middle classes in several provincial cities as a political and cultural elite, where they became leading voices promoting reform. Facing prejudice, they frequently earned respect by demonstrating integrity, personal frugality and charity to those in need.[4]

Those Dissenters who in the later eighteenth century were imbued with or influenced by the wide liberal education of their academies became known as Rational Dissenters. Hannah was close to many of their leaders and shared may of their views and aspirations. They were to play a major role as radicals fighting to overcome prejudice against their faith, and as reformers in politics. They shared a liberal and intellectual outlook and had several fundamental aims: first, the support for unfettered enquiry, for freedom of thought and for the essential role of reason in the quest for truth; second, the toleration of other people's viewpoints, which were to be received with candour; third, they supported education as a liberal force. They shared three further aspirations, which were political: the reform of constituencies to provide a fair representation of the people, annual elections and universal suffrage.

The Dissenters' vocal support for the French Revolution in its early stages was a gift for their enemies. By 1790 there was a real fear that Dissenters across the country had the intention and the means to stage a revolution in Britain. It is easy to see how excited the would-be reformers were at the fall of the Bastille, just as they had been glad to welcome democratic government in America as an outcome of the War of Independence.

As the Revolution in France turned to the Terror, loyalism was strongly and successfully promoted by the government and by the Anglican Church. There was also a great deal of affected indignation and concern designed to stir up loyalist feelings, and to use them to marginalise the reforming intentions of Dissenters. As a result, many Dissenters lived in the shadow of hostility within their communities – a feature of Hannah's early married life. It is remarkable that she was able to sustain her faith in religious and political progress in the face of this, but she was sustained by the knowledge that her ancestors had also been harassed and persecuted for their faith.

All these connections and currents were part of Hannah's upbringing. The confident, pious and unostentatious era of her parents was replaced, in her time and in her circle, by a thirst for knowledge, for action and for change. On her return to Liverpool in 1786 these Enlightenment ideas were current and optimism was in the air. She could see all around her improvements in science, medicine and technology. The town was being enhanced, its trade expanded as new worlds were being opened up. Debate was encouraged, and her gender was no barrier to her being included.

It is hardly surprising that Hannah should resolve to record her immersion in this world on her doorstep in the form of a diary.

Three

'A history of my own heart': Hannah the diarist 1787–90

We can trace some of Hannah's youthful aspirations, resolutions, disappointments and moments of elation as she noted them in her diary for the years 1787–90. It records glimpses of life in Liverpool, inside the houses of the merchants, and into the life and thought of some leading citizens at a time of vigorous commercial and cultural development. Some entries describe the life of the mind and comment on some of the big questions in life; others, by way of contrast, describe a stimulating social world in which she joins in gatherings of family and friends, all no doubt looking to find her a suitable husband.[1]

As do so many young diarists, she begins with a litany of good intentions, as though there were rules in life that could ensure composure, benevolence, morality and good relationships. This is followed by descriptions of the social and intellectual activity in Liverpool. The record of books devoured and sermons heard is not long sustained, but there are accounts of visits to London, to her sisters in Leicester and Lancashire, pious and philosophical reflections, and records of intense discussions.

We read her impressions of events and gatherings, though there is surprisingly little information about fashion or shopping –

passions for most women of Hannah's age. For all its uneven-
ness, the diary narrative provides insights into the circles and
culture of a Dissenting family at a dramatic moment in British
history, when reformers were initially excited by the revolution
in France. We see the young Hannah concerned about the roles
of women, and insisting on their independence of mind being
respected. She was absorbing the thoughts of her friends, including reformers and radicals such as James Currie and William
Rathbone; taking an interest in medicine and health; discussing
issues of faith, morals and taste; and, above all, broadening her
mind by reading, reflecting and debating.

Although Hannah states at the outset of the diary, 'it is for my
eyes only', it is clear that she was conscious that others might
read it, which may explain why it contains few intimate revela-
tions and little insight into private emotions.

The diary starts on New Year's Eve 1786, with girlish earnestness:

> Amongst other resolutions made and forfeited is that of keeping
> a Diary, a sort of Register of those actions which have left a trace
> behind them by impressing my mind, and of those sentiments
> and feelings that have led to or accompanied such actions, that
> by occasionally perusing an abstract History of my own heart I
> might remark thereby learn to avoid every circumstance, situ-
> ation or pursuit that had proved unfavourable to its virtue or
> peace – … that by noting the motives that have caused, and the
> consequences that have followed particular actions and events I
> may, when in similar situations recollect them to my advantage
> … the world would laugh at the absurdity of writing so insignifi-
> cant a life as mine but it is for my own eye only, and in the hope
> of being useful to myself.

The diary narrative goes well beyond this moralistic aim, revealing how Hannah's mind and character matured, modelled to an
extent by her discussions, reading and travelling. She could be
observant and empathetic as well as enthusiastic.

In between the moments of piety and introspection, there lurks a self-deprecating sense of humour, but at other times she failed to see the comedy latent in situations which, in her earnest way, she had got herself into. She could sometimes see that youthful enthusiasm could be a shortcoming: 'Dr C called and said tranquillity must be my Motto – of which I had always been sensible but incapable (or vice versa).' And she could be tactless: 'talked to Mr Yates of the misfortune of being deaf; always unlucky in my observations.'[2] As Hannah explained in a pencil noted added later, both her host Mr Lowndes and Mrs Yates were 'quite <u>deaf</u>'.

There are similar moments when she ruefully admits she had been silly: she can laugh at herself for a childish sulk: 'Walked and quarrelled about venison pasty. Drank tea at Mrs Grey's; and next day Walked about Enville – low and vexed. Dined at Walsall and laughed about the Venison Pasty.' She is cross with herself for being a coward: 'Went to Racquet Court to have a tooth drawn – had no resolution to get out of the Carriage, angry at myself for being so childish.'[3]

But there are other entries that reveal a streak of determination, a critical opinion and even arrogance. She did not like being patronised, which she found insulting:

Mr Marsden (then Secretary to the Admiralty, and a man of much learning) did not please me, always appearing to think it necessary to level his conversation to his Company and trifle with the Ladies. As he is a man of acknowledged abilities it was quite uncomfortable to see him take pains to make himself a fool to amuse me – and very offensive too.[4]

She could be pithy in her dislikes. When there was not much to be said in favour of Buxton, she wrote simply: 'Hate Buxton'; the reader can picture the dreary weather, the spa's pretentious social scene, and the sophisticated town girl stranded there with elderly relatives. A number of other things vexed her. For example, missing seeing her new friend Samuel Greg: 'Came home – found Mr Greg had been at Liverpool – much mortified. Went to the Concert – very uncomfortable – a trial of temper ill-sustained.'[5] Hannah's enthusiasms are also displayed: they include long walks down to the seashore, talking with friends, listening to music, looking at pictures and going to plays.

As well as being a self-portrait, the diary also gives brief glimpses of some of the personalities in her circle. She could observe with insight, as when portraying Edward Crisp, the brother of her London headmistress. She describes him as:

> Philosophic, profound, and studious – airy, trifling and indifferent. After 20 years residence in India he seemed a Child on his return to Europe. In Sumatra he had sometimes lived a considerable time without the sight of an European – and had had at any time very little social intercourse – London was to him a new world … a man of most invincible taciturnity but when known affectionate, honest and sensible.[6]

Hannah's social and family circles

The family network was the fundamental framework for Hannah's social world. Growing up without the guidance of her father, Hannah was offered all the more affection and support by her numerous relatives.

The families of Hannah's sisters were also close to her. In 1781 both her sisters had married Anglicans, but it was not unusual for Dissenters to marry outside their faith, especially if there were some tempting inducements. Elizabeth Hodgson and Agnes Pares frequently invited Hannah to stay, arranging for her to meet their circle of friends, taking her to their local assemblies and balls, and no doubt doing their best to find their sister a suitable husband. The Pares moved in the rather grand echelons of mercantile and landed society in the East Midlands, while the

Hodgsons' social rank was more commercial, based in Liverpool, but not at that time tainted by their association with many Africa traders. There were also many suppers with her uncle's family, the Lightbodys, and birthdays and wedding anniversaries were celebrated, often with communal meals. Hannah also made herself useful to her sisters, often looking after their young off-spring. She took her duties as an aunt seriously, caring for her sister's children when they were ill.

In this period there was a distinct consciousness and even pride in belonging to the middle class. As John Aikin wrote of his circles: 'Your natural connections are not with kings and nobles. You belong to the most virtuous, the most enlightened, the most independent part of the community, the middle class.'[7] Inevitably, Hannah would have been expected to marry within such circles.

Hannah's chapel provided a supportive circle. Dissenters in Liverpool at this period tended to belong to chapels where they had their own pews, but were frequent visitors to neighbouring chapels, and even to the Anglican churches, to hear and judge alternative preachers. As there was no set liturgy, they would appreciate the nuances in the sermons and prayers between different ministers. At Kaye Street Chapel, founded in 1707 by the older merchant families, Dr Currie, a new arrival, was rapidly becoming a prominent member of the congregation, alongside many fellow Scottish émigrés. Dr Currie's father-in-law, the linen merchant William Wallace, had long worshipped there, as had the Nicholson and Lightbody families.

The culture of these circles could be pervasive, and Mrs Elizabeth Lightbody and her children would have been much admired by very many of the congregation and respected for their family connections as well as for their good works. As an unmarried heiress, Hannah was no doubt favoured with special attention. The Lightbodys contributed financially to their chapel as well as to the town's main charities. In addition, Hannah's mother cared for the poor in her neighbourhood.

For Hannah and her mother, a wide cross-section of Liverpool society was within their orbit: linen merchants, bankers, insurers, medical men, literary figures, and the cream of that society – wealthy merchant families who had wielded civic power over several generations, such as the Hardmans, Brooks, Tarletons, Gildarts, Earles and Smyths.

Domestic life

Hannah's diary reveals that the centre of her universe was her home and home life. There are private pleasures and duties, trips to visit sisters, and routines interrupted by a social whirl and by the demands of friends.

Home for Hannah was the company of her widowed mother. During the summer months Mrs Lightbody, like her friends the widow Arabella Nicholson and the spinster Anna Cropper, was often to be found at her country home. The rest of the year, the location of her Paradise Street house in Liverpool's town centre was no longer as salubrious or fashionable as it had once been and, looking to help her daughter entertain friends and to keep company with others in the first rank, a move to a more fashionable part of the town centre seemed desirable. This was already mooted only a couple of months or so after Hannah's return from London, when she recorded: 'conversed about my Mother and I coming to live in town.' A year later they had set their sights on a new house in Bold Street. Hannah records her expectations with some concern: 'looked forward to our settlement in Bold Street with anxiety when we should have formal Company to entertain.'[8]

Bold Street later became a street notable for fashionable shops, but it was planned as a residential area and attracted professional people such as Dr Binns, who contemplated living there in comfort and discreet style. The development's character is captured in a description by Jonathan Binns a few years later:

Then father built a house in Bold Street ... At the upper end of the street where the beautiful church is now, the green fields were open to the street without any fence, and cows used to stray down the street ... A cow occasionally troubled my father by rubbing its neck against the lower part of his house, such was the state of that part of Liverpool in 1790.[9]

On 23 February Hannah prepared for the move – 'Readied my bookcase'– and then on 17 April 1788: 'Came to live in Bold Street – felt very solemn.' By 20 April 1788 she had settled in and 'Felt very comfortable to spend a Sunday at home after moving about so long'.

In May, Hannah's mother was planning to sell her harpsichord, no doubt to make way for a fortepiano – to keep up with the fashion. While Dissenters would not wish to be thought of as showy or extravagant, a home of taste with scope for entertaining would be a vital asset for a mother in her class with a marriageable daughter. And at Bold Street the Lightbodys now had a home where Hannah's friends could be entertained in some style. It was not long before Hannah recorded: 'Had a pleasant little dance at home.'[10]

There are occasional anxieties: concern for her sisters during childbirth was a frequent one. Illness was a constant fear, and recovery a cause of thanks to God: 'Jane Pares is this day 2 years old, and is just recovered from the Small pox.'[11] Epidemics were prevalent and on 11 February 1788 Hannah remarked that several friends had died that week: 'felt grateful that it had not entered our own family.'

There are anxieties about the health of friends no less than of family members. One group was feared lost on a ship crossing the Atlantic – but after weeks of waiting, the fears proved ungrounded. The loss of friends was keenly felt. Hannah recalled with sadness and sentiment the loss of an early school friend and Anna Cropper's health was a frequent source of worry, too, as the diary pithily records: 'Express came from Manr. about Miss C's seizure.'

Then, the next day: 'A day of unrelieved and most painful anxiety with just hope enough to keep suspense alive.'[12]

The material world brought its share of anxieties too: the fear of financial embarrassment was especially disturbing as it undermined the achievement of respectability. The diary records a moment in the summer of 1788 when the news first reached Hannah of a large loss incurred by the Hodgsons in a trading venture. They suddenly faced financial ruin. Hannah's immediate thought was for her sister:

> Dr C called and looked anxious and distressed – went to see my Sister H. She told me of Mr Hartley's failure, and their consequent distress – was much shocked – Returned home ... Lost my voice.
>
> Sat with my Sister H all day – much charmed by her behaviour – called upon Dr Currie in the evening.[13]

This was an act that deceived Hannah, for in reality her sister Elizabeth was in an agony of anxiety. She set out her feelings in a note describing how she feared the disgrace of losing everything, yet found comfort by thinking of her blessings, and relief that she was spared the company of her mother and sister while such disgrace threatened:

> Four days have I spent in the most cruel suspense, nor is it yet near an end, though my impatience encreased with every hour since yesterday morning & towards evening became so painful that the certainty of the worst seemed preferable to it. Not an hour passes in which my mother's and my sister's absence does not make me rejoice, as to save them from suffering under the suspense makes my deprivation of their society a comfort.[14]

In the event, the family rallied round, and John Pares quickly bailed out his brother-in-law, so not all was lost. This was a close family, bound to each other often through adversity, and one that was well connected and well regarded.

The social round

Hannah's diary records a round of events and entertainments beyond the confines of the family. Some were those of a dutiful daughter, and others were in conformity with the social calendar, a framework that could hardly be ignored by an eligible young woman. The main social seasons – often centred on the races, assizes and assemblies – were from January to March in Liverpool, in the summer months at Wavertree, late summer in Buxton, September and October in Leicester, November and December in Manchester, and London throughout the winter.

The assemblies were formal gatherings where the respectable citizens met to dance, play cards, talk and have tea, often – as in Liverpool – in handsome new buildings designed for the purpose, aiming to provide opportunities for young women to meet eligible men. As Hannah recorded, they were often not much fun, unless her brighter contemporaries such as Benjamin Arthur Heywood[15] or the Tates were there. Yet it would have been inconceivable for Hannah to miss such events; participating in them helped to define her position in society, confirming her standing and her good taste.

In January 1787 she records: 'Went to the Assembly where my feelings were strongly contrasted to those of the preceding evening,' referring to when her intellectual friends had dined and shared thrilling conversations: 'Fatigue in my Limbs, confusion in my head and dissatisfaction in my heart.' Hannah's friends were invited to stay during the Liverpool season and Hannah was later invited back, to go to assemblies in Lancaster, Leicester and Manchester. The trips that she made to see friends and relatives were in fact usually connected to the seasonal round of assemblies and parties: so for example, when visiting Caton and then the Lakes, Hannah went to the assizes and assembly at Lancaster. In Manchester, she stayed with the Percival family and then the Kennedy family during the season, attending assemblies, suppers and plays.

Hannah was an active participant in the social life of her home town, enjoying the theatres, the concerts and the art exhibitions. A highlight was the occasion of the King's recovery from mental illness, when the loyalist Common Council laid on celebrations. A contemporary account records the centre of Liverpool illuminated, a cannonade, and 'coloured lamps and transparent paintings' in front of the Exchange building.[16] The following month she was again delighted by the splendour of the decorations for the Grand Corporation Ball.

The annual visit to the baths at Matlock and Buxton, usually with her mother and her mother's elderly friends, was less stimulating: a fixture that seems to have been dreaded by Hannah. All these trips took her away from Liverpool for long stretches of time: she was absent for the second half of 1787, from September to November 1788, and in 1789 (even when betrothed) she was travelling in much of July, August, September and October – perhaps as a determined attempt to make the most of her last weeks of freedom.

The normal social round in Liverpool was strenuous, with many calls to be made. For example, on 5 February 1787: 'Called at Miss Loxham's, Miss Heywood's, Miss Copland, Miss Ashton, Miss Hodgson's, Mrs Smith, Miss Clegg's, Mrs Case and Mrs Currie. Mr [Sorre?] dined with us. Played Piquet with him.' Then, on 16 April 1787: 'A large party supped here. Misses Brooks, Sandys, Payne, T Percival, Lightbody, Bailey, Mr L Heywood.' And, from 7–9 May 1787: 'T Percival and I drank tea at Allerton – called at Woolton – promised to supply Anne Leigh with Books. 8th: T.P. and I dined in Paradise St – met my Uncle's family and Mr R Coleman. 9th: Dined at Dr Camplin's. T.P. and I staid supper.'

Amid these routines a trip to London with her mother promised to be a highlight. Serious Dissenters of the older generation regarded London, with its concentration on fashion, leisure and consumer spending, to be a centre of iniquity. There is no evidence that Hannah shared these reservations.

Besides, she had teachers, school friends and cousins to see, as well as the fashionable sights. She was feted at her old school, and enjoyed the company of her former teachers.

She entertained and was entertained by the Rogers family and by many of the leading London Dissenting radicals of the day. She and her mother were already familiar with Dr Price, the radical minister and preacher who still lived at Newington Green, near his old friend Thomas Rogers. But Hannah also met other prominent radicals there; she also went to Clapham to meet the Thorntons and to see Dr Kippis, the leading Dissenter and writer, and the central figure in the current campaigns between 1787 and 1790 for the repeal of the Test and Corporation Acts. These may have been merely social visits, but Hannah was not shy about engaging with such august figures, who were all articulate and passionate promoters of political and social reform and learning.[17]

Hannah was not intimidated by men – or women – of scholarship. For instance, she shared her enthusiasm for Johann Lavater, the poet and physiognomist, with Dr Hunter, the translator of Lavater's *Physiognomy*, when they met over dinner. Hannah and her mother had tea and a literary conservation with Mrs Barbauld: 'Called at Hampstead upon Mrs Barbauld – was much pleased with her chearful [sic] friendliness – read *Vathek* in the evening recommended by Mrs B [and] *Castle of Otranto*.'[18] The poet and essayist, Mrs Barbauld had settled in Hampstead earlier in 1787, where she produced her effective public campaigns for social reform. Hannah later quoted aphorisms of Mrs Barbauld's in her books of *Maxims* and kept up an intermittent correspondence with her.

Would Hannah find society in Liverpool provincial by comparison, as she threw herself into the party season, with plays, concerts and parties? There is little evidence. She also enjoyed the style of John Pares, her brother-in-law, whose Leicester house, The Newarke, was:

a noble looking house, like a mansion, which boasted of a paddock with an avenue of very fine trees … Besides two parlours and a study on the ground floor, there were two large drawing rooms above and some twenty bedrooms. Adjoining the house on the North West was a two story warehouse in which the hosiery business was carried on.[19]

On her visits Hannah enjoyed shopping in Leicester as well as walking and riding across parkland and open country on the various estates recently bought by John Pares's rich and ambitious father. But she also appreciated unspoilt nature such as the countryside of the Lune valley, which greatly appealed to her whenever she visited her elder sister there.[20] There too she met the local gentry and manufacturers.

Beside the events, names and places encountered in Hannah's diary lies a hidden narrative of a mind being widened by reading, by debate and by experience. All these excursions and social trips were formative, enlarging Hannah's confidence and broadening her into a thoughtful, well-read and inquisitive person. It may be that some of her Liverpool contemporaries sometimes found her opinionated or stuck-up, qualities that would hardly endear her to an average suitor, but she seems to have been determined to acquire and to be recognised for those elusive and desirable qualities of taste and sensibility. At the same time, she was attentive to current political debates and carefully considered contemporary issues, such as women's roles in society.

Developing views about politics, morals and society

A diary entry for a Sunday in April 1787 gives an idea of the range of Hannah's enthusiasms:

All morning read Interesting Memoirs, a very serious book, in the afternoon wrote a Catalogue of Books, a Country dance in my Music book, some Scripture passages and read a discourse on the Love of Praise, full of instruction for me.[21]

Hannah was clearly anxious to cultivate the unusual gifts of a good fortune, a family with a committed faith, a desire to help others, combined with an appreciation of beauty in art and nature that she found uplifting and inspiring. She realised that the best opportunity for her to pursue her personal development was before marriage.

As Hannah's father had died when she was 11 years old, she naturally looked to male role models to guide her in matters that she thought a father may have done. There was at that time no impropriety in men discussing philosophical or literary matters with an unmarried young woman on her own or in company. The diary provides ample evidence that a number of the most gifted men in north-west England drew Hannah into their circles and conversations: among these were Dr Currie, Dr Percival and William Rathbone IV. What motivated them? We can make a number of suggestions. There is no evidence that any of these men might have found Hannah's mind, personality or presence attractive, but perhaps these are factors that should not be ruled out: she was a willing pupil, ever ready to learn and absorb information. These three men were didactic by nature. They were also all prominent Dissenters who held the enlightenment view that there was nothing intrinsically inferior about women's minds. Then there was the fact that no further-education establishments admitted women. Those women who wanted to extend their intellect and satisfy their curiosity had to tune into the advice and tutoring of their family or learned friends, in private. Finally, they were aware that she was a direct descendant of one of the revered founders of their faith.[22]

The most remarkable of these role models was James Currie. His name occurs in Hannah's diary with greater frequency than any other.[23] Hannah was impressed by Currie's mind: 'Dr Currie and Mr Godwin dined with us and had an argument on Materialism on which Dr C shone very much – Mr Godwin was a very liberal defender of this doctrine.' Currie was starting to share his views with Hannah and communicate his taste and his enthusiasms: 'Dr C re-called in the afternoon and read to us Miss Williams' Ode to Peace of which he pointed out the beauties.'[24]

The following week, Hannah let him see her commonplace book. This was a personal selection of epigrams and extracts from her various readings, and she must have felt sufficiently confident in his judgement to let him see it, as in it 'he found some of his own works'. This interest was maintained, and Hannah was flattered, and to judge by this note she wrote about him after he treated her for a mild illness, quite affected:

> Restored and confirmed health presses on my heart a sense of my obligations to Dr C to whose attention I owe the blessing. Long may he enjoy the ease he dispenses prays with warmth of heart his ever obliged and respectful H.L.[25]

In spite of Dr Currie's constant fight against tuberculosis, he was a striking figure. His son described him as: 'tall, well-built, and dignified, with piercing, dark blue eyes. Although he could be playful he was also melancholy.' He liked women and, as he told Hannah Rathbone, found it easier having conversations with them than with men.[26] As though in confirmation of Hannah's own admiration, she recorded the opinion of the rural intellectual William Cockin:

> Called early on Miss C – found her and Dr C engaged in an argument on Independence of Mind – When I returned Mr Cockin was talking highly in praise of Dr C's Character saying he was a Man of a capacious Mind, powerful eloquence, clear perception and noble feelings.[27]

Thus it is little wonder that Hannah admired Dr Currie and enjoyed his company. The relationship between Currie and

Hannah developed with his serious interest in broadening her education, his keenness to communicate his enthusiasm for contemporary literature, and in his work for the abolition of the slave trade. Hannah was aware of his passion for political reform, his campaigns for peace and his mature view that for reason to prevail in all these fields, time and patience may be required. He also encouraged her to support the voluntary fundraising efforts for the Infirmary.

Following Currie's recommendation, Hannah devoted three days to absorbing Thomas Reid's *Essays on the active powers of man*.[28] There cannot have been many young women at this period who were prepared to study and take on board Reid's thinking on morals, and in particular his conviction that it is our conscience that directs our moral sense. In a letter to Hannah Rathbone dated I October 1806 she recalled: 'I have both Reid and Stewarts' large works from which I have formerly experienced more pleasure as well as improvement than perhaps from any books I ever read.'

Hannah also seems to have learnt from Currie (and from Dr Percival) an understanding of the basic precautions and provisions for health in communities, which she was to apply in later life with skill and confidence. This was a subject that was of great interest to her and it was a sphere in which women could develop useful roles.

How was it that Hannah, when young, was also on familiar terms with Thomas Percival, one of the great minds and personalities of the Enlightenment in Britain, a friend of the French philosophers Voltaire and Diderot, a pupil of the Scottish philosopher David Hume, a correspondent of America's Benjamin Franklin?[29] In the midst of Percival's busy career as a physician, campaigner, writer and reformer, he found time in the 1780s to come over from Manchester to Liverpool, where he spent whole days with Hannah, and had her to stay at his home in Manchester for several weeks, where his daughter Fanny was one of her close friends. In the late 1780s he was in middle age and at the height of his powers and influence.

He campaigned against slavery, fought to reform the ossified medical establishment in Manchester, and was the first to take up the cause of the health of the young employees in the new cotton mills. His lasting influence on Hannah was probably in developing her interest and skills in supervising the health and welfare of the Quarry Bank Mill workforce and in her approach to the education of her children.

Hannah was also flattered by the attention she received from William Rathbone IV.[30] His mind was penetrating, his character mercurial and quixotic, his sympathies liberal and often radical, and his determination courageous. He stood out against the transatlantic slave trade, one of only a handful of Liverpool merchants to do so publicly, criticising 'the unexampled cruelty and aggression of our commerce with Africa'. Motivated by an unshakeable faith in reason, he fought for municipal reform in Liverpool, and in consequence was attacked more than once by dangerous crowds. Among causes dear to his heart were free trade, universal suffrage, reform of the poor law, and freedom of speech. His letters to Hannah engaged her in all these issues: they show a mixture of what he would call 'enthusiasm', and a tinge of dark pessimism. He was positive and, despite his faith in reason, sometimes excessively idealistic about the improvability of human nature, and was carried away at times by his own imaginative rhetoric, speculating optimistically about society and mankind. Though frequently ill, possibly with migraine or a depressive illness, he was a resilient campaigner, initially welcoming the revolution in France. William Rathbone recognised Hannah's instinct to teach and preach and encouraged her. It seems to have been his idea that she should raise herself above her taxing round of maternal and household duties, by starting to write. Although fond of William, Hannah was not easily carried away by all his excitable enthusiasms, though he probably helped develop her thoughts on Ireland and on a range of political reforms to secure a more liberal and fair form of government, both locally and nationally.

Hannah acknowledged her debt to these role models. They recommended books and encouraged her learning. Books furnished her mind at an impressionable age and were used as a mine of information for her own commonplace book. She had developed the practice of copying out passages from her reading, and she seems to have treasured these quotations, reflecting on them and eventually assembling selections of extracts for the benefit of her family and friends. Only a few fragmentary drafts of these extract books have survived but, with her published compilations, they provide evidence of an exceptionally wide range of sources.

Her reading during the period of her youthful diary is remarkable enough. Taken as a whole, the diary reveals Hannah's considerable appetite for topics that go beyond 'safe' titles or fashionable magazines and novels. She also studied the arbiters of contemporary thought on sensibility and taste.[31]

Cultivating sensibility and taste

One of the strongest impressions left by Hannah's diary is her sensibility to nature and the countryside. For her, nature could be a solace, an inspiration and a religious emanation. It remained an abiding passion throughout her life. The busy seaport atmosphere in the centre of Liverpool where Hannah's family lived and where she was raised may not seem a likely location for stimulating this love of nature, were it not for the vivid contrast provided by the rural scenery within a short walking distance. In Hannah's youth, Toxteth Park was unspoilt farmland lying close to the southern edge of the town. There she discovered walks down to the shore and dramatic views across the River Mersey to Wales; she often went rambling alone, or with her good friend and distant kinswoman Arabella Nicholson who lived at a country house in Toxteth Park:

The day was bright and I may almost say my spirits high of course. Walked to Park and in my favourite dingles ...

Rode out in the morning. It was a delightful day and produced in my mind those agreeable sensations which a clear atmosphere, sunshine and the appearance of Spring never fail to create ...

Walked through the Lodge fields to Park – much delighted with the Scene – Ever charming, ever new ...

Good Friday spent chiefly in the Dingles –very happy to be in the country – such a day ...

And exercise in the fresh air was part of the pleasure: 'a charming day and very happy – rambled about Otterspool – walked 13 miles.'[32] A young woman's passion for long solitary walks may have been less unusual than it sounds, and Hannah seems to have relished being alone. In Derbyshire and Leicestershire she spent a great deal of time wandering around the large estates of Thomas Pares at Ockbrook, Hopwell, Bradgate Park and Groby, sometimes on foot, sometimes on horseback. In the Leicestershire countryside: 'Walked 7 miles with Sister P in the morning and narrowly escaped being shot' – it was the first day of the season for the partridge shoot. Similarly, in Lancaster, Hannah: 'Walked 6 miles in the Evening to see a fine view.'[33]

She cherished the religious or spiritual value that she absorbed in the countryside. This was frequently endorsed by the Rev. Joseph Smith with whom she discussed her convictions and developed her thoughts:

In (the) tranquillity of the Country your thoughts rise without interception to the Creator of that beauty so liberally spread before you – every surrounding object is an Auxiliary to their assent, and you throw off for a time the incumbrance of a connection with the world.[34]

Hannah was also inspired – perhaps through her reading – by nature's renewal:

Went to Park and walked in the Dingle – my favourite scene –
I sat up on my beloved rocks and enjoyed almost with rapture
the renovated state of Nature now just bursting from the impris-
onment of Winter – expressive, striking emblem of that renewal
of our mortal body when it shall burst its prison, the Grave.[35]

As the poet Mark Akenside suggested in *The Pleasures of the
Imagination*, by identifying with scenes in nature the poetic soul
can find inspiration and solace. The consoling powers of nature
and poetry were felt by Hannah and her response to nature
often seems to reflect current literary, philosophic and artistic
movements of the time. She liked to walk in the country and
recall poetry whenever she was upset, and she identified herself
with her natural surroundings, promoting this philosophy to her
friends and family:

How useful to People immersed in worldly concerns is occasional retirement from the despotism of care to refresh the mind
with solitude and tranquillity – to give the mind air to breathe
as well as the lungs. So far do I carry these opinions as to think it
our duty to live in the Country.[36]

She wrote some maxims of her own on this theme and included
them in her books. In conversation with Hannah Rathbone in
early 1787, for example, she 'persuaded Mrs R that there was a
propriety in letting her husband know of anything that was so
necessary to her happiness as living in the Country', and could
probably claim some credit in ensuring that the Rathbones took
on Greenbank in Toxteth Park.[37]

With her appreciation of the countryside, her wide reading and
her enquiring mind, Hannah would have been regarded as a polished young woman – in any decade in any provincial town. But
in the late eighteenth century a further veneer of refinement was
thought desirable. This was 'taste': a prized attribute, even if hard
to define. In her pursuit of taste, Hannah enjoyed visiting famous

houses and looking at works of art; she made tours of the Lakes and saw the sights in London. Her mother had been a keen visitor to collections and by the 1780s such activities had become very fashionable among the middle classes, and this was the period when guidebooks began to proliferate. Following the example set by her mother, Hannah was keen to cultivate her sensibility to nature and art, and to appreciate how it might be equated with moral virtue. How to identify, cultivate and refine taste seemed to her to be a useful topic of conversation and a worthwhile pursuit in a woman, no less than in a man. 'It is such a sensibility of heart,' wrote the philosophical writer Alexander Gerard, 'as fits a man for being easily moved and for readily catching, as by infection, any passion that a work is fitted to excite.'[38]

The pursuit of taste and sensibility was a growing preoccupation of middle-class men and women, who valued the distinction that these accomplishments brought to them, especially those living outside the metropolis. Sentiment and sensibility were not confined to the arts: people of greater sensibility were thought of as more morally virtuous. It is clear that Hannah, who was dedicated to the cultivation of her mind and to the acquisition of taste, judgement and knowledge, pursued these goals ardently between leaving school and getting married three years later. She not only saw the sights, or read the books and poems, she was thoroughly familiar with the theoretical and philosophical works that underpinned this whole movement.

Instinctively and passionately fond of natural scenery, Hannah was already familiar with Jean-Jacques Rousseau and his romantic sensibility. Her reading was extended to include the Graveyard poets, Ossian, the plays of Richard Cumberland, and new novels such as *The Man of Feeling*, by Henry Mackenzie. Her travels sought out romantic scenery such as that to be found in the Peak District and the Lake District. Her conversations and diary entries reveal these developing interests, which she reinforced by reading the philosophical treatises on which these perceptions were based, such as Hume and Gerard.

Hannah also developed an interest in music while at school in London. She learnt to play the piano and later the harp, and could compose music. On her return home to Liverpool, she threw herself into the seasons of concerts and plays, writing occasional pithy comments on the performers.

She was close to a circle of collectors and connoisseurs of art in Liverpool. The acknowledged leader was William Roscoe,[39] but Hannah also knew and liked William Tate, a painter living mainly in Manchester between 1787 and 1803. He was a friend and former pupil of Joseph Wright, so it was no surprise that Tate should show Hannah some masterpieces of Wright's as well as his own paintings. Hannah also admired old master paintings in her tours of stately homes such as Hagley Park and Burleigh House.

London offered the excitement of seeing the Tower, St Paul's and the British Museum, as well as the studios of the fashionable artists such as George Engleheart and George Romney. Another thrill was seeing the work of the mechanical genius John Joseph Merlin, who made and exhibited musical automata. Yet the highlight of this feast of metropolitan culture were her visits to the theatre at Covent Garden – where she had the best seats in the house.

Hannah also enjoyed visiting gardens and designed landscapes, another very fashionable medium for those who wanted to be appreciated for their discerning eye. Hannah was drawn to the romantic landscapes pioneered by the poet and writer William Shenstone, whose literary work she knew and admired.[40] In August 1789, when already betrothed, she was 'impatient to get to the Leasowes', and finished her walk there as darkness descended. The farm and estate at The Leasowes, in Halesowen in the West Midlands, had been planned and planted by Shenstone in a new naturalistic and romantic idiom, which by then was highly fashionable. She also admired nearby Enville and Hagley, where the designed landscapes were much influenced by Shenstone's naturalistic and atmospheric approach.

Hannah talked to Joseph Smith about theories of art and taste, to Dr Currie about ethics and romantic poetry, to various kinsmen and ministers about aspects of her faith and to William Rathbone about political reform and the afterlife. In between these conversations, many of the men were meeting on a regular footing in private societies, where normally there was no access for women. But it was a reflection of the enlightened times in Liverpool that Hannah was welcomed among several of these distinguished and mainly masculine circles.

Liverpool's intellectual reputation in Hannah's time was enhanced by the Literary Society, with its high standard of debate on literary, moral and political topics. Its members included William Rathbone IV, Edward Rushton, Dr Yates and Rev. William Shepherd.[41] The group's focus was not solely literary; they often discussed the political aims common among Rational Dissenters, becoming known further afield as the 'Friends of Freedom'. Suspected of Jacobin sympathies, they were forced to disband in 1793. It seems that no women were ever admitted to their meetings.

The Octonian Society on the other hand seems to have been a more literary and domestic discussion group, in which Hannah and her mother were welcome to participate. Its members (who presumably totalled eight) included Joseph Smith (of Benns Gardens Chapel), Edward Rogers (who at that time was president of the Liverpool Library), William Rathbone IV, Matthew Nicholson and Thomas Moss Tate (or possibly the painter William Tate). The balloonist Thomas Baldwin attended in January 1788, presumably as a guest. Hannah recorded some of the Octonian gatherings with youthful excitement:

> 3 Jan 1787: We spent the afternoon in playing quadrille, and in the evening, Mr Smith, Mr Rathbone and Mr Rogers were the only members of that selection, of learned, wise and good men called the Octonian Society who attended the meeting at our house.

17 Jan 1787: This evening I spent with the Octonian Club at Mr Rathbone's, a Society of Men who bring together in their various characters, Learning, Science, Vivacity, Seriousness and solid Worth. In their conversation the heart and head share profit – and I would rather bring a young person to spend an evening in the Company than give them a whole year's common School education. The sort of luxury enjoyed in such company is exhilarating instead of fatiguing – you are grieved when it ends and enjoy it again on Reflection.

31 April 1787: The Octonian Society supped with us – they conversed on the different religious persuasions that divide Mankind.

These were such memorable occasions that Hannah recalled them later in life. They provide a short glimpse into an intellectual and enlightened world. More than twenty years later, Hannah established for her own children a debating circle based on the Octonians. She called it the Duodecimo Society.

Women's roles and spheres

Hannah's upbringing in Liverpool and London coincided with a confusing time for intelligent and ambitious young women. At this period, the traditionally submissive wife's position was being challenged. Conventions, fashion and the law demanded wives to be subservient and limited the spheres in which they could flourish and nurture their talents. Hannah's mother, like her forbears, nevertheless played an active and influential role in her husband's life and work: she had her own circle of female friends and kinsfolk, and developed her mind with reading and travel. But married women of that generation would not normally be brave enough to publish their thoughts, or develop intellectual or artistic skills, unless they were exceptionally gifted and courageous.

Acceptable roles for women in the public sphere in Mrs Lightbody's generation could include trustee roles in their local chapel, and no doubt also in the hospital charities. Widowhood or spinsterhood seem to have been more liberating. While practical skills were acceptable and even admired, intellectual brilliance in women could be regarded as embarrassing.

In her youth Hannah had absorbed some of the work of daring female writers such as Mary Wollstonecraft and Helen Maria Williams, and she seems to have agreed that the subjection of women in marriage was degrading and indefensible, while asserting that women's minds were intrinsically not inferior to men's. The point had been made by John Aikin: 'virtue, wisdom, presence of mind, patience, vigour, capacity, application are not sexual qualities: they belong to mankind'.[42] So it would be surprising if Hannah – after her extensive education – had not questioned the assumptions that women's minds were of little account, and that it was unnecessary and maybe even dangerous to encourage their development. She believed that education could make a woman more companionable as a wife, but was wary of the rights of husbands to demand submission.

Hannah then developed her own ideas about the rights of women. Her starting point was the independence and indissoluble value of the female mind. This was a foundation stone noted by Rational Dissenters who derived it from earlier philosophers such as Locke. This led her to insist that women's education need not and should not be inferior to men's. In her first book of maxims, she argued that:

> Nature has, perhaps, made the sexes mentally equal, but fortune and man, seem to have established an oppression which degrades woman from her natural situation; and it may be observed that in this, as in other instances, the crime creates the punishment, inasmuch as a slave is less useful and valuable to man as a friend. The books that are intended for the instruction of the female sex, are commonly addressed to them as women, not as rational, accountable,

individual human beings; their duties are made to refer to their connexion with men, and those are most insisted on which are most important to them, as those of wives, housekeepers, mothers, daughters, etc, whereas wisdom and virtue are the same to both sexes and will make a woman a good wife, a true friend, a tender mother, an active mistress etc as they will render a man a good merchant, statesman, or minister, a good husband, father or brother.[43]

The advantages of spinsterhood were apparent to her. There were role models such as her friends Miss Cropper and Miss Kennedy, women whose independence of action and expression she admired. From time to time in her diary Hannah reflected on the case for remaining single.[44] She was clear that in several respects women had superior strengths, and that men conspired to deny or ignore these 'for their own convenience and amusement':

Were the other advantages equal, … superiority would be frequently found on the side of women, in whom affection is a stronger motive of conduct; who possess therefore greater disinterestedness and sensibility, which, when strengthened by habit, often enables them to dare and to endure, more than mere manly wisdom and courage.[45]

Having been trailed around the assemblies and matchmaking gatherings of Liverpool, Manchester and the Midlands, it was understandable that Hannah should question the prospect of having to give up much of her prized independence of mind and self-determination in exchange for the conventions of marriage. In this situation, Hannah, as any other girl in her position, would turn to her closest advisers and mentors for advice. While her sympathetic male supporters such as James Currie and William Rathbone encouraged her to make the most of her talents, she could also turn to a group of wise female role models. Her mother, her own sisters, her best friend Mrs Rathbone, and the godmother-like figure of Anna Cropper and her sister Arabella Nicholson all acted as sensible sounding boards.

From her mother, Hannah would learn a sense of proportion, good works and self-denial. She was a good model of the capable woman who, entering upon marriage and becoming a dutiful wife, could still find personal fulfilment and intellectual stimulation, while keeping alive the family tradition of caring for the spiritual and physical health of others in the community. Perhaps the most significant legacies that Hannah derived from her mother were her faith and vocation to help the poor in her neighbourhood. Self-deprecating yet firm, her mother seems to have expected the poor wherever possible to help themselves, to heed the Bible, and to do what they could to improve their condition.

Hannah was also naturally influenced by her elder sisters, who presented her with enviable examples of companionable marriages, with close and affectionate family lives. They were fulfilled and happy bringing up their children and managing their households. Hannah was heartbroken when the eldest, Elizabeth, died in 1795, and felt thrice orphaned when Agnes died in 1812.

Hannah Mary Rathbone (1761–1839) was already happily married to the quirky William Rathbone by the time of Hannah Lightbody's return to Liverpool. Though concerned for her young children, her fragile health and her husband's demanding preoccupation with work and radical politics, she was a person of wise counsel and sympathetic affection. For forty years Hannah Mary was a constant and intimate friend of Hannah, a person to whom Hannah could pour out her hopes and fears, discuss the nursing of children, their illnesses and their death. It was a relationship in which emotions were not concealed. Hannah Mary Rathbone's home at Greenbank in Toxteth Park represented a model to which Hannah probably aspired. It was an elegant base in which to entertain scientific, literary and political visitors from afar, as well as Liverpool reformers, while at the same time offering a rural haven for the children.

Among Hannah's warmest and most intimate advisers of an older generation were the sisters Bella Nicholson (1736–1815) and Anna Cropper (1739–91). Their father Edward Cropper had married well and had been a successful merchant in the Africa trade.[46] Bella lived at Toxteth Park, where Hannah's frequent visits were a constant and reliable tonic. Hannah loved the country setting, and frequently met with Bella's children, her contemporaries and other friends for breakfast, teas and suppers, often also staying the night. Bella, by then a widow, was a senior figure in the Kaye Street Chapel congregation, but her main distinction – one recognised by her wide family – seems to have been a sympathetic heart and being 'always at call in family illnesses and in times of trouble'.[47]

Bella's sister, Anna Cropper, was also a stalwart of the Kaye Street Chapel and an old friend of Hannah's mother. A confirmed spinster, she lived out of town in the country village of Everton. Hannah found her to be kind, if at times forbidding. Often in fragile health, she was undoubtedly clever, and could be critical. Anna Cropper acted as a godmother to Hannah, often providing advice: she knew Hannah well and was widely respected for her kindness and good judgement.

It was Anna Cropper who raised with Hannah the question of her absorption in intellectual matters. Had she devoted herself too much to the cultivation of her mind, Anna enquired, instead of to the acquisition of those practical skills that a future husband would more greatly value? She struck a chord, and Hannah was stung and reflected on it in a long passage in her diary. She wrote:

Held a long interesting conversation with her [that is, Miss Cropper] on the 'lower order of accomplishments' as domestic management &c. which she was friendly enough to tell me she feared I was too much disposed to despise, or at least not to consider as sufficiently important – & that the present mode of educating females too much excluded an attention to what was nevertheless a most valuable part of a woman's character and substituted in its place accomplishments which might indeed render them <u>agreeable Companions</u> but not <u>useful Wives</u>, which two

characters should always be joined – that Men whose affection
I should be ambitious to gain, however they might delight in
the first would select for a Wife accomplishments peculiar to the
female province in domestic life –[48]

All were familiar with the anxieties about young women being
over-educated. It was a theme for cartoonists and theatrical
comedies, but it had its defenders too. Hannah admits there is
some truth in Miss Cropper's assertion, but she draws on some
well-considered arguments to counter this accusation:

> I contended that it was not only more <u>common</u> than was gen-
> erally approved, but that it was certainly <u>natural</u> that they should
> be found joined – that a woman of Sense and taste was likely to
> apply those faculties to whatever duties her situation presented,
> and that the minutest & vulgarest occupation of ordinary life
> would certainly be better performed when their performance
> was under the direction of a cultivated mind – that for my
> own part, if it should fall to my lot to figure in domestic life, I
> should perhaps not keep what in Liverpool would be esteemed
> <u>an elegant table</u>, or an elegant equipage – but tho' my <u>Style</u>
> might have less <u>shew</u> I ventured to hope it would not have
> less <u>true taste</u> than those which now pass for models in this
> gay town – Hospitable plenty neatness, simplicity, unaffected
> friendliness, <u>rational conversation</u> and <u>tranquillity</u> I should ever
> be carefully solicitous to preserve … – that tho' I was ignorant
> at present of matters relating to household management yet if it
> ever became my <u>duty</u> to know and practice them I should find
> them interesting and attainable – if my heart would prove equal
> to learn it.

Anna Cropper had clearly identified an area where Hannah felt
vulnerable, for in the same diary entry she went on to defend
the cultivation of her mind:

I thought Men too hasty in forming judgments – and concluded that if a woman had a <u>turn for reading</u> she must of course neglect or despise that sort of knowledge – most applicable to ordinary life – but I thought a Woman of Sense would always have ambition to perform her duties whatever they were creditably and well – and that a sensible liberal Man would not esteem her less for being capable of being his <u>companion</u> as well as his <u>housekeeper</u>. I thought I should never prefer the <u>dulce</u> to the <u>utile</u> when they became incompatible, but that I thought now was the time to give to those pursuits that might form me into the Companion before the more useful and importunate cares and occupations of domestic life claimed all my time – that however, I ought not to throw away all the advantages of such an education as I had received by neglecting those pursuits it had favoured – and that I would never marry a Man who did not value them in a wife – that a woman who merely provided her husband with the <u>conveniences</u> of a <u>clean house</u> and a <u>good table</u>, while he sought abroad the pleasures of <u>Society</u>, was no better than a slave … a <u>moderate</u> share of abilities well cultivated and united to the conscientious desire to do what is right and the ambition to be approached by those we love form the best foundation of virtue as well as happiness – and is surely what a wise and rational Man would <u>wish for</u> & be <u>satisfied with</u> in a companion.

It was understandable that Hannah should expect to make the most of her education, to crave intellectual stimulation, and to claim that when the time was right, she should strive to master the art of domestic management. And that if and when married, she would expect companionship from a husband who would value her education too. But did Hannah really understand the need for Anna Cropper's advice? There is perhaps some unintentional irony in the confident manner in which Hannah brushes it aside.

Hannah's own beliefs

The religion of the Dissenters in Hannah's circle was not dour. It was a way of living entirely compatible with an enquiring mind, a developing sensibility, wide reading and a convivial life. It gave Hannah confidence and it promoted tolerance across religions and classes. It also provided its adherents with a moral framework.

Many aspects of the Dissenters' faith were continuously evolving and openly debated. Hannah grew up in this climate, encountering challenging variations, no doubt, when at school in London and in the circle of radical friends of Thomas Rogers. On her return home in 1786 she engaged in discussions with her family and friends on conduct, charity, worship, the afterlife and doctrine. While the main framework of Hannah's beliefs were unshakeable and central to her daily life, she happily debated religious questions and confided her conclusions in her diary.

According to her youngest son, she saw herself as a follower of Joseph Priestley.[49] In 1788 when a group of Manchester Dissenters who, unhappy with the direction being taken by their minister at Cross Street Chapel in Manchester, established a new chapel at Mosley Street, it was in the mould of Priestley's faith (and akin to Yates's creed and practice at Kaye Street in Liverpool). Hannah joined Yates and the Kaye Street elders on their visit to Manchester to attend the opening of this new chapel. Priestley came there to preach a few years later and Hannah remained loyal to Mosley Street for the rest of her life, having all her children baptised there. It is clear from Hannah's books that she knew the works of the leading Dissenting writers, and she retained a framework of clear personal beliefs throughout her adult life, resisting complex debates on doctrine or dogma. Hannah also thought about the afterlife; following Priestley's ideas, she understood that the development of the mind was justified as a step towards the 'perfection of our faculties' in the next life. She also quoted the following paragraph from John Jebb which probably represents some of her core beliefs:

The religion which God requires of all is at once simple and it speaks an uniform language to all nations – it is intelligible to every sensible being – it is clear, and engraved on every heart in indelible characters – its decrees are secure from the revolutions of empires, the injuries of time, and the caprice of custom. Every virtuous man is its priest, errors and vices are its victims, the universe its altar, and God the only divinity it adores. Morality is the sum and substance of this religion: when we are rational we are pious; when we are useful, we are virtuous; and when we are benevolent we are righteous and just.[50]

Among Dissenting communities, individuals were encouraged to study and interpret the Bible, and Hannah was very familiar with it. Scattered throughout Hannah's diary are brief entries noting conversations with ministers, lay friends or family on matters of belief and the interpretation of the Bible.

Hannah's convictions about ethics and morals evolved throughout her life. Through sermons, discussions and the example of her mother, Hannah learnt that in her fortunate position it was her duty to help the poor and to support charities. Hannah often found her visits to help the poor to be rewarding occasions. 'The greatest of human pleasures,' she later wrote, 'and the most effective cordial for grief, is procured by active and personal benevolence.'[51] Many middle-class people doubtless helped the poor in this way, but Hannah maintained a close interest in the minds, characters and potential of the working classes whom she met. She respected them, encouraged them, and perhaps understood them. Like her mother, she could help care for them in terms of diet and health, and also teach them to read so that they could find solace in the Bible. Hannah probably concluded, like her mother, that the poor will always be poor, but she gave much practical advice and support with the aim of encouraging them to improve their lives by learning reliability, frugality and the rudiments of health. The problems that she saw, but did not mention, were no doubt fecklessness, drunkenness and profligacy with money – vices that it was believed exacerbated their poor health and could lead to unemployment and crime.

Characteristically, there is hardly a surviving shred of evidence of Hannah's donations and charitable giving during the rest of her life. It is likely to have been constant, and well directed towards her chapels and other causes dear to her, but always anonymous, so that the cumulative total of the wealth she gave away in her lifetime was never known.

Hannah among the campaigners for the abolition of the transatlantic slave trade

Rational Dissenters of Hannah's generation took the long view that improvements in society would in time make the world a better place; such confidence was a source of comfort to Hannah during the Napoleonic wars. Although at times pessimistic about the future of her country, she was by nature an observer and a commentator on the prospects for change in politics and society. While confining her views on politics to her family and close friends (she deplored women taking on political roles in public), she had trenchant views on the failings of successive governments and their policies. On the big issue of her time and place, the campaign for the abolition of the transatlantic slave trade, she probably shared the conviction of James Currie that this aim could be achieved gradually. Nevertheless, this question became a private source of anguish.

The campaigning of William Wilberforce and Thomas Clarkson in the 1780s had highlighted the inhumanity of the slave trade. Even in a ports such as Bristol, which had a long connection with the trade, merchants recognised by the 1780s that it was not humane and should be stopped. While Bristol and Manchester produced large popular petitions opposing the trade, no such support for abolition could be expected from Liverpool, where the council's view was reflected in the pulpit and the press. In Liverpool, the merchants, councillors, MPs and ministers of the Church combined with the seamen and port workers to defend the trade that the town depended on.

The number of Liverpool abolitionists was small: they were publicly vilified and, not surprisingly, their impact was muted. The town's Dissenters were leading opponents of slavery, but the few of them who did speak up have had a poor press.[52]

As the congregation at Kaye Street Chapel settled in to listen to Dr Yates's sermon on Sunday 28 January 1788, they heard an astonishing public condemnation of the slave trade, and a call to stop it. The sermon had been carefully timed. Following Clarkson's fact-finding visit to Liverpool in the autumn of 1787, the parliamentary and public campaign for abolition was getting under way. Petitions from Bristol and Manchester had been publicised. No one then expected a leading minister to call on his congregation to review their actions and connections. It was an act of great individual courage, probably deeply considered and carefully prepared by Yates, deliberately timed to coincide with Wilberforce's parliamentary strategy, and the promotion of abolition in Liverpool by its small committee of which Yates was a prominent member. It exploded like a mine among the congregation, taking by surprise many families, such as the Lightbodys.

This is what Hannah reported:

Heard Mr Yates discourse on African Slavery from 2nd Malachi 'Have we not all one Father? – and hath not one Lord created us? – why do we then deal treacherously every Man with his own Brother' – he began by general observations on the equality of Mankind being all equally the Children of God, tho' distinguished by difference of lot, some being fostered in the lap of indulgence during their infancy – in youth amused with all the pleasures natural to the season – all the pursuits of their maturer years crowned with success – and their old age comforted by every alleviation of Infirmity – Others thro' every stage of life were alike unfortunately nursed in poverty, trained to labour, pursued by want, disease and Calamity – yet have we not all one Father – The Wise and benevolent Governor of all things intended the abundance of one Man to supply the necessities of another, the treasury of the rich to be the granary of the Poor, the Power of the strong to be the safeguard of the weak, the house of the wise to be the school of the ignorant.[53]

Hannah later added a note to confirm that 'Mr Yates formerly preached excellent Sermons – he wrote them carefully'. Her account goes on:

What opinion were the poor victims of our Avarice to form of that Religion whose votaries practiced such inhumanity? – how would they abhor a system which they would suppose from the conduct of its professors gave a sanction to Cruelty. Did we but follow that short and comprehensive precept of our Great Master – Do to others &c. this inhuman traffic, this oppression of our brethren could never have taken place – he was unhappy to say that 2/3rds of the Slave trade carried on by Britons was by his Townsmen – 27000 he calculated were exported yearly by Liverpool Merchants.

In the afternoon he preached on the duty of Self Examination – said that those who were satisfied with their own conduct would find pleasure in receiving it – and those who thought themselves in danger could not set about it too soon.

There were considerable aftershocks. Hannah was close to the leading Liverpool abolitionists and spoke about African slavery the next day. Meanwhile, across Liverpool as arguments between abolitionists and merchants broke out; people were discussing and maybe even reconsidering their links with the Africa trade and its future. Hannah's brother-in-law was a leading and well-known Africa trader. Many of her friends had connections with the trade: her cousins the Nicholsons, her uncle William Lightbody and even her father had traded in cloth for Africa merchants to sell. It was hard for anyone in business in the town to claim that their trade was not in some way implicated.

Physical threats were made to abolitionists, and Dr Binns suddenly and unexpectedly gave up his successful practice, almost certainly as the result of pressure. Currie admitted that he lost many patients and a high proportion of his income as a result of his views - that is no doubt the reason why he felt it prudent to conceal his role on the Liverpool Abolition Committee.

The Liverpool abolitionists used literature among their strategies, believing that popular poetry and ballads could be effective in stirring up public opinion. In the abolitionist campaign as a whole, the country was inspired by the pathos of the anti-slavery poetry of William Cowper and Hannah More. So in March 1788 Currie and Roscoe produced their short poem 'The African' and Currie had it printed anonymously in London. Roscoe added his poem 'The Wrongs of Africa' (in two parts: 1787 and 1788) and a pamphlet. Edward Rushton wrote frequently on these themes, publishing *The West Indian Eclogues* in 1787.

Currie faced moral dilemmas, which were described by his son in his biography:

> His position in Liverpool, was one of extreme difficulty and delicacy. He was in the midst of many friends, who were embarked in the slave-trade, with whom he was in habits of daily intercourse and intimacy, and from whom he experienced much kindness ... he had an opportunity of knowing that to be in the African trade did not necessarily render a man either unfeeling or dishonest. He knew that many of them (his own friends) were generous, affectionate, and humane, in private life; liberal, enterprising, and intelligent, in public, and it did not escape his

observation, that the general indignation against the trade itself was equally directed against the individuals concerned in it, without allowance for the circumstances in which they might be placed. He abhorred the slave trade; but he was anxious that excess of enthusiasm and ardent feeling (where, indeed, it was scarcely possible to be calm) should not injure the cause, which they were striving to promote.[54]

These perceptions were doubtless shared among others in Currie's circle. Currie, who knew and respected a good number of Liverpool merchants and slave traders such as the Earles and the Hodgsons, had confidence that a reasoned and gradual approach would in time yield dividends.

How did all these questions affect Hannah? She was in Leicester and London when Clarkson visited Liverpool on his fact-finding mission in the autumn of 1787 and she may not have read or heard about the newspaper articles from Manchester in that period, or seen the local newspaper debate. Yates's sermon at the end of January 1788 attacking the slave trade took her by surprise. She discussed it at length the next day with Rev. Joseph Smith, and on the day after that she 'lay wake endeavouring to recollect the Negroe's Complaint', Cowper's moving poem.

On Sunday 2 March she was with Currie, Smith and William Tate, hearing and discussing Currie and Roscoe's poem 'The African'. On 16 March she was with Dr Currie and Mr Trench, discussing Roscoe's poem 'The Wrongs of Africa'. Hannah's diary reveals that a number of Dissenters were able to discuss abolition in private, and spread the word. But campaigning was dangerous, and most of such activity was covert. In late February 1788, and throughout March, the Privy Council heard the witnesses for and against abolition and, in early April, concluded with the recommendation that the trade should be more strongly regulated, though not abolished.

Currie wrote: 'Men are awakening to their situation and the struggle between interest and humanity has made great havoc

in the happiness of many families.'[55] He could have been thinking of the Lightbodys and the Hodgsons, united in marriage,
but potentially divided on the issue of the slave trade. Hannah's
diary does not reveal that she raised the matter within the family
circle, but there can be little doubt that she was caught up in
these agonising discussions.

The abolitionists often talked about this issue in Hannah's
presence and there are enough clues to suggest that Hannah
was on their side. Hannah's friends such as the Rathbones freely
shared with her their opposition to the slave trade.[56] We have
only a few scraps that reveal Hannah's own views. In a letter
dated 1798 to William Rathbone she had written: 'Surely in
Ireland, in India and in Africa the English name must be for ever
odious – expressive of Injustice, Arrogance and Cruelty.'[57] This
reference to Africa could only be understood as shorthand for
the transatlantic trade in the people of that continent. But there
was also equivocation and Hannah still had to mix socially with
old family friends who were opponents of abolition. Historians
of the abolition movement from Clarkson onwards have tended
to dismiss the idea promoted by Currie and others that the
best solution would be a phased approach, an idea that had the
backing of Thomas Hodgson and probably a good many other
merchants known to Currie, and one that Hannah may well
have supported too.[58]

Hannah's ethical dilemma grew more acute after her marriage. At a period when women in Manchester in all levels of
society were joining campaigns and signing petitions in favour
of abolition, Hannah was constrained in expressing her own
views. The reason was that her husband Samuel was in line to
inherit his uncle's slave plantation in Dominica. There is no evidence that he had any sympathy with the abolitionist cause, and
her loyalty to him demanded her silence on the matter of slavery.

In 1791 Wilberforce's Bill was defeated, but the debate continued. The opprobrium experienced by slave owners was
aggravated after 1807 when the abolition of the Alantic slave

trade had recently been passed by Parliament. This must have caused Hannah considerable anguish, and there is just one piece of evidence that confirms this: a small scrap of paper with a handwritten quotation from Thomas Clarkson's *History of the Abolition of the Slave Trade* (1808), which was written in Hannah's hand. The quotation is from the end of a famous speech in which Bishop Horsley, an outspoken critic of the slave trade, refers to the eternal damnation awaiting those who produced arguments to defend it. Below this Hannah has written: 'some things one cannot resolve to utter from fear.'[59]

What Hannah meant by this seems clear. It is that for two decades, the fear of contradicting or compromising her husband had prevented her from objecting to the slave trade. Hannah appears to be admitting that being married to a man who was not only the heir to plantations but who tolerated slavery prevented her from speaking her own mind on the subject. Now she had realised that her tacit acceptance of slavery had been not merely unacceptable, but could lead to eternal damnation. Few of the painful debates and discussions in the Greg family have come to light, and it may well be that this scrap of evidence points to a deep and lasting scar, one that was too divisive to be discussed in the open. It was a reminder that the independence of mind of an educated woman was still constrained within a marriage.

So Hannah, who understood much about ethics, and was a believer in practical action to relieve distress and injustice, was fettered in her response to some of the great Enlightenment challenges of her time: the abolition of the transatlantic slave trade and the emancipation of slaves in North America. While many of her friends and contemporaries were vocal and vigorous campaigners for abolition and then emancipation, she was generally silent on this topic. We can only guess how much this may have hurt.

Hannah had learnt much on her return to Liverpool after her schooling in London. Her diary shows her pursuing literature, taste and ethics under the guidance of exceptionally gifted tutors. But she seems to have been little exposed to life's lessons, and was emotionally quite immature. Her aim was to acquire a sense of personal equilibrium, but Liverpool's violent rejection of the abolition campaign disturbed this process. Her world was also destabilised when she fell in love for the first time. The next phases of her life provided further experiences that made her into a mature woman: the painful early years of marriage and the finding of her vocation to teach and look after the poor. In many ways she still had a lot to learn.

Four

'The differing changes that await you':
courtship, marriage and Manchester family life in revolutionary times, 1789–98

Samuel Greg courts Hannah

Amid all the strands that made up Hannah's youthful diary, in its last few pages one theme eventually came to dominate: her increasingly close relationship with the young Manchester merchant Samuel Greg.

A young girl's diary might be expected to reveal feelings, hopes, fears and excitement, but Hannah's says remarkably little. This may be significant. The entries in the diary are usually brief and they simply record encounters. Some furtively refer to correspondence, which we assume to be with Samuel. Several entries, however, suggest a raised emotional level, of both happiness and often also of anger, for example when they miss meeting each other, or when they disagree. Finally, a day after the wedding, Hannah wakes up and records that she hardly knows this man whom she has married.

The diary reveals a degree of innocence about marriage and conventional wariness about men and their motives. Hannah was impatient with men's shallowness in society, and aspired to find a companion who would value her mind and her accomplishments. We do not know whether men were put off by Hannah's bookishness and appetite for learning, but she could sound as dismissive and arrogant as any teenager. She wrote what she thought: 'what a troop of shallow brained fellows the young Men of Liverpool were.'[1]

Long before she met Samuel Greg, Hannah wrote:

> Men I knew were in general, selfish and unreasonable and instead of being satisfied with and making the most of those excellencies a woman <u>had</u> they were apt to expect she should excel equally in everything – expecting from what their pride terms the weaker sex an exemption from even human infirmity when it becomes inconvenient to themselves – Tho' an Enthusiast on many subjects I am not a romantic Girl likely to be misled by fancy or absolutely blinded by passion, I may hope therefore not to marry anyone whose disposition will not suit me and from whom I may not reasonably expect an addition of happiness.[2]

A year later, she was quite suddenly swept off her feet. At times elated, at times impatient, she does not seem to have taken a great deal of effort to understand Samuel's nature and personality. It did not occur to her that he might not appreciate as much as she did a dip into Homer's *Iliad*. In terms of faith and charitable inclinations, she imagined him to be a man after her own heart, and was upset when these notions turned out to be groundless. The courtship seems to have been conducted partly though letters, some marked by arguments, disagreements and anxieties. So perhaps she was fashioning in her own mind an image of her betrothed, and getting ready to embark on a life with him based on a slender grasp of reality. Where reality intrudes on her dreams, the result can be seen in outbursts of temperament and frustrations with others or with herself.

The diary briefly records the start of Hannah's relationship with Samuel. On 8 November 1788, after spending September in Leicestershire and October in Buxton, Hannah set out alone for Manchester to stay with the family of Thomas Percival for the social season. There she was often in the company of old friends such as the Heywoods and the Scottish fustian manufacturer and Dissenter William Kennedy, with his daughter Rachel, who was a close friend of Dr Currie's.

On 12 November she noted: 'Supped at Mr Kennedy's – met Mr & Miss Greg – was much pleased with the latter and surprised I should never have heard of him before – sat by him all the evening.' Kennedy was probably a business associate of Greg's; Samuel Greg was looking after his unmarried sister Margaret, who normally lived with her widowed father in Belfast. She was two years older than Hannah.

Then at the assembly the next day, 'Mr & Mrs G Philips made their appearance. Miss J. P fainted away – great confusion.'[3] What happened next was a turning point: 'Engaged to dance with Mr T. Philips. Mr Greg came and desired Mr P would let him dance with me – had a very pleasant evening.'

Hannah next met Samuel and Margaret Greg a fortnight later among a large party at a conjuring show where the Italian virtuoso Signor Pinetti astonished his audiences with his 'Capital deceptions' and 'philosophical experiments'. A few days later Hannah was invited by Samuel's aunt, Mrs Hamilton, to join them for tea and supper. Samuel Greg called on Hannah a few days later, on 6 December. On 11 December Hannah went again to the assembly: 'and danced again with Mr Greg – very happy.'

Perhaps this marks the start of the attachment, for a few days later as she was leaving Manchester she records: ' – saw Mr G – had a note from him, and next day: Left Manchester with much regret.'

They wrote to each other, it seems, over the next two weeks, but did not avoid a misunderstanding – probably their first. On 30 December, after staying for a few days with the Rathbones at Greenbank, Hannah wrote: 'Came home – found Mr Greg had been at Liverpool – much mortified. Went to the Concert – very uncomfortable – a trial of temper ill-sustained.' This episode seems to have made Hannah realise that she was in love. On 5 January she records: 'Wrote to Mr G Manchester – and was much affected.' Then, at the end of the month, the diary records 'a long conversation with Miss Cropper' followed by some kind of emotional crisis. 'Long explanation in my room – was much distressed. Dr Currie supped with us and his Conversation raised me a little above those cares.'

For the next three months there is no mention in the diary of Samuel Greg, his sister Margaret, or any correspondence with them. During that time Hannah had recovered her spirits, and records going to concerts and assemblies, as well as enjoying the onset of spring and spending time with family and friends.

Then, in April 1789, she went to stay for a month in Manchester at the Kennedy's in the company of Miss Cropper. On the 23rd they saw the Gregs and in May there was a flurry of visiting friends in Manchester, suggesting that the attachment had been resumed, though the diary reveals very little. Perhaps Miss Cropper finally gave her blessing. In the next fortnight they met up at least nine times, going to the theatre and having meals with mutual friends.

Over the next month, Samuel Greg came frequently to Liverpool and met members of Hannah's mother's family who had come over from Chester. The betrothal of Hannah and Samuel was probably agreed at this time. In June, Samuel and Margaret stayed in Liverpool for a week. Then, when he was briefly ill, he was looked after by Hannah. They left on 24 June, and two days later he wrote a letter to Hannah, attempting an ardent and amorous tone to express his impatience to overcome her reluctance to set an early date for their marriage. Astutely, he refers to the verdant landscape of Quarry Bank as an inducement:

> Oh, how little justice my friends do me when they suppose me insensible to your merits, because my words are not loud in your

praise – my friends & yours all alike – abuse me – & still, I can only answer them with a smile … My delight is great in imagining future days, & the spot visited yesterday (QB) I regard as the seat of many promised Joys. I hope to see you more enthusiastically fond of it than of any places now dear to you … It appeared beautiful yet I saw it with a regret that your not being present can alone account for: many of its beauties are passing unseen by you. The weather & injury done the foliage by the late storm would almost delude me into a belief that winter was at hand had you not so strongly impressed it on my mind that two seasons must first past. Why will you insist on two lingering seasons intervening & why make me impatient of the duration of an autumn which you can so peculiarly bless – thus we might spend a few months free from the impertinence of a busy world & form our schemes of future life before winter invited a return to town …

… Be particular in the mention of your health I beg of you – mine is much better & I am indebted for it to you. Make my kindest compts to your mother & other friends & believe in the unalterable affection of

S Greg[4]

On 1 July, when she Hannah almost 23 years old, she sat for her portrait to be painted in miniature – possibly a further clue to the timing of the betrothal (see plate 3). Hannah records seeing Samuel on several occasions in Liverpool that month, once with his uncle Robert Hyde, but the course of true love did not always run smoothly. Hannah was due to go away with her family to Buxton for the summer months, and this forced absence may have been the cause of 'a very unhappy morning with S.G'.[5] A frequent, almost daily correspondence followed, as Hannah moved with her mother and aunt to stay with her sister at Grooby near Leicester. Only one of Hannah's letters survives: which is rather cool and formal. In it she hopes and expects that Samuel is attending Mosley Street Chapel, her preferred Dissenting chapel in Manchester. She chides him for being a poor correspondent and tries to arrange the training of a maid, presumably to attend her in her new married state in Manchester. She goes on to refer to arrangements for Samuel to stay with her sister at Caton, where he was planning some form of business collaboration with Hannah's brother-in-law Thomas Hodgson:

> I rejoice to hear of anything that is likely to prove an advantage to the Caton Mill. So many are made happy by Mr Hodgsons' success that it is most desirable indeed – they are so extensively useful, & so ready at all times to assist the unfortunate, & to help the widows and fatherless that it would be delightful to see them <u>rich</u>. I feel obliged by the interest you take in their affairs.

Hannah finally turns to domestic arrangements for the management of her new home in Manchester:

> Whenever you can spare the maid from Wilmslow, I shall be glad you will send her here any time after the middle of this week –. I wish to procure her some instruction in those things in wh she may not be completely accomplished – as I am finical about washing I want to try her performance that way … this week you find I shall be a poor Correspondent – but tho' I am silent why you should be so – your pen is much in my debt and you may shew yourself generous by taking this opportunity of repaying me – … but if you have any leisure it would be kind to shew me that you wish to <u>oblige</u> me. I hope you see Miss Kennedy often. Present my dear love to her. I remain your true friend H L.[6]

On 14 August she started her tour of the great sites of the Midlands, and was pleased to have Samuel join her on her return on the 19th, but on the 21st another tiff or misunderstanding is recorded: 'Mr G went to Leicester with Mr T.P. Was very unhappy all day – and Mr G hurt.' Samuel was no doubt on a business trip. He and John Pares left together a couple of days later.

In early September Hannah set off on her last sightseeing journey, this time to Burleigh House. Her autumn tour now took her to stay with her sister Elizabeth Hodgson at Caton in mid-September, passing by Derby en route to order a tea and breakfast set at the Derby china works, then picking up Samuel who joined her as far as Preston.

On 21 September Samuel came to stay, but on the 24th there was another 'long painful conversation with Mr G'. Hannah records a few days later, 'Sat with Mr Greg and read Paley'. If this is a reference to William Paley's *The Principles of Moral and Political Philosophy* published in 1785, then Samuel Greg must have been made fully aware of the serious and religious side of Hannah's character.

Hannah returned home to Liverpool in October, where she was busy with preparations for the wedding. These included an unsuccessful attempt to improve Samuel Greg's attendance at chapel. Hannah also tried to convince him of her views and those of Dr Yates about the roles and duties of the fortunate to those who needed their charity. It was an uphill task, one of many similar conversations that would follow:

> Sat up very late. Conversed with Mr G on the objects of Charity – thought he expected too much of the Poor and that more allowance ought to be made for their bills than for the more trivial faults of those who have the advantages of good Education and good Society.

On the eve of their wedding, rifts of misunderstanding still opened, illustrating that Samuel might not have shared all Hannah's enthusiasms, and yet he had the gift of making amends where there was a risk of discord or disappointment. October ended with the following entries:

> 30: Sat all morning with Mr G. Had a long affecting conversation with him and was made very happy.

31: Went to Everton. Disputed with SG about the *Iliad* – was vexed to be so warm about it and secretly vowed not to hold any Arguments on such sort of subjects when I was married. [By then the date had been fixed.]

Nov 1st: Mr G sat with me all morning – thought on the entrance of this month of the event that was to take place in its course and prayed that it might make both S.G. and myself both happier and better.

The next day, friends and family members started to gather round: Samuel's youngest brother Cunningham; Mr Hibbert, his Manchester business colleague; and William Pares, Hannah's brother-in-law who was an Anglican rector from Leicestershire. The financial arrangements and deeds were formally signed on 2 and 3 November.[7]

On 5 November, after the deed was signed and witnessed, there was a wedding breakfast provided by Mrs Arabella Nicholson at Toxteth Park amid snow and driving rain. On the 7th the cake was cut, and on the 8th, the couple went to chapel. (They could not be married there as Dissenters were still required to be married in the Anglican Church and according to the Anglican ritual.) Then on 9 November there was a large reception, and the couple appear to have stayed in Liverpool until 23 November.

The day before their departure to live in Samuel's large old house in King Street, Manchester, Dr Currie called in the evening '– gave me many charges as to health &c, and evinced the most friendly interest in my welfare'. Then Hannah records: 'Left Liverpool – my heart sinking within me.'

Samuel Greg's family background

Amid the wedding celebrations and in a moment of painful lucidity, it dawned on Hannah that she hardly really knew this man whom she was marrying. This is the way she put it to herself, writing her diary entry for 19 November:

> That day in the preceding year had never even heard of Mr Greg till in that evening had met him at Miss Kennedy's … Felt ashamed … at the short acquaintance … neither of us having any mutual <u>intimate</u> friend from whom we might acquire any previous knowledge of each other's habits, tastes and real character and never having seen each other till under the influence of mutual prepossession …

Samuel Greg had swept her off her feet, and she might well ask herself about his character and background.

Like the Lightbody family, he came from a line of merchants of lowland Scottish Presbyterian stock, initially devout, latterly enterprising. Samuel's father Thomas (1718–96) was an energetic and successful self-made merchant and ship owner who, in the mid-eighteenth century, played a leading part in the transformation of Belfast from a sleepy town into a major trading port. Thomas and his family belonged to the New Lights, which could be compared with the Rational Dissenters, in that they represented the more radical and intellectual wing of the Presbyterian denomination in Ireland. Thomas Greg traded with Jamaica and New York in linen, butter, salt meat, rum and passengers, making an additional fortune during the Seven Years' War by trading with the enemy.[8]

In 1742 Thomas Greg married Elizabeth, the eldest daughter of Samuel Hyde, establishing a connection with the Lancashire Hyde family's trading empire. Four brothers inherited it: Samuel Hyde and his brother prospered in Belfast in the mid-eighteenth century, while the other two brothers, Robert and Nathaniel, were established as merchants in Manchester, the former in partnership with Robert Hamilton, his brother-in-law.

Thomas Greg, by now a man of wealth and influence in Belfast, invested in an estate outside the town, a plantation in the West Indies, as well as land in the Catskill mountains in the province of New York. He speculated in mining and manufacturing ventures in Ireland, in docks and canals, with mixed success. He must have been bold and tough: by getting the local militia to bring in his harvest in 1771, he provoked the wrath of local farmers who attacked the barracks; three farmers were killed and in retaliation Thomas's house in Castle Street was threatened and his youngest brother's house in Belfast was burned and ransacked.

The Crown, however, recognised Thomas Greg's enterprise and contribution to the economy of Belfast and its region: in 1783 he was offered a baronetcy but refused it. Thomas and Elizabeth Greg had thirteen children. When the eldest boy, Thomas, was sent off to London in 1766 at the age of 15 to start his career in insurance, his younger brother Samuel was packed off with him. Although Samuel (who was born on 26 March 1758) was only 8 at the time, his parents may have been responding to a suggestion from his uncles, Robert and Nathaniel Hyde, in Manchester. They had no heir to take on their business and would naturally look for a nephew to take under their wing, and to be trained up to succeed them.

So Samuel lodged with the Hydes, probably in King Street above the shop in Manchester town centre, and was sent to school in York. Later, he had a gruelling experience as a border under Dr Parr at his school in Harrow. This may have strengthened his character, for he emerged determined to join the firm of Hyde & Co., brushing off Nathaniel's attempt to provide him with a living as a parson.[9]

In 1778 Samuel duly joined Hyde & Co., and was sent abroad to learn the business of a textile merchant, travelling widely in

Spain, Italy and Germany. Based at their King Street counting house, the Hydes were one of the leading textile firms in Manchester, contributing to the town's commercial growth and to its reputation as a dynamic trading centre. They had developed large markets at home and abroad, including in all probability goods that were shipped during this period on the triangular route via Liverpool to Africa, as part of the outbound cargoes that were exchanged for slaves.

Portraits of the Hydes show them as upright but somewhat colourless men who surely imparted to their protégé Samuel a spirit of correct business practice, reliability, integrity and trustworthiness. Robert Hyde died in 1782, the same year that Samuel had been made a partner. Robert Hyde Greg, Samuel's son, takes up the story:

> Nathaniel Hyde being given to occasional long fits of intoxication, almost immediately on his brother's death handed over the entire business to my father and a sub partner of the Hydes, John Middleton.
>
> 1782 – war with America ended: father made £12–13,000 on the rise in value of the stock, and this with a £10,000 legacy, £7,000 sale of reversion he launched into life.[10]

So, in 1782, Samuel, at the age of 22, found himself in control of a large company with branches all over Lancashire, Cheshire and the Midlands, and trading connections in the Americas and on the continent. He took on the Hydes' former home, warehouse and offices in King Street. This was a large site, probably covering more than an acre at the heart of the smartest residential area of Manchester.

Samuel quickly realised that customers were increasingly turning from linen to cotton. He saw how merchants were attracted by the pioneering example of Arkwright at Cromford, who was licensing his cotton-spinning machinery to manufacturers. They were building large water-powered mills, and the operation was initially so profitable that it was worth them submitting to the large licence fees demanded by Arkwright. John Pares' mill at Calver was started in 1778, the Strutts' mills at Milford and Belper not long after. Recalling those pioneering years in his old age, Samuel's son John wrote: 'At that time 1782/83 Manchester was intoxicated with the idea of cotton spinning, Samuel found a Mr Massey and posted about the country to find a spare water power.'[11] Massey was the vital technical expert with experience of manufacturing and of the cotton-spinning machinery. In 1783, they had found the place of their choice: a site on the River Bollin near the village of Styal, 1 mile north of Wilmslow and about 8 miles south of Manchester.

The land was leased from Lord Stamford and building started. Setting up this spinning enterprise cost Samuel £16,000 overall, a considerable part of his newly inherited fortune, and far more than he had originally intended. But his spirit of enterprise paid off. His manager had to recruit and train his workforce, and to provide the discipline of repetitive – yet safe and conscientious – work that was characteristic of mills powered by machinery, a business challenge that was new at that time. Quarry Bank Mill soon became known for efficient production of coarse cotton yarn, and within a matter of years was among the major cotton spinners. Samuel Greg was thinking about expansion. It was also a time to be thinking of marriage.

What did Hannah see in Samuel Greg?

Samuel had attractive qualities and was known for his 'rather easy and buoyant disposition'. His youngest son recalled:

> With the steady perseverance and tenacity of the Scottish character, he united the readier and more suppler faculties of the Irishman. He acted from instinct and with great courage … He was handsome in person, and his manner was singularly

polished and courteous. He had the genial sparkle that comes
from an ever ready sense of humour. [12] [See plate 5.]

According to the painter and naturalist John James Audubon's
journal, Samuel 'addresses his children in the most patriarchal
style I ever heard and with a kindness only equalled by my friends
at Green Bank'. He was demonstrative, if not always refined, 'yet
there is a bluntness in his speech at times.'[13]

He liked women. John Greg, his son, told the story of how
Samuel, at school in York, had 'amused himself' by shooting billets
doux though the window to pretty ladies across the street, for which
he was reprimanded, as also for squeezing his partners' hands at
dancing lessons. There is only one slender confirmation that he was
gallant in his relationship with Hannah: in a letter, she thanks him
for the woollen stockings that he sent her; describing with a rare
hint of suggestiveness, 'the cheering sensation of drawing on a pair
of such stockings after walking in wet feet over your eternal Farm'. [14]

Though no advocate of new roles for women either in political debate or in the public sphere, he valued and indeed came to
rely on his wife for her quality of judgement in many aspects of
his business and social life. Hannah's sister, Elizabeth Hodgson,
confirmed that Samuel was 'truly sensible of your Intellectual
Endowments'. Writing to his daughter Bessy in his old age,
Samuel reflected: 'always selfish, we throw the burthen on our
own shoulders, on those termed the weaker sex – but in truth in
all but muscular strength, yours is far superior.'[15]

Late in life in a moment of unaccustomed introspection and
sadness, he wrote to William Rathbone VI, his grandson, admitting that when in polite society with his wife and Hannah
Rathbone, he felt a lack of polish and self-confidence. While he
could not share Hannah's enthusiasm for the classics, he admired
her independent spirit, her inquisitive mind and her religious
vocation. The books that he liked having read to him on Sunday
evenings at home were not too serious, nor too flippant, certainly
not philosophical, poetic, profound nor too thought-provoking.

To judge by the letter he wrote while courting Hannah, describing the late summer scene at Quarry Bank Mill, he understood and shared her love of nature.[16]

It was probably due to Hannah's influence that he joined the Manchester Literary and Philosophical Society in 1790 soon after his marriage. As far as is known, he made no contribution to its debates, but he would have appreciated the liberal political views of many members at that time. Hannah's influence may also be detected in his election to join the first Committee of the Portico Library in 1810.

In the same way that Hannah tried to influence Samuel's views about religion and charity, she probably encouraged him to play an active role in the political causes dear to her heart, a sphere of activity reserved for men. Samuel became a campaigner for free trade and for peace, but like many men of action, he was probably impatient of committees. He was prepared to give his support to some of the important reforming movements of his day, but did not share his wife's 'enthusiasm' for the reform of the suffrage, nor for the wider toleration of Dissenters. Like other Dissenting business leaders in the 1790s, he argued for peace with France, a vital but by no means popular cause during the Napoleonic wars, and he consistently championed the liberalisation of trade, with strategies such as breaking the monopoly of the East India Company. He was prepared to stand up for this cause in Manchester in the early 1790s;[17] this was risky and he was suspected of sedition and investigated in a witch-hunt in 1794–95.

The Gregs were unable or unwilling to conceal their sympathies for the Irish, though they had to be careful when Samuel's radical and outspoken sister Jane came to live with them in King Street after the Irish Rebellion in 1798. Although later in life Samuel became more conservative, he was a critic of the cover-up of the Peterloo massacre. He was among the earliest backers of the *Manchester Guardian* – he owned shares in 1823 and was also one of the very few radicals of his generation who was active after Waterloo in the campaigns to liberalise trade and to reform political representation. As Archibald Prentice wrote about the formation of the 'small but determined band' of reformers who first met in 1815 in Richard Potter's warehouse, Samuel Greg was there with them at the inception of their reforming campaigns and he 'remained true to his early principles'.[18]

All of these views of society and political change would have appealed to Hannah. At a simple level, Hannah would have been pleased to meet a man of warm character who at the same time came from a similar background and with a business vocation similar to her father's. Had she been conscious of status (and few Liverpool women of her age and class would have been impervious to subtle social stratification), she might have recognised that Samuel was eminently respectable and that he was emerging into the first rank of Manchester society. He was well educated and well connected. He was ambitious and had already made the most of his good fortune by hard work. In a word, he was eligible.

She could discern a combination of conviviality and maturity; an enterprising streak, as well as clear-sighted discipline. He loved company, was a good host, entertaining and attentive to his guests. Informality suited him; he enjoyed letting his hair down when staying with his relatives in Ireland. He was down to earth, liking few things better than taking his family and guests tramping round his farm at Styal to admire his pedigree herd of cattle.[19] He had no desire to shine in smart society, nor ambition to parade his wealth or appear ostentatious.

In business Samuel could be an astute investor, shrewd rather than intuitive, considering steadily and often at some length the merits of the issues and personalities involved. He was one of the first shareholders in the Liverpool and Manchester railway and he invested judiciously in land in central Manchester. But as he grew older, the sense of initiative was replaced (as in so many) by doubts and resistance to laying out money speculatively. He consistently refused to buy from Lord Stamford the land on which Quarry Bank Mill stood, stubbornly insisting that it had been overvalued.

He embodied a quality he sought in his partners, business associates and sons: integrity. He regarded it as a key to success; the personal quality that earned respect, that enabled a business to prosper, credit to be advanced, and reputation to be gained. He put it like this: 'our greatest gratification is to deserve & possess the respect of those among whom we live & who can judge of our merits.'[20]

His interest in the personal quality of individuals enabled him to pick outstanding partners and associates, and to delegate to them. The ablest of these was Peter Ewart, one of the greatest mechanical engineers of his age. We might include Hannah herself among his close business associates: her mind and judgement were often consulted on business as well as on wider issues, and he relied on her to keep an eye on the business when he was away. He also had that quality so necessary among business leaders, a clarity of direction and an ability to express himself plainly. His letters are models of clear and economical expression.

While he directed a fast-growing and profitable business empire, he remained unostentatious, and in an age of unprecedented social mobility, he did not care to give up his home in central Manchester even though his contemporaries and neighbours had long moved away from what had become a commercial quarter. His son John recalled: 'I have heard my father say he lived 69 years in the King Street House which belonged to his Uncle Hyde.'[21]

Although a Dissenter and, through his wife's connections, close to a number of active abolitionists, Samuel's inheritance of a sugar plantation in Dominica in 1796 does not seem to have disturbed his equilibrium or reputation. (The Hillsborough Estate there, acquired by Samuel's uncle, John Greg, remained in the control of local managers and became the responsibility of his widow, Catherine, until her death in 1819.) The growing recognition that it was morally unpardonable to trade in slaves does not seem to have been discussed by him, although abolition was a popular public cause across Manchester. Indeed, some of his close associates such as the Hibberts were large and committed plantation owners, while his brother-in-law Thomas Hodgson was highly active in the Africa trade.

So Samuel was a man in a man's world, and there is little evidence of his sensitivity to Hannah's interest in ideas, or her growing desire to write and teach, to promote social reform or to have their daughters well educated. If Hannah had ever aspired to meet and marry a 'man of feeling', as did many of her contemporaries after reading Henry Mackenzie's famous novel, Samuel Greg's character did not match that model. He expected his wife to conform to conventions, to say nothing in public about politics, to limit her social work to her own community, and to say no more about the oppression of women in their relationships with men. In addition, Hannah was probably required to be silent on one of the great issues of her day, the abolition of slavery, an issue on which they probably had opposing views.

Although it was by no means a pre-arranged match, Hannah must have considered that Samuel was a good catch. For his part, Samuel may have admired her good nature as well as her mind, and of course her fortune. These points aside, there are numerous clues that Hannah was smitten.

A marital crisis and its resolution

The Gregs' marriage started on a spectacularly low note, with the interminable, jolting carriage ride from Liverpool to Manchester in appalling weather on a November evening in 1789. Hannah wrote in haste in her diary about her fatigue and dismay on arrival, feeling too wretched even to see her friends Fanny Percival and Rachel Kennedy:

23 [November 1789]: Left Liverpool – my heart sinking within me – my Cousin and me in our Chaise – Mr G and his brother on horseback.[22] Dined at Warrington and could not

persuade the Gentlemen to move after dinner till nearly dark and the road from Warrington to Manchester so very bad as to require 4 horses – we were 4½ hours upon it in the dark and in perpetual danger of being overturned – the extreme fatigue I had undergone in first finally leaving my dear home and then being mortified, disappointed, and terrified so overpowered me as to disable me from seeing Miss K and F. P. that evening – the only friends I had in Manchester.[23]

Worse was to follow. The next day, Hannah recorded with horror that she had overlooked some vital advice given by her older sister, on taking charge of the household:

The Chambermaid gave me warning saying that she thought there were servants enough in the house without my bringing in more (meaning my Maid who came with me) – I ought to have allowed her to lessen the number, but knowing she had lived there several years, dared not till I had spoken to her Master, who said he should be sorry to lose her and I had better keep good servants &c. My sister P's earnest advice then came to my remembrance and sunk deep into my heart viz: 'before I married not only to have the servants dismissed but the very house changed in which their Master had so long lived a Bachelor'.

Hannah was not only homesick; she was trapped in an alien household among staff who she was expected to manage but who seemed to have no wish to be managed by her. Although she and Samuel had previously discussed training a maid of her own, Hannah was quite unprepared for the trials ahead. They included formal receptions for all Samuel's uncles, aunts and cousins, as well as his business associates. Samuel's young sister Margaret was fortunately on hand to help entertain, and Rachel Kennedy helped explain the customs of the town. But Hannah was upset to see her own dear friends, and could hardly contain her emotions the morning after her arrival:

At 11o'ck Mr and Mrs B.A H.[24] called – and my eyes were so swelled that I dare not for some time go down and when I did, the sight of one who had been an old acquaintance at Liverpool from infancy again nearly overset me. Miss K and Miss F.P. called – not pleased at having been refused admittance the evening before and I dared not wholly explain the reason lest they should read my disturbed mind.

Tuesday: Mr G received Company. Miss K telling us how to follow the general custom – a long table in the Dining Room – covered with cold Meats, Turkey &c. a Great Bowl of Milk Punch &c, the Plum Cake and Chocolate on a side table – all very new to me – the room full of Gentlemen all morning. And the large Hall, over which there was no painted cloth, very dirty with so many feet out of the dirty streets.

Wednesday: My Cousin, Miss K and I sat up for Company – very formal – no Gentlemen – and me not even knowing the names when we heard them – should have been much embarrassed if Miss Kennedy had not been with us.

It is a sign of Hannah's dismay and disorientation that her diary entries at this point are in a hurried script, and omit any reference to the date or the month. Frequent underlinings also indicate how Hannah's poise and confidence were replaced by signs of anguish and at times desperation: ... 'Saty: Returned visits in Mr Hyde's Coach. Mr Greg's footman refused to go behind the coach – but was obliged by his Master.' It was a depressing and disturbing period. The servants at King Street were often impertinent: 'the Groom refused to bring in Coal – and was dismissed. I wished the footman had met the same return for repeated insolence.'

Samuel's uncles and other relations called and their hospitality had to be returned. Samuel was indebted to the Hydes for his good fortune, his education and his start in life. They were virtually his foster parents, but to the young Mrs Greg, the in-laws were numerous, demanding and critical, while the regular formal visits to the Hyde aunts and widows at Ardwick Hall every Monday were clearly a strain. The household, with its business premises, garden, stables and warehouse attached, must have seemed of a formidable size and complexity. Hannah's youngest daughter Ellen recalls her mother being 'engrossed with the work and cares of a large … household … under the surveillance of her husband and aunts, so strict and formal about all the conventionalisms of Society'.[25]

Hannah's ordeal continued and it was often hard for her to maintain her composure. She noted that Mrs Hamilton complained to her mother:

> … that I never called or seemed to care for Mr G's friends – a charge the <u>most</u> unjust that <u>could</u> have been found – for I should have pleased more had I <u>cared</u> less – my attempts being marred by the cruel consciousness of the <u>importance</u> of succeeding – one day she enquired when I had heard from my friends at Grooby – and on replying that all the family were now met there but me, which was very tantalizing to me, she very sharply observed 'I think you have no joy with us for you are always wishing to be somewhere else'. I retired as soon as I could – and always to depressing comparisons, and remembrances of the different treatment I had been accustomed to.

It was not long before the scales began to fall from her eyes, making her look at her new husband in a fresh light. The alarm was caused by Samuel being brought back from a cricket match in Lancashire by a well-known local Methodist preacher. Samuel was drunk, and unable to ride. Hannah recorded her dismay in her diary:

> … knowing <u>nothing</u> as to former habits &c … – tho' learning his character only from himself how <u>impossible</u> it seemed to me that I <u>could</u> be deceived. His kind sister only laughed at my distress – for she knew better.

It is easy to imagine Hannah's homesickness for her family and like-minded friends in Liverpool, which she still thought of as her true home. 'I seldom ever wrote home without having my eyes swelled with weeping, and did it as little as possible.' It only made it worse that this upset Samuel:

> Mr G displeased at finding me in tears over a letter home. I assured him I only wanted his kindness and approbation to make me easy and happy and should have it if he would judge & feel for himself but not if thro' others who did not know me enough.

Hannah had to come to terms with the reality of her situation and her surroundings. Her married status diminished her discretion, her freedom of action and thought. Her position as manager of the household was burdensome, exposed and lonely. This was to be a test of character for which her education and enlightened upbringing provided little preparation. Alas, the first months of her marriage showed how wise Anna Cropper had been, and how little Hannah had absorbed her advice. Her hopes that her diary would become a record enabling her to learn from advice and experience proved hollow, too.

Apart from the difficulties of marriage and home life in King Street, Hannah found it hard to come to terms with Manchester. She had often been there as a visitor, knew a number of the Dissenting community as steadfast friends, and had a supportive network around the new Mosley Street Chapel congregation. So why did she still compare the town unfavourably with Liverpool?

For reasons that will become clear, Hannah never learnt to love Manchester, but she did manage to overcome the emotional crisis at the start of her marriage. She was homesick, surrounded by insolent staff, and longing for the companionship of her Liverpool family and friends. Samuel had come home drunk. She was pregnant. What was she to do?

There was a possible answer: she had an elder married sister to support and guide her. As the youngest of the three, Hannah had relied on her sisters for advice on a wide range of topics, not least on what to expect in marriage. So she sought advice from her eldest sister, Elizabeth.

Characteristically, the first thing Hannah asked for was a book. Mrs Raffald, the well-known writer, teacher and caterer in Manchester and Cheshire had died in 1781 but her book, *The Experienced English Housekeeper*, first published in 1769 was still widely used not just for its recipes but also to instil domestic economy. Hannah also sought guidance on her rights as mistress of the household. Elizabeth's response was affectionate and tactful:

> I am sorry that you should have wanted Mrs Raffald – I luck-ily had Mrs Cole which I think a superior Compilation.[26] What a change diversity of situations makes? That a Cookery book should be the only one you should wish for – be not ashamed my dear Sister, nothing discriminates more justly the excellence of the understanding than adapting judiciously the studies and habits to the differing changes which await you –[27]

Elizabeth Lightbody had been married to Thomas Hodgson for almost ten years and they had five children. Now she seems to have had a real concern for her youngest sister, and while not claming any intellectual distinction herself, saw how Hannah's could become an impediment to the give and take that marriage requires. She went on to advise her to take up the reins and run the house, securing her husband's domestic comfort, rather than start by arguing. It is a subtly phrased word of sisterly advice:

> This my dear sister you wisely consider as the season when the seeds of domestic happiness are to be sown – & it is the season when thousands make shipwreck of it for ever –. It is a good rule … not to contradict their Husbands the first twelvemonth, relying upon it if they did so they wd never afterwards be in danger of it … yet I think a Wife has much to do besides passively to obey – & a course of conduct infinitely harder. Not to contradict a

husband, … yet it is merely a negative goodness – & various, nay increasing are the occasions in which active thoughtful minute Attentions are requisite on the part of a Wife – & from women with such powers as you possess from Nature and Education much may be expected – You have married a Man truly sensible of your Intellectual Endowments, & disposed to pay you all the respect & deference they entitle you to; on the other hand you are well acquainted with the right which Men possess from Custom & I may say from Nature too – of the superiority which all ages have acknowledged to be theirs – & therefore the season which is that for securing domestic happiness, is not that for deciding the different rights of the two parties – but for laying down a plan for the Management of Domestic affairs, for giving a Wife who comes into a strange Town & among servants who are strangers an opportunity gradually to assume the reins of governing. You have not one part of Management to exert & that very often the hardest of all, & that is to make home so pleasing to their husbands as to prevent them from spending a very large portion of their time absent from it –.

Elizabeth adds further advice to Hannah on the attainment of marital harmony, and ends the letter with commissions.

Within a short period, matters improved. Hannah still missed her circles of family and friends at Liverpool, but learned to cope with her household duties at King Street. She was probably accountable for the domestic management of the whole site, including counting house, warehouse and several cottages, as well as the large principal house. She was also becoming involved in the growing Greg textile business. She found it all onerous and time-consuming, and relations with Samuel's family remained stressful, but before long she mastered the art of managing the household to such an extent that she entertained the cream of Manchester's intelligentsia, the members of the Manchester Literary and Philosophical Society at her home after their meetings. But just as she was recovering her poise, the political upheavals of the time changed her whole world.

Stresses and strains of family life in Manchester in the 1790s

Manchester continued to present Hannah with challenges. As a visitor before her marriage, Hannah had stayed with the Percivals in their civilised home on the fringe of the metropolis, visited other smart households around the town, and enjoyed the company of the Dissenting circles that she knew. The swarming, crowded, dirty town centre was new to her and the company of its merchants and manufacturers less appealing. Manchester was a busy, prospering, expanding manufacturing town. 'The smoke and dirt on the approach to Manchester was abominable,' wrote a contemporary, 'Manchester is a dull, smoky, dirty town in a flat, from whence the black soot rises in clouds to overspread the surrounding country.'[28] While Liverpool was bounded by the estuary on one side and parkland or farmland surrounded the town centre, by 1790 Manchester's centre was ringed with factories and increasingly crowded areas of workers' housing. The unplanned growth in the periphery made the town centre even more crowded. The atmosphere there could be volatile and even threatening.

King Street had been a highly fashionable location, but it is unlikely that a fashion-conscious young woman from the new and smart environment of Bold Street in Liverpool would feel comfortable in a bachelor's forty-year-old Manchester town house. Outside the front door Hannah often confronted poverty, mud and squalor. Nor was there any charming, unspoilt countryside within walking distance.

Early in 1790 Hannah was pregnant and about to find her carefree youth replaced with the ever-present responsibilities of a family. None of her interests or pursuits, her reading and absorption in nature and art, had prepared her for these challenges. One light on the horizon was Hannah's feeling that the site of Samuel's mill at Quarry Bank could be a country refuge. Attracted by the romantic landscape of the beech-clad river valley, she had fallen for the place when Samuel took her there while courting her. Now looking at it from the perspective of her new home in central Manchester, she writes:

> The romantic beauty of Q.B. delighted me and the possibility of occasionally escaping from Manchester to such a place renewed my hopes, vivacity and sanguine disposition – which the constant rain, confinement and constraint &c of Manchester (very heavy on one <u>accustomed</u> to Country Air and high bred Society) had for some time wholly discouraged.[29]

Then a number of political events shattered the framework of many Dissenters' lives, and Manchester became a battleground where, for almost three decades, Dissenters lived under suspicion and even under the threat of persecution. Having enjoyed the companionship of a community of lively minds in Liverpool in a climate of optimism, Hannah found herself if not isolated, in Manchester, then ostracised in polite and conservative society, and at times fearful for the safety of her family as a result of their faith, as well as their Irish connections and sympathies. The story of how she came through this stressful period, bringing up a large family while Samuel managed to develop and extend his business empire, is all the more remarkable.

Reform and repression

In the last two decades of the eighteenth century, cotton textile manufacturing was being transformed. From the 1780s, following the example of Arkwright, there was scope to make heady returns by investing in the new water-powered spinning machinery, which was almost invariably located in mills in river valleys in the countryside. By 1790, however, the first mills to be powered by steam engines were erected in towns, where there was a ready supply of labour; this different revolution was to have profound effects on urban life and work.

The scale of the workforce demanded by the steam-powered mills was a new phenomenon. It provided a livelihood for workers who were often drawn in from the surrounding countryside, but this quickly provoked problems of urban overcrowding, which in turn led to dangerous epidemics.

This was further compounded when trade cycles resulted in slumps when workers were laid off; poverty, starvation and unrest ensued – all on a scale that was unprecedented. The authorities recognised the threats to social order but were ill-equipped to provide solutions, and as the population and manufacturing importance of the town grew, it became apparent that its lack of political representation was a national scandal.

Meanwhile in 1790 Thomas Percival and his Dissenting friends at the Literary and Philosophical Society were actively engaged in renewed efforts to remove the impediments faced by Dissenters, following the failed attempt in 1787 to overturn the Test and Corporation Acts. James Currie described the feelings of Dissenters at this time:

> The French Revolution proclaimed universal freedom of conscience to all sects, foreigners as well as natives. Could it be long endured in England, that a large body of the most industrious and enlightened of the people should have privileges offered them in a foreign … country, which were denied them in their native soil?[30]

Currie wrote to Hannah on this issue and, perhaps inspired by Hannah, Samuel Greg became a member of the Literary and Philosophical Society and an active supporter of reforming and mercantile pressure groups. It was provocative of Currie to refer to France as a model, as revolutionaries in France were already seen as a threat by the British establishment. This was the start of a long period when Hannah and Samuel, along with many Dissenters across Britain, and in Manchester in particular, were met with suspicion, rancour and at times outright hostility.

In October 1790 the Manchester Constitutional Society was founded with the aim of promoting constitutional reform. The reformers were united in their support for the French Revolution and determined to defend civil rights and to promote parliamentary reform. Among the prominent figures supporting the new society were merchants and manufacturers, including many leading Dissenters and radicals. They were now joined by their mutual friend, Samuel Greg.[31]

Opponents of the Dissenters were quick to question their loyalty to the British Crown and State. Government propaganda made much of external threats and supported the formation of loyalist Church and King societies set up in north-west England. Attitudes, however, remained polarised and clashes soon developed between radicals and loyalists, as the government classified Dissenters as Jacobins. Following a loyalist public meeting in St Anne's Square on the birthday of George III on 4 June 1792, a mob attacked Cross Street and Mosley Street chapels. As the atmosphere of suspicion developed, the fear of sedition spread across Manchester. Witch-hunts gripped the town.[32]

This was an uncomfortable time for the Gregs, several of whose friends, such as the Rathbones, had been enthusiastic supporters of the early stages of the French Revolution. But then, in the summer of 1792, the revolution in France was transformed into a regime of terror and the September massacres followed. As events there became ever more violent, the minority in Manchester favouring peace and reform came under increasing attack, while the local press stirred up patriotic feelings.[33]

As hunger and poverty increased, so too did the violence of the populace. Provoked by a government that feared internal disloyalty, Britain was entering a period of irrational, polarised and sometimes violent internecine conflict, in which Dissenters were frequently the object of attack. Manchester was one of the areas where these attacks were the most unpleasant, and the Gregs were caught up in them.

By the end of 1793 it was generally understood that the private letters of suspects were being opened. The radical and reforming elements of the Manchester Lit & Phil came under suspicion, and it started to drop all aims or publications associated with reform, focusing instead upon scientific and economic topics. In Manchester, local persecution was led by the Tories' branch of the Society to put down Levellers. They identified, took away and examined in secret thirty-four suspects. Thirteen of these were members of the Manchester Lit & Phil and, inevitably, many were members of the two main Dissenting chapels.[34] Samuel Greg was caught in this sweep and he, too, was interrogated. It must have been alarming for him and terrifying for Hannah. It was no comfort to provincial reform groups that an Act was passed to suspend habeas corpus.

The climate of suspicion in Manchester seems to have cut off the Gregs from many of their former friends. Feeling ostracised there, Hannah still missed her circles of stimulating friends in Liverpool. She wrote of her perception that in Manchester, unlike Liverpool, she had to watch with extreme care what she said and to whom she spoke, complaining about 'the want of Candour, Charity and Trust in the Society which turned me back (as it always does) to the Remembrance of those friends and that society where they all abounded'.[35] She corresponded with Currie and the Rathbones, and took opportunities when she could to visit Liverpool. She wrote to William Rathbone of her continuing spirit of 'Enthusiasm', regretting the climate of 'prudence, coldness and selfishness' that she detected in Manchester. This suggests that a number of Hannah's liberal Manchester friends had by then detached themselves from their earlier ardour for reform and, in the light of the French Revolution and its atrocities, were adapting to a more pragmatic view of the future. Hurtfully, they disassociated themselves from Samuel and Hannah too.

As the political situation in France deteriorated, the position of the Dissenters and radicals in Manchester and Liverpool became exposed and increasingly uncomfortable. Abandoning their agenda for reforms, the Manchester Dissenters were accused of pusillanimity.[36] The uncomfortable truth is that the Manchester Dissenting elite were often only lukewarm supporters of universal rights, and stood away from the increasingly vocal masses of starving, unemployed and disillusioned workers, a proletariat that the more radical leaders saw as potentially powerful allies.

From the mid-1790s the Gregs would have been wise to keep a low profile, but the future of Ireland concerned them greatly and, at further personal cost, they became involved. Samuel and Hannah visited Ireland in the summer of 1794 so that Hannah could meet Samuel's extensive family and enjoy a break from the tensions of life in Manchester, as well as a tonic, as she had been ill. She reported her pleasure in:

> seeing Mr S G such a different Being to what he left home, he looks twenty years younger and in such delight from morning to night … and I am pleased to see Mr G proud of his own children even among those he has been accustomed to consider as Standards.[37]

But Hannah was also unsettled by the condition of the poor in that country and blamed the British government: 'one must be infected with indignation when in contact with this oppressed and engaging people'.[38] Her father-in-law and especially Samuel's radical sister, Jane, would have left her in no doubt that the cause of Ireland's problems was the decades of oppression at the hands of the British. It was probably after her return that she wrote:

> Certain will be the day of retribution – the crimes of this country and the crimes of old France are crying out and will be visited … to be Irish has always been sufficient to make anything obnoxious to the English Government.[39]

Hannah's friends James Currie and William Rathbone had strong and intelligent sympathy for the Irish and it is likely that Hannah's views were influenced by them as well as by her husband Samuel and his Belfast relations. Currie, asked by Jane Greg for his view of the future of Ireland, wrote to Hannah: 'Ireland is kept under by the sword, and by the sword only can her bonds be cut asunder.'[40] At this time in Manchester there was violent prejudice against the Irish, who were seen as disloyal immigrants seeking work. Hannah was aware of the strength of anti-Irish feeling, quoting a magistrate who told her 'he thinks it very well the Irish all inhabit one quarter (about Newton Lane) or else they would be murdered'. She knew that Samuel was considered as the most senior representative of the Irish nation then living in the town, which was a dangerous distinction.

On Hannah's visit to Ireland in 1794 she met keen reformers such as Samuel's sister Jane and Lady Londonderry; they had inspired her feelings in favour of a more liberal regime for all Irish. In spite of the isolation and risk, Hannah supported the Society of United Irishmen in their romantic hopes for an Ireland where Catholics, Protestants and Dissenters would be tolerated and the country united in freedom from oppressive government from England. In the summer of 1797 she sent William Rathbone an Irish pamphlet promoting a united Ireland: *The Appeal of the people of Ulster to their countrymen*. This was risky, as were her frank comments on recent food riots in Stockport. Currie heard of this and feared that, as with this own circle in Liverpool, her letters were being intercepted. He was horrified and advised her to be a great deal more prudent.

Support for the Irish was deeply embedded in the Greg household. Hannah was incensed at the increasing anti-Catholic and anti-Jacobin fervour in Manchester at this period. Individuals were being persecuted and, in April 1798, she wrote to Hannah Rathbone of her anxiety 'for one friend and acquaintance and another being taken up in the next street', and of her relief that a mutual friend had been released from prison. More astonishingly, she ignored the advice of Currie and William Rathbone to be more prudent in what she wrote. Writing to Hannah Rathbone, she revealed the identity of an *agent provocateur* and spy in their midst. This was Robert Gray, a cotton manufacturer who had infiltrated the United Englishmen and was employed as an informer by the Manchester magistrate. She explained that he provoked a meeting of a radical group so that he could report seditious behaviour and blame ensuing violence on the 'Jacobins'.

This story confirms that Hannah's courageous radical convictions remained unaltered. It also demonstrates that, in spite of her protestations to the contrary, she would communicate her firm views on politics. By now her dismay was very clear:

> Surely in Ireland, in India and in Africa the English name must be for ever odious – expressive of injustice, arrogance and cruelty … Let we mothers … endeavour to fortify our children for the rough scenes through which they must pass.[41]

Though aware of the risk of being associated with the Gregs' Irish connections, Hannah was not deterred even when there was civil unrest in the town centre, as she later recalled to her married daughter Bessy: 'with regard to personal safety nor was I much given to it [alarm] in some of the more serious situations of the sort even in Manctr when the populace have been in the next street.'[42]

Meanwhile in Belfast, Samuel's sister Jane, already well known as an outspoken radical and friend of several leading British and Irish radicals, was playing a leading role in a number of dissident female societies and was prominent in the United Irishwomen's organisation established in Ulster from 1796.[43] She was one of a group of educated and socially prominent women who, it was claimed, used their charms and connections secretly to convey messages vital for the United Irishmen's cause. But the post was being regularly intercepted and Jane was implicated when, in

May 1797, the Belfast postmaster reported her activities. Jane's father, Thomas, successfully protested her innocence, and spirited her out of the country to lodge with Samuel and Hannah in Manchester. Consequently, at the very time when hostility to the Irish was intensifying prior to the 1798 rebellion, Jane Greg, a rebel if not an outlaw, was being harboured secretly by the Gregs in Manchester.

Jane's outspoken nature can only have increased the risk to the Greg household. Further, she had brought with her compromising letters showing that Lady Londonderry, the wife of the Chief Secretary in Belfast, was in strong but secret sympathy with the rebels.[44] So the Gregs in Manchester, by sheltering a voluble and committed Irish rebel, incurred a real risk that all of them could be arrested for sedition.

According to Hannah's daughter, Ellen:

> They were anxious times then … they had feared at one time domiciliary visits; for my father was the only Irish gentleman in the town, and his sister Jane had been obliged to leave Ireland, being a friend of Lady Londonderry and her letters might bring suspicion upon him. Invasion too was feared, and my mother kept all ready for flight along with her children.[45]

The Irish Rebellion exploded on 23 May when rebels attacked Dublin. It came as a surprise to Hannah, as she later recounted:

> … for a few weeks before the Rebellion of 1798 broke out I was always writing as you do now to our friends in Ireland to enquire the truth of such & such reports, and their answer was, even within the last week that the reports were quite false and they never in greater tranquillity – when the mine exploded.[46]

Barely a month later, the uprising was put down with widely reported cruelty; the following year Ireland was put under martial law and, in 1800, subject to the Act of Union. These events and the Napoleonic war caused widespread fear and further repression, bringing down the curtain on the decades of optimism among Hannah's circle of enlightened friends. But Hannah was resilient: she wrote to William Rathbone 'we will hold fast our <u>Enthusiasm</u> whatever betide and I believe it is at least one means of holding fast our <u>Integrity</u>.'[47] As the pressure on the Greg household continued, the prospect of living at Quarry Bank near the peaceful village of Styal must have had a particularly strong appeal to Hannah.

Family responsibilities and concerns

With the stress of life in Manchester, the first ten years of Hannah's time there were taxing enough but, in addition, she had borne eight children by the time she was 34. At the same time Samuel's business grew, but managing it was increasingly fraught with risk. Hannah, maturing fast as a wife and mother, was also becoming the confidante and support for her husband in his business. She had been aware and indeed proud of the professional standing of merchants since her youth, when her father, uncles and cousins were among the merchant elite of Liverpool, and she probably knew something of the mercantile world, its risks and procedures, long before she married Samuel. She applied her mind to the issues that he had to address, and seems to have acted partly privately as a sleeping partner, partly as secretary and amanuensis. Ellen, her youngest daughter, recalled: 'My mother was cognisant of all my father's affairs and would not have allowed any to be neglected.' She was 'always ready to help my father, or at a moment's notice to accompany him'.[48] She was entrusted to buy raw cotton and to hold the fort while Samuel was away.[49] Writing to Hannah Rathbone on 18 December 1792, she inserted Samuel's business brief between her own personal news and greetings: 'Mr Greg having desired me to talk to (Mr R) about the East India business I will now say what I have to say about it which I will thank you to give him.'[50] She ends this business brief for William Rathbone, writing 'I believe I have now done as a Woman of Business', before ending the letter with a note about turning to a new book of poems by her London cousin, Samuel Rogers.

The early 1790s were vital years for the textile business that Samuel was investing in. He had been a pioneer importer of American-grown cotton. It was said that the first consignment of four bales and three bags was imported by the Rathbones for use at Quarry Bank Mill in 1784 (and that Hannah frequently wore a neckerchief made from this cotton). In the following years, the Rathbones developed this trade, which soon became of exceptional importance to Liverpool and indeed the whole north-west of England. But trade fluctuated: 1789–93 were good years for the cotton trade, but European markets were affected by the wars of the next twenty years. There was a banking crisis in 1793, and relations between textile leaders and their workforce were coloured by increasing concerns that mechanisation threatened the livelihood of thousands of handloom weavers in the region.

Among all her other concerns, Hannah experienced a family tragedy when her eldest sister, Elizabeth, died unexpectedly on 30 November 1795, at the age of 37. The cause seems to have been diphtheria. This was a tragic loss, as she left seven children for the elderly widower Thomas to look after. The youngest was barely a year old.

Surviving letters paint a harrowing picture. There had been a worrying premonition. In the spring of 1792 Elizabeth had felt some pain or constriction in her throat and, in her anxiety, drafted a farewell letter to her children. It remained unfinished, as though Elizabeth broke off at a point when she was overcome:

> I have had reason for some days past to think that the disorder in my throat would soon cut me off from the discharge of Maternal duties. I therefore now in a hasty manner shall address a few requests to my Children …

> You my Eliza and Isaac have already given proofs of your deserving the Care already bestowed upon you, ... Your affectionate behaviour ... brings tears into my eyes & makes me long for the tender farewell. Whether I may ever see you again is known only to God but if I do not let my ...[51]

Elizabeth recovered and the family moved to Mount Pleasant on the fringe of Liverpool's town centre, where she established a happy house. The health of her children was a matter of constant concern, but when a diphtheria epidemic hit Liverpool in the winter of 1795/96, Elizabeth succumbed to it. Her younger sister Agnes was heartbroken and wrote from Leicester to her mother, via Hannah, who added her own note. The two elder sisters were near each other in age, were married in the same year and obviously had been the closest of companions since their youth. Agnes planned to come from Leicester to Liverpool for the funeral and to comfort her bereaved mother. She remained worried, not least as Thomas, the youngest of Elizabeth's children was also infected, although apparently not in danger: 'We rejoice that little Thos is likely to be spared.'

Hannah added this note to her mother on the same letter:

> My dear Mother, Yr account of Thomas is truly distressing – how strange so young a child should sustain so cruel a disorder so long – his constitution must have been very strong – Think, my dear Mother, of the importance of your own life not only to your remaining children but to the children of our beloved Sister who would have thought herself happy in leaving them in your care. We are now a small family, we must draw still closer together and each become more dependent on the others.[52]

A few days later, Hannah forwarded to Agnes a grim letter from their mother in Liverpool, with a note to say: 'I am grieved to forward you such a melancholy letter – the poor infant's sufferings seem to have been protracted beyond what one could imagine even a strong person to have borne.'

This is the melancholy letter from the distraught grandmother Elizabeth Lightbody:

> be assured we use all precautions, & we commonly see those that are useful, providence takes care of – or what would come of physicians &c – we take bark & wine & burn gunpowder & sprinkle vinegar …
>
> I wrote the above this morning, tis evening and my dear child's short Life draws near a close; may his sufferings (which seem to have been prolonged four days by great care) be closed soon & he have an easy passage to the Bosom of his father & his God yrs EL.

> Friday
> I shall now resume my melancholy narrative. The Dear Infant continued much the same … but was weaker every time til almost one he ceased to breathe … it was a painful night indeed … I beg my dear children will not think of coming till not only our part but the whole town is more healthy … Never was parent blessed with three such Daughters, … your loving m'r EL.[53]

Elizabeth Lightbody was probably the one to feel most pain at the loss of her eldest daughter, and even though lame and feeling her age (she was then 60 years old), she saw it as her task to care for the motherless grandchildren. There was a family meeting in Manchester in December and it seems that Hannah suggested some scheme, probably to help ensure the Hodgson children were looked after by the Pares and Greg families, especially in the school holidays.[54] From then on, Hannah certainly acted as a godmother to Elizabeth's children.

Hannah was also feeling the increasing political pressure affecting Samuel. Years later, in a letter to her friend Mrs Rathbone, she recalled:

> ... one of the bitterest passages of my life – when in the midst
> of similar alarms from an <u>opposite</u> cause tho' resembling the
> Birmingham Riots when your Father attended meetings and was in
> the most violent & daily agitations, my poor sister Hodgson died –[55]

A fine portrait of Hannah was probably painted at this period, when she was about 30 years old (see plate 4). Here the vivacity of youth is replaced by grace and poise, while the gaze is still discerning: it shows a young woman who is both alert and mature, a character capable of unwavering determination.[56]

Recurring illnesses from about this time affected Hannah at intervals, amid childbearing. Although she had a governess to help look after the children, the responsibility for the family and the house was a considerable burden. Hannah looked increasingly to Liverpool visits to recuperate. Though she had mastered the art of household management, she found the responsibilities time consuming and physically arduous:

> Life in Manchester ... had become a very serious thing ... hard
> work, painful illnesses etc to me they are the duty of my station.
> Except my regular letters to my one sister, I never sit down to
> write but on business; and except to write or with company, of
> which we have enough (far, far too much), seldom sit down at all.
>
> I am enclosed in a busy noisy town amidst employments so
> pressing and unmitigated that my nerves & my strength had nearly
> sunk under them and a week ago I concluded I should have been
> obliged to go to Liverpool to recover my natural state.[57]

She also found herself isolated in Manchester when mutual suspicion replaced free discourse among friends. Years later she recalled: 'Society was destroyed after the French Revolution at Mancr and wholly so after the Irish Rebellion.'[58] Among radicals in Liverpool she did not need to be guarded in conversation, whereas in Manchester, if a group of Dissenters and radicals came together, there was probably a risk that this would be reported to the authorities. So she missed the freedom that she had found in Liverpool society, where she felt she belonged, as well as the stimulating company of family and friends there, and particularly the easy access to the surrounding countryside. She was also returning to the question that she had posed in her diary several years earlier: given capable minds, what might women *do*? Her household duties, child bearing and the business and social round were not in themselves fulfilling:

> In youth I was fond of reading books that required deep attention and of having my critical faculties exercised to their full speed − then came the dark ages − those middle years when household cares − bearing, feeding, clothing, teaching young children brought me down from the skies.[59]

Hannah probably continued with her charitable work, helping the poor and providing anonymous donations to good causes, but she did not join any of the public women's committees then starting up in Manchester, fighting (amongst other things) for the abolition of slavery.

Although burdened with family and household responsibilities, and with her health at times fragile, Hannah craved some activity that was more mentally stimulating and rewarding, confessing to Hannah Rathbone at about this time following a visit to Liverpool:

> I want … a little <u>mental</u> medicine and there is something in that place that gives animation and speeds a sort of circulation though my whole system. I shake off there what Dr Johnson calls 'the dust of life' (and I think there is more of that dust, as well as all other dirt and dust in Manchester than anywhere else).[60]

Two projects formed in her mind, both encouraged from the start by the Rathbones, who were concerned for her safety as well as for her health. The first was to establish a family home at Quarry Bank. Hannah Rathbone might have reminded her of a conversation in 1787, when it was Hannah Greg who had urged her to establish a home in the countryside in Toxteth Park. Hannah, though then barely out of school, argued that 'a Wife has scarce a right to keep her husband in ignorance of what is necessary to her comfort'.[61]

There was a tradition that the Gregs spent some of each summer renting rooms in Oak Farm in the village of Styal, but it was not until July 1798 that Samuel agreed to provide a family home of their own nearby. Hannah reported to Mrs Rathbone:

> I look forward to being less in the town (which of late has become almost insupportable to me) as Mr G seems to intend seriously building 3 or 4 rooms in the Country this year – which will enable me to keep my family about me all summer.[62]

The Rathbones warmly supported this project and frequently asked about progress. They were right to anticipate that this would be a beneficial transformation for Hannah, her family and for her health and peace of mind.[63]

There was also a second project conceived at this time, for which William Rathbone probably deserves some of the credit. Hannah had occasionally written to him of the frustrations of being a woman, and of her regret that, being married, she might not be able to use her mind and energies in a way that a man could. William recognised that Hannah probably had a serious vocation and the ability to do something about it. 'When you were last at Liverpool,' wrote William, 'you appeared so much out of health and so much disposed to gloomy impressions ... I promised it should not be long before you heard from me.'[64]

His perception was penetrating:

> I sometimes figure to myself how you would have been distinguished and mankind benefited if the fates had decreed you to

have been a female Preacher, and who will say that this may not yet be the character for which you are destined? The genius of inspiration always hovers over you ...[65]

Hannah regarded it as inequitable that men alone could claim the qualities of, for example, courage or self-possession; women, being born with equal potential, should be entitled and recognised accordingly:

If I had, I believe, your description of my rough chin and hoarse voice, it could hardly deter me from exercising it if with that chin and voice I could assume masculine qualities and virtues, with their enviable properties (and exemptions), courage, independence, self possession, talents, dignity ... ![66]

William responded with characteristically excessive support:

Whether for instance <u>you</u>, when you wish to be unfettered by the common offices, cares & employments that form a Woman's province ...

When you think that if you were a man, how much easier and pleasanter it would be to realize the perfection of our nature and ... to be useful on a more enlarged scale & to extend to thousands the energies of that benevolence which appears to you to be chiefly limited to the exercise of domestic duties.[67]

Hannah was firm and clear in her beliefs, but was not inclined to be strident in expressing them or in promoting them to others. But William Rathbone had faith in her and persevered, and in early 1798 he put forward a project probably related to the education of the apprentice children at Quarry Bank. In their letters they refer to a new 'scheme':

I rejoice with you in the successful advancement of your valuable scheme which ... will be conducive to the happiness and comfort of those primarily intended to be served. And to the satisfaction and improvement of the benevolent friends to the institution who may join their labours and influence to yours[68]

What was the scheme, and what was the institution? The clue is in an undated letter to William from Hannah:

You kindly wish, I know, to engage me in something that may refresh and invigorate my mind, may prove some counterpoise to the busy worldly harassing occupations that now often overpower me … My expectations respecting my little book are really so moderate … and my utmost hope has been to supply what to my immediate experience is a want, and were it even to have been published, as well as printed, my ambition would have been more than gratified to have seen it in the use of schools, and to have ranked with some of the Editors of 'Reading made easy'.[69]

The scheme – or a major part of it – was to be a book, addressing the education of the mill children. This was a project that Hannah could undertake from her new base at Quarry Bank; it implied that Hannah was already interested or involved with the apprentices and other mill children. A catalyst for this new interest was undoubtedly the time and trouble she had been taking over the education of her own growing brood: Bessy, the eldest, was by then a precocious 9 year old.

In the first ten years of her marriage, the world in which Hannah had grown up had changed dramatically. She had come a long way from the optimistic climate in her circles in Liverpool, as confidence in human progress, led by reason, could hardly survive the terrifying phases of the French Revolution; the breakdown of civil society in Ireland and in her own neighbourhood in central Manchester were also deeply disturbing. The demise of the intellectual and liberal reputation of the Manchester Lit & Phil was an example of the disintegrating vision of an ever-expanding Enlightenment;

even more ominous was the threat of the potentially violent rabble that took to the streets in pursuit of their grievances. Rational Dissenters still occupied the moral high ground, but had not so far demonstrated that they caught the imagination of the working classes, nor shown any inclination to do so.

All these experiences, as well as marriage and motherhood, had made Hannah more mature. She retained her positive Dissenting faith, a liberal outlook and an interest in political reform, but for the sake of her children she would hope to spend part of the year in her new home at Quarry Bank, where she would further cultivate her mind, and focus her uncommon abilities and fervent faith to educate those around her employed at the mill.

Saddened by the demise of the enlightened spirit that illuminated her social relationships before the French Revolution, she had also decided to use her well-furnished mind and her remaining contacts to secure for her children an education in her faith, in her love of literature and the arts, in business, and in the polish of her circle. She would pursue, for the first time, her new vocation as a writer, promoting her principles and ideals.

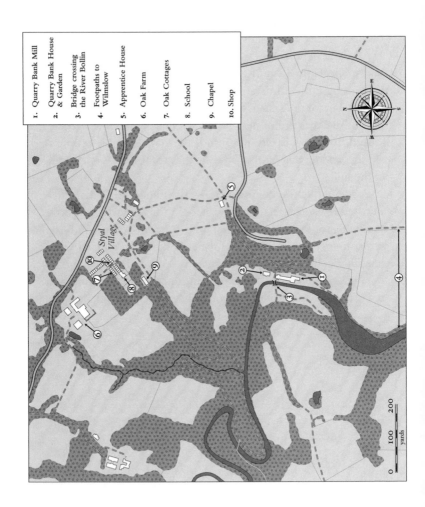

1. Quarry Bank Mill
2. Quarry Bank House & Garden
3. Bridge crossing the River Bollin
4. Footpaths to Wilmslow
5. Apprentice House
6. Oak Farm
7. Oak Cottages
8. School
9. Chapel
10. Shop

Styal Village

0   100   200

yards

2 Map showing the River Bollin flowing north-west, Quarry Bank House and mill near the centre, and the factory community of Styal to the north.

Five

'The diffusion of knowledge and morals':
Hannah as teacher and preacher, 1798–1810

A decade of war and social conflict

The years between 1798 and 1810 were demanding times for both patriots and reformers in north-west England. The shadow of Napoleon and the threat of invasion coloured the daily lives of middle-class families no less than those of the increasing numbers of poor workers who flocked into Manchester and Liverpool looking for food and work.

It was a period of tension and disappointment for many Dissenters, whose Enlightenment aspirations for a fairer and better world seemed shattered in the wake of the French Revolution. The impetus for reform was set back decades, while patriotism, the defence of the realm and the support for the Anglican Church were commitments required of all British citizens. The government seemed unable to distinguish the rational reform proposals put out by Dissenters from the radical views that were capturing the attention of the masses. To the government, all were dangerous, destabilising and disloyal. Petitioning was still an option for reformers, but the government feared the power of mobs; riots were increasingly frequent means of making a political point. When starvation and epidemics threatened, as they frequently did in the north-west in the early years of the nineteenth century, mobs were seen and heard clamouring for action, relief and remedies. Yet there were moments of hope in this gloomy decade, such as the Whig election victory of 1806, when William Roscoe was elected as a Member of Parliament for Liverpool.

In Manchester, the Greg family were closely affected by many of the political issues. While fears about invasion fluctuated and then waned, the powers of the mob continued to cause the authorities anxiety. To add to their woes, fourteen of the harvests between 1793 and 1814 were poor. Trading conditions were also tight at times, leading to economic crises and rioting in the winters of 1799/1800, 1800/01 and 1811/12. A consequence of the Napoleonic wars was periods of lengthy unemployment and extreme poverty among thousands of mill workers in the north-west.

While local government seemed incapable of addressing this major problem, towns such as Manchester were at risk of being controlled by either the mob or by the militia. On several occasions food riots brought these towns to the edge of civil disorder.

These events led to a determined attempt by a small group of young liberal merchants and business people to address the risk of ever-increasing social unrest, win back control of town affairs, and address the social problems of the day. They were interested in fairer representation, social reform, free trade, education, public health and welfare, and the reform of the Corn Laws, imposed in 1815. The Gregs, whose commitment to their liberal values remained undimmed though the years of attrition, were from the start closely associated with this 'small but determined band' who in time became influential as the leading exponents of Manchester liberalism and free trade.

While Hannah was immersed in the care of a large and grow-ing family, she observed these developments and remained determined to sustain her vision for a better society. Though pessimistic about improvements in her own lifetime, she looked to the next generation and worked on three practical strategies. The first was to take a detailed interest in the development of her children's minds and characters. The second was to assist in a practical way in the development of the mill children at Quarry Bank, so that, in addition to their role as workers in the mill, they would learn skills and acquire the ability to lead a decent life. Finally, she aimed to influence a wider audience with her ideas: by writing, by inspiring others, and by being a successful and influential hostess, cultivating a wide range of men of letters.

Establishing the family home at Quarry Bank

In 1796, after Peter Ewart, the noted millwright and engi-neer, joined Samuel Greg as a partner, a project was started to enlarge the mill and increase its production capacity. To achieve this, Greg had to plan, finance and construct an extension to the building, doubling its length and erecting an additional storey, as well as a weir, a new mill pool and a second mill wheel. These were complete by 1801 (though the children observed that this spoilt their swimming for a season: 'They have begun the new Weir by the cave as a preparation for the grand lake, all that sweet walk is now a scene of busi-ness, there is no bathing in the cut.').[1]

Quarry Bank Mill continued to prosper, even during the period of the Napoleonic wars, but the side of Greg's mer-chant business that managed handloom weaving operations at Eyam was becoming uncompetitive and eventually closed in 1807. Reflecting the inexorable impact of technology, at about the same time, in 1806, Greg and Ewart invested together in a new mill in Peter Street, in the heart of Manchester, which was equipped with mules for spinning fine cotton, powered by a steam engine. By 1811, the Greg enterprise was highly profitable and one of the leading cotton spinners in the country.

The situation of Quarry Bank provided the greatest contrast with the Gregs' home life in Manchester, and it is not difficult to see why Hannah loved the landscape and threw herself into making her home there the base for the children's holidays. At Styal, the River Bollin carved a deep sandstone valley through the Cheshire plain; cliffs were exposed by former quarrying activity and beech hangers clothed the slopes. On an old salters' route, a bridge crossed the river close to Quarry Bank, where a small old house next to the north end of the mill overlooked the most dramatic part of this landscape. The Gregs' new home there turned its back on the mill and faced the valley. Its gardens and grounds provided a striking setting, and the opportunity of creating a romantic garden in the newly fashionable taste for the sublime. Hannah was well-versed in this style and grasped the opportunity to bring out the dramatic aspects of her setting, with its steep banks, wooded slopes and long view of the meandering river. Over the next few years, attractive arbours and seats were sited among the paths to offer framed views; flower beds were created with judicious planting, with lawns enhancing the lower areas. High above, on the plain, new fruit and vegetable gardens were laid out as well as the children's plots. Further up the valley, away from the garden, lay the mill pool, a man-made lake constructed as a reservoir of power for the mill waterwheels when river levels were low; Hannah's garden afforded a picturesque view of the water cascading over the weir.

The Apprentice House stood at the top of the hill above Quarry Bank. In the nearby hamlet of Styal there were scattered houses across the fields near Farm Fold, and further away at Oak Farm. The whole estate meant a great deal to Hannah and her children. It was partly a holiday retreat: from the outset Hannah saw the potential for recovering her poise and settling her mind after the pressures of life in Manchester. Quarry Bank was also a home where she could write, as she explained to Hannah

Rathbone in January 1806 after a period of ill health: 'when once there [back in Manchester], I have little time, facilities or inclination to write.'[2] The contrast with Manchester could not have been more complete:

> Yet is a spring evening worth coming here for – it is truly a renovation of life, natural and moral – to change the long confinement among brick houses for such a scene – to deliver the oppressed frame and immured mind – to transport the heart itself where it can recover room to breathe and expand, after being so imprisoned, and sinking under the fetters fastened by care and labour. In this lively scenery – this incomparable seclusion – gazing on a splendid sky.[3]

The Gregs' move to Quarry Bank was at first tentative. Although the business was very successful and the family was prosperous, this was certainly not intended to be a demonstration of status. Among the successful Manchester business entrepreneurs, some such as the Duckwaters and Lloyds took on large country houses and a gentrified lifestyle. But self-advertisement and extravagance, as shown by Arkwright in his prominent new house and park in Cromford, would have been out of keeping with Hannah and Samuel's personality and principles. They were not interested in statements or symbols that conferred status. The Gregs, like some cotton masters of this period such as the Oldknows and Ashworths, built comfortable but unpretentious family homes near their mills.[4] When, in 1802, Samuel Greg bought Oak Farm at Styal, it was a practical solution to a business problem – a way to keep his rural workforce reliably fed, and fit to work.

The seasonal move to Quarry Bank had practical advantages for the family: it took them out of the violent environment still experienced sporadically in central Manchester and it enabled Samuel to keep a close eye on his major investment, a business that required further capital in the increasingly competitive world of cotton spinning.

But progress on extending and equipping the cottage at Quarry Bank into a family home, agreed in 1798, was frustratingly slow. By the summer of 1800 there was still building work to be done on the house: 'Our House is not yet quite in order but every day does something – every day there is less to do, so in time we may hope to finish & I hope our patience will last out.' However, they had found a housekeeper for Quarry Bank as well as a retainer for the house in town – 'Mrs Dobson is come here – she is stout & good humoured & your Mama is pleased with her & she has got an old deaf inconvenient woman to take the care of the house in town.'[5]

Quarry Bank, as the family always called the house, seems at this stage to have been plain, rectangular and modest in size. There were a kitchen and cellars at the lowest level; an entrance hall, business room, dining room and staircase on the main floor; and several bedrooms above. It was not until around 1802 that a drawing room was added to the north, and a bow on the west elevation (with further extensions to the cellars underneath). A few interior details and refinements were probably completed in this phase. Stables for the horses and carriage were not built until 1803, on a level site near the mill.

The family at first visited in the summer and autumn season, but were soon spending weeks there in the spring and then also at Christmas. It was only after 1815 that more time was spent at Quarry Bank than in their King Street home in central Manchester; the country house was then further enlarged and it became a hub for the family and for entertaining.

For Hannah, Quarry Bank provided a society 'so secluded as to know, see, and scarcely to remember anything of the "spites and turmoils" of the world'.[6] The landscape and the peace were appreciated: 'Our evenings are very long, in Autumn I think longer than in any town, the window being covered with trees whose leaves do not fall till Xmas, Oaks and beeches.'[7]

Hannah made this place a haven for her family, devising domestic routines and entertainments: reading aloud, sewing, weaving plaited bonnets, mending, playing music and singing. One Christmas when Bessy, the eldest child, was away in London, Hannah encouraged the children to write verses to send to her, to remind her of the home that she was missing. They all loved the river valley landscape and described it vividly, while revealing also their cherished family life:

> Far in a vale remote from public view
> From earliest youth a prosperous family grew,
> Their manners simple and their hearts sincere,
> Friends to the poor, and to each other dear.
> Eleven youths of various ages stand
> To bless (we hope) and serve their native land
> Their revered sire in all their joys takes part
> And views his Children with exulting heart
> He goes from home to toil throughout the day
> And then returns to chat the eve away.

There is a note of solicitude, of concern for mother's frail health:

> A most dear mother next on stage appears
> And full of Care her peaceful sceptre rears
> Who with good children hoping to be blest
> May she in granted wishes thankful rest.
> Experienced well in every worldly ill
> Also expert in swallowing a pill.
> We all together from one Mother learn
> What we must do our daily bread to earn.
> Where Bollin wanders o'er his stony bed
> This family their lives contented led.
> Deep in a sheltered vale their mansion stood;
> Whose sheltering hills were crowned with waving wood.[8]

They also referred to domestic pastimes such as music, games and charades round the fireplace. Hannah's own poem regretting Bessy's absence lists some of her activities, adding her own explanatory footnotes (which are transcribed below). It provides a picture of light-hearted family domesticity:[9]

Then Xmas wiles no longer mirth inspire,
Games ingenious miss their wonted jest;
No longer Sally's • blunders we admire
And pointless falls your Thomas' witty jest[2] ♥.

For now no Bessy folds the <u>Cramboline</u>[10]
By questions 10 the hidden thought detects
Performs <u>Old Poz</u>,[11] or King <u>Canute</u> so fine
As with the dark charade our brains perplex.

'A blazing ingle and a clean hearth-stane'
And candles snuff'd (thy mother's luxuries) ♠
To chear her heart no longer power retain
For now they shew not thee to her fond eyes.

The silent instrument provokes regret
No longer 'Just like Love' I hear thee play,[4] ᵛ
Nor see thee stockings mend, nor watch-chains net, ◊
Nor 'Lyrics' read, nor repetitions say.

• Sally rather pedantic, so making ridiculous mistakes.
♥ Tom a punster.
♠ No one that does not live with me can imagine what a fuss I
make about it.
ᵛ 'Just like Love' was oftenest sung as being Mr Rathbone's
favourite.
◊ Favourite or usual employments of Bessy's.

The children were encouraged to make the most of the setting of their country home. The sandstone caves in the Quarry Bank garden were irresistible, and the children spent happy days there with their cousins, the Hodgson children, and with the children of Hannah's surviving sister, Agnes. Bessy wrote to a cousin at the age of 11:

> Papa has given Thomas, Robert and me the upper cave and we have put up a ladder of ropes but Mama says we must not get up it … Robert gets forward very fast in learning both to read and write … Sam has just become a scholar of Miss Bates … Sally is quite a tyrant … Hannah Mary is very cross for her teeth hurt her.[12]

The next summer Thomas wrote to Bessy, who this time was staying with her uncle in Leicester:

> Do you remember when you were saying that you would get the cave ready for me but I think it is just the contrary for I think it will be me that gets it ready for you.
>
> Poor Elizabeth has broke her arm, it is much swelled but doing well, Thomas was drawing her round the garden in a little carriage and overturned her.[13]

Thomas later described a routine day – a combination of boredom, flashes of interest, moments of duty, and family banter, against a background of being in the open as well as studying indoors:

Journal of a Day

Waked from a sound sleep – no dream

Half past seven

Walked for half an hour & grew tired

Debate with Mama concerning the bad management of Mary Anne to be considered as a warning to others NB meaning no disparagement to the hearers.

Half past eight

Walked in the garden and mowed.

9 o'clock

Made a bench for the cave; sawed, planed and painted. NB took 5 hrs

2 o'clock

Dined

3 o'clock

Battle between the pygmies and infants with grass. Combat doubtful.

Half past three

Sitting in a chair was pulled backwards by Miss Agnes and my hip bone hurt. NB pain enrceased by walking.

4 o'clock

Went a walking with Papa over his farm; grew tired & thirsty, my head wet through, caught a blue butterfly & carried it home in my hat. NB I was not under my hat but my hat under me.

Half past six

An infectious disease prevalent in the room, called the vapours. Sally dreadfully ill of it.

7 o'clock

Saw Maryanne coming down the hill & was first with her. NB had the good sense to take an umbrella which cousin Anna was too slow to get hold of.

Half past seven

Worked at Mama's account till half past ten and brought them right.

Half past ten

Went to bed much tired after having in vain tried to persuade Robert to spout. Good night. [14]

The romantic setting of Quarry Bank was appreciated by discerning friends too: Hannah Rathbone recorded in her diary for 10 September 1805 a party of close friends boating on the mill pool with 'a fine moonlight'. [15] The only shadow upon this idyllic family was Hannah's own poor health. A trip to the Lake District in 1803 was planned as a tonic but to little avail. [16] These anxieties were to increase.

Maintaining her faith in reform through testing times

During this productive period, Hannah suffered some severe personal losses as her close and influential friends died: Thomas Percival in 1804 at the age of 64, and James Currie in August the following year, barely 50 years old. Then William Rathbone, whose health had long been fragile, died in 1809 at the age of 52.

For Hannah, the death of her mother, Elizabeth Lightbody, in 1801 at the age of 66 was a very great loss. She had bravely soldiered on in her Liverpool home, helping to look after her grandchildren, especially the children of the widowed Thomas Hodgson.

The death of children was still common even among the most watchful families. The loss of the Hodgson's infant son in 1795 and similar tragedies had deeply affected Hannah and others in her circle. The Percivals and the Curries as well as the Rathbones each suffered the loss of several children. Then Hannah suffered the loss of her young son, Samuel, shortly before his seventh birthday in May 1806. She was consoled by Hannah Rathbone, who wrote:

> you are my dear Friend so much the companion of my thoughts that I cannot help addressing you, tho' I cannot express the sympathy, the solicitude I feel for you, weakened as you were by illness ... trust in the generous Being, but still there is a feeling which only Mothers know, and only those who have lost a child can conceive ... I mourn, tho' in secret, over those who are taken away. I hope we are not the less resigned because our sense of suffering is acute.

At this point the writer was 'so poignantly affected I might almost say overcome by her own feelings' that William Rathbone, taking up her pen, 'persuaded her to decline the effort of proceeding ... We have thrice had to drink of the same bitter cup.'[17]

There were anxieties about epidemics such as diphtheria, so every child who developed a swollen throat was the cause of heightened concern. In 1805 her friend Hannah Rathbone's health had worried her and she wrote:

I never felt so much anxiety about the health of my friends as in this inclement weather surrounded by instances of daily mortality and in this town (when the body of inhabitants are the Poor) always with so much distress.[18]

In June 1807, shortly before the birth of her next child, Hannah was seriously ill again but her child, Ellen, was born safely and Hannah recovered. Her last child, William, was born in January 1809 when Hannah was 42. He was named after Hannah's old friend and mentor William Rathbone IV, who died after a long illness when the baby was barely a month old.

With the death of William Rathbone in 1809 a formative period in Hannah's life came to an end. William had suffered increasingly from depression and illness; his death was not unexpected. But from then on Hannah found herself alone, the lone survivor of a group of enlightened and deep-thinking friends who had helped to form her views.

From her peaceful situation at Quarry Bank, she observed and commented on an embattled new world beset with new and difficult economic and political issues. But the threat of invasion seen off in 1801 was renewed in 1803 and lasted until 1805, when English naval victories averted it. Napoleon, now emperor, had defeated British allies at Austerlitz and Jena in 1806 and was aiming to throttle Britain by stopping all maritime trade.

While British merchants found ways to deal with continental customers, the working population was hard hit when harvests failed. Famine was a frequent threat, bringing misery, disease and food riots. The national situation was so serious and the public mood in Manchester so patriotic that in 1803 Greg and many of his Dissenting and reforming colleagues decided to demonstrate their loyalty to the Crown by subscribing generously to the Manchester General Defence Fund.[19]

The urban populations of Manchester and the mill towns were affected by the wartime economy as well as by the poor harvests. Hannah had long experience of poverty at first hand, from visiting the poor and giving alms with her mother; she had very likely contributed to the soup kitchens established in central Manchester during the harsh winters of the Napoleonic wars. In the winter of 1805/06 she reported a harrowing incident when she took in a pauper woman she found ill on her doorstep: 'yesterday a poor woman fell in a fit on our steps and in less than two hours after I took her into the house expired almost in my arms – an affecting circumstance before the eyes of my Children and Servants.'[20]

In 1806 she witnessed starvation almost at first hand: 'The distress at Manchester increases. I find one whole family quite within knowledge starved to death during the last week – much worse at Stockport ... and distress such as has not been known since there was a nation.'[21] She was pessimistic, even after the victory of Trafalgar.[22]

One underlying cause of the mass distress, unemployment, poverty and starvation was the increasing investment in power looms. Thousands of hand-loom weavers found their means of livelihood shrinking, and many joined the ranks of a working-class radical movement. The most radical were Luddites, machinery breakers, but the unemployed weavers evoked much public sympathy. Any evidence of practical or moral support voiced by the leaders of Dissent was, however, limited. Representing to a large extent the middle ranks and commercial classes, they were often seen as the capitalists responsible for putting so many out of work.

Hannah was silent on this aspect, but she was gripped by anxiety about the world that her children were to inherit. Hannah's comments on the convulsive events in this period at times reflect her mood, her poor health, her maternal instincts, and her desire to awaken in her children a consciousness of the qualities required to maintain their faith and to conduct themselves with integrity in a world of increasing turmoil. Recovering from severe illness, she wrote to her son Robert in December 1807 to say she would try to be more resigned:

> I have been very much to blame for allowing such extreme anxiety to lay hold of me and destroy my health as it has done ... I shall now soon see you my dear fellow but instead of being lively and making your home and your evenings always pleasant and amusing, I can do nothing, and now you must help – alas my strength fails and my mind is also weakened as is usual with bad health.[23]

Her letters to her elder sons and to the Rathbones show that Hannah was passionately interested in politics, supported the Whigs, feared the Tory government and detested the way it dealt with unrest in the towns of the north-west. Like the Rathbones, she was highly critical of the corruption still prevalent in local government elections, and saw the need for reform.

When, in April 1808, Napoleon sided with the Danes and there were once more fears of an invasion, Hannah wrote to her son Tom, aged 15, then at school in Birmingham:

> An American War seems less likely than it was but the prospect for the country in general more gloomy than ever and as Bonaparte is hiring the Danish sailors for his fleet it seems not impossible that there once more be a Descent on the waves on these Kingdoms and no adequate defence. How necessary all fortitude and patience be for the times which await us & how much the neglect of Ministers seems to indicate their being instruments of the fall of the country. Mr Philip Henry amongst many wise sayings used to say: '<u>Duty</u> is ours; <u>events</u> are God's.'[24]

Writing to Tom again the following year she was still pessimistic:

> You ask me what I think of politics now; as I have done, my dear friend, for some years past, that tho' England is left the last, it will

as surely be conquered & more surely severely dealt with, as the rest of Europe …[25]

Hannah was well informed about the political pressures felt both locally and nationally, and worried about the world that her children would inherit. She hated the thought of her boys being conscripted. But in spite of her pessimism, she had underlying faith that in the future a more perfect world would emerge. As she wrote to William Rathbone after the Irish Rebellion in 1798: 'we who have children and live in the future may I think look at the gloom to even a brighter day than our fathers knew.'[26]

Hannah's ablest disciple was her daughter Bessy, but she too had to fight prejudice against women taking a leading part in welfare and social reform. Hannah's hopes for social and political reform was darkened at times by foreboding that the world facing her children would be painfully unpleasant, either as a result of political corruption or foreign invasion.

By 1806, she had grown more pessimistic about the future:

… have not indeed fluctuated with Events, but in Victory and Defeat, the strong unhappy impression has invariably dwelt on my mind that it is in the scheme of Providence that Revolution accompanied with War and Civil Tumult shall proceed – and that this Govt & Country are ripe for these purposes. I look certainly to Good as the final & perhaps not distant Result, but to dreadful scenes for our Children, if not for ourselves in the present time.[27]

Hannah's ambitions and ideas as an educator

Hannah was always conscious of the benefits that education could confer for her own family and to a wider community. She shared with Dr Currie, Thomas Percival and with her enlightened circle of Liverpool friends the convictions of Rational Dissenters that education could be an effective investment to achieve social and moral progress. She did not believe that these benefits should be confined to men, nor to the middle class to which she belonged. With other leading Dissenters, she believed that there was nothing wrong with women undertaking deep study: if they were to fulfil useful roles in society and in their families, they would indeed need to develop themselves through education.

Hannah probably enjoyed discussing these ideas with Thomas Percival before her marriage. Among his other considerable talents, Percival was a gifted teacher who wrote to entertain and educate his own children, making his points through memorable 'moral fables', usually involving the young.[28] He believed there were four main aims of education: to refine the feelings of the heart, inspiring the mind with the love of moral excellence; to awaken curiosity and the spirit of enquiry; to enlarge the understanding; to give strength and solidity of judgement.[29]

As Hannah's young family grew, she also turned to William Rathbone and James Currie for their thoughts on education. Currie's advice was clear and short: let the child learn from experience. 'The great secret is to teach a child to teach itself,' he wrote to Hannah.[30] Hannah imagined setting out a 'plan of education' for her children as early as 1794, when she wrote to William Rathbone:

> Tell me really if you think <u>Enthusiasm</u> so bad a thing as you used to do? So much pleasure has it yielded me beyond the pain it may have exposed me to that I am almost disposed to admit the cultivation of it into my plan of education for my Children?[31]

Hannah also read the educational writings of her mother's friend Mrs Barbauld, with whom she corresponded from time to time, and she was familiar with the works of the philanthropist Hannah More. She read the writings of Mary Wollstonecraft and was influenced by her ideas on the potential of women's minds. Hannah was also aware of Rousseau's ideas[32] and was taken also with foreign writers on educational themes, keeping abreast with contemporary thinking from abroad, such as *Adelaide and Theodore* by Madame de Genlis, probably in the translation by Maria Edgeworth, which provides an outline of an educational programme for boys and girls that values the countryside and recognises the scope for developing values that are far removed from the false sophistication of the metropolis.[33]

The greatest influence on Hannah's ideas about education, however, was Maria Edgeworth. In 1798 William Rathbone commended her *Practical Education* as 'the best mental medicine I could prescribe' and claimed that he would go to heaven for the good deed of suggesting it.[34] It is likely that Hannah welcomed this writer's ideas about children's development through practical instruction rather than solely through book learning, its focus being on fresh air and exercise, and on morality learnt through play and encouragement, rather than punishment or coercion. The Edgeworths' theory of education was based on the premise that a child's early experiences are formative and that the associations they form early in life are long-lasting. They also encourage hands-on learning and include suggestions of 'experiments' that children could perform and learn from.

While absorbing many of these ideas in the plans for her children's education, Hannah was also inclined to use her talent for selecting excerpts and copying aphorisms that she valued. These filled a growing number of her 'extract books'; and she formed the habit of calling to mind appropriate sayings for the right occasion. She wrote that 'in the instruction of youth, [she] has found nothing more calculated to open the mind and form the judgement, than reading and examining maxims or opinions'.[35] Her mother was good at this, and no doubt her pious ancestors on her mother's side were also frequent users of the appropriate pithy maxim. This form of academic training was not, as far as we know, a system favoured in the programmes of education for other Rational Dissenters of Hannah's time, but is perhaps a leftover of medieval humanist educational theory and practice, where the distilled thoughts and aphorisms of great writers and politicians are valued as a source of wisdom.

Hannah's circle of family and friends might have been impressed or even deterred by such displays of scholarship and memory, but Hannah could be disarming, and when teased by them, wryly acknowledged that she was regarded as singular in this respect. Her first books were compilations of aphorisms, extracted from her reading, interspersed with other efforts of her own. They had clearly been tried out first at home, and found to be effective. Following encouragement from William Rathbone, Hannah used similar material as a guide to the upbringing of the mill apprentices. She called it *Virtue Made Easy*; as she herself admitted, much of the material in it was pillaged directly from a similar book no longer available. It was intended to be of use for the mill children, as Hannah's preface explains: 'having had many opportunities of observing how much the poor suffer from ignorance and prejudice,' she hoped the present publication would prove 'useful to a small set within her own acquaintance.' 'Instruction through <u>proverbs</u> and <u>sayings</u> is of great antiquity,' she went on to explain, 'and to those whose laborious lives exclude study and reflection, and whose opportunities of acquiring knowledge must be very limited, they still form the best vehicle of important truths … the moral lessons they contain are generally most strongly impressed, easily remembered and easily applied.'

Hannah's persevered as a writer, even though her first book was neither original nor a success. When ill in 1817, she set out a long list of her manuscripts that she wanted to see preserved.[36] These unpublished collections included 'A Tour of the Lakes', 'A Catechism of Health and Safety', excerpts from her letters, her youthful diary and a large amount of guidance to her wayward son Tom. She omitted two of the four books published and privately circulated by then. The last book of aphorisms, entitled *The Monitor*, was published in 1804, and is an altogether more mature and carefully assembled compilation than her earlier efforts, though still based on a structure of chapters addressing topics such as Virtue, Truth, Fortune, Ambition and Happiness. It combines aphorisms written by well-known writers among her own efforts, all clothed in anonymity. The fact that *The Monitor* was used in class by Lant Carpenter and, no doubt, by other Dissenting teachers, is evidence of her growing ambition and ability. In her last book, published posthumously, she returned to the theme of alleviating the suffering of the sick, where she contributed with her fellow authors a distillation of a lifetime's experience. The most remarkable and original chapter stresses the value of what we might now refer to as psychology: the need for doctors and nurses to recognise and use the mind's influence over the body to promote recovery.

One of Hannah's educational aspirations was that her children should absorb and carry on her aims and ideals, as well as her religious faith: 'of late my sympathies and pleasures here leaned chiefly to the young on whom my heart and hopes repose and who command my thoughts and anxieties and expectations,' as she expressed it to her nephew John Pares in 1811.

She was determined that her girls should be given the same chance to develop their minds as she had: 'My advice and instruction (in relation to the education of daughters) will be ... in the notion of their being individual and rational and immortal beings.'[37] Marriage and motherhood had done nothing to temper her observations on the potential among women that a male-dominated society repressed. She wrote:

Were the other advantages equal ... superiority would be frequently found on the side of women, in whom affection is a stronger motive of conduct; who possess therefore greater disinterestedness and sensibility, which, when strengthened by habit, often enables them to dare and to endure, more than mere manly wisdom and courage.[38]

In another Maxim she added:

> Women are in general less selfish and more generous than men;
> if nature had reversed their fate in respect to personal suffering
> and exemptions, would they have cruelly aggravated the partial
> distribution by artificial distinctions, formed for their own con-
> venience and amusement?[39]

Such convictions were widely tempered and mollified in the
later versions of her books after 1800, reflecting the prevailing
conservative climate with advice on the need for a wife to exercise tact and diplomacy.

The education given to Hannah's children

Hannah was her children's first teacher. Ellen, the youngest
daughter, testified in her old age how her mother taught her:

> We often spent Sunday afternoon in the parlour, with my
> mother, and I remember in answer to some questions, she walk-
> ing up and down the room as was her custom, and I with my
> pencil in my little chair, noting down her clear, concise account
> of the people of the Jewish nations and history.

Ellen recalled how, years later, she 'was often surprised to see how
little [she] found to add and nothing to correct in the information'
which her mother had given her 'so simply and pleasantly.'[40]

The children's schooling had already been the subject of
correspondence, debate and sometimes argument among their
parents over several preceding years. For Hannah, to put her
ideas into practice meant that ideals and philosophies, inevitably
perhaps, turned into compromises and sometimes disappointments. It is of note that both the boys and girls were exposed
not only to Dissenting ideas on ethics, but also to new curricula

on geography, geology and the sciences. They were taught the rapidly expanding universes of scientific knowledge that were already a feature of their generation, and were made to think about how these related to society.

The younger children were often placed in the care of their elder siblings, who were sometimes expected to help teach them as well as look after them. Then they were entrusted to the governess, Miss Bate, who acted *in loco parentis* and taught them some basic lessons, as the children themselves put it in 1808:

> At home the seven next are taught to know
> where foreign countries stand and distant rivers flow.
> And dear Miss Bate her friendly aid imparts
> To form their judgements and to mend their hearts.[41]

A letter from a youthful Thomas confirms this: 'I like being in school with Miss Bate in an afternoon … mostly we write letters and Maryanne does her netting and then we read and find places on the maps.'[42]

The *Catechisms of Safety and Health* survives as an incomplete manuscript, which had been clearly devised as a text for Miss Bate to use to teach the children. Hannah referred in her preface to a theme that she returned to in her last book; the 'irremediable and mutual dependence', and the vital influence of the mind upon health.

Turning to the catechism section, the twenty surviving pages of questions and answers are a mixture of simple suggestions for diagnosis of illness based on symptoms: for first aid and for dealing with emergencies:

Q   What would you do for example, for a Burn or Scald?
A   I would apply spirit of turpentin, or mix limewater and sweet oil half and half.
Q   What quality is first necessary … before you can either save yourself from danger or be of use to others?

A Presence of mind

Q What is presence of mind?

A The triumph of reason over the passions of surprise & fear.

The emergencies imagined by this anxious mother included being caught in a riot, a runaway carriage, clothes catching fire, falling through ice while skating, being bitten by a mad dog, or chased by a bull: 'look steadily in its face, which always makes it stop.'

This sound approach breaks down when the cause of the ailment is found to be self-indulgence, imprudence or intemperance. While a warning may have been needed, Hannah's remedies are more daunting:

Q What painful operations must children often submit to if they are disobedient, imprudent, inattentive, intemperate, passionate etc?

A They may be obliged to have blisters, leeches, emetics, teeth drawn, bones set, cupped, amputation etc, tied in bed, blinded, etc etc etc.[43]

Boarding schools were considered for Hannah's boys and girls. After making enquiries within their circle of friends, as parents often do, the first choice for Hannah's eldest son was the school in Birmingham run by the Rev. John Corrie. Adam Hodgson wrote to Thomas in his first term and enquired, as an old boy, if the curriculum remained stimulating:

I wish you would let me know what your studies are … I mean particularly The Evidences of Natural & Revealed Religion, Natural & Moral Philosophy, Metaphysics &c. These are subjects to which I think Mr Corrie is much attached & which he is extremely happy in illustrating.[44]

But the choice of his next school was fraught, as Samuel took time over his decision. Hannah later recalled 'the 4 months suspense between Mr Shepherd's and Mr Tayler's school which almost cost me my life'.[45]

Robert, their second son, went to the Rev. James Tayler's school in Nottingham,[46] where he met the sons of several Manchester radicals and reformers and became a friend of John Tayler, the son of the headmaster. A studious and clever boy, he managed the Latin and Greek in the curriculum. John and Samuel junior went to Mr Carpenter's school when it moved to Bristol in 1819. William Rathbone had met Lant Carpenter, a gifted teacher and Rational Dissenter, in Liverpool many years earlier. When, in 1804, Carpenter accepted the post as minister to the Dissenting congregation in Exeter, he set up a class and taught grammar, composition, history, language and philosophy, and built a reputation as a teacher.[47]

All the boys except the eldest, Thomas, finished their education at Edinburgh University. This was the outstanding centre for a university education in Britain at this time, and a magnet for the children of Dissenters who were still prevented from obtaining a degree from Oxford or Cambridge. Robert described his university course, which includes chemistry, natural philosophy and mathematics, as well as fencing, and a Spanish master:

> I am sure I have got more from one month here than I should have done from a year at home. If you were tolerably ready on the six books of Euclid, trigonometry and some little knowledge of conical sections, you might attend Playfair with very great advantage and pleasure …[48]

Bessy and then Mary Anne, Agnes, Sally and Margaret also went to Mr Tayler's school in Nottingham.[49] Hannah suffered when sending the two eldest girls away: 'From two of my children I am separated almost wholly – my dear Mrs R will understand this mortification.'[50] Hannah believed that 'distance from one's friends throwing one so entirely on one's own is one of the great improvements of a school education'. So Hannah thought the pain of separation was worthwhile; she went on: 'I hope to procure it for a short time even for my girls not having forgotten its advantage to myself.'[51]

> The single circumstance of being thrown wholly among strangers comprehends more of real education and improvement than whole years of common book learning and instruction, and every youth of either sex, who has never experienced this great trial, is unseasoned as a result. This is the great advantage of distant schools and one for which there is no compensation.[52]

The daughters spent not only long terms away at school, but also long holidays away from home staying with relations. All the older children spent weeks in the summer of 1800 with Hannah's sister Agnes at their Leicester home. This also was an educational experience, as Hannah lost no time in pointing out in a letter to Bessy when she was 10 years old:

> I often lament, my dear Bessy, that you do not write better and then you and I could have more intercourse when we are separated. I hope in another year you will be able to write me a <u>pretty</u> letter both in <u>matter</u> and <u>manner</u> – in <u>substance</u> and <u>dress</u> – that is, in thoughts, language and penmanship.[53]

Some weeks that Bessy spent as a teenager at Greenbank with the Rathbone family are recorded in the surviving pages of a diary, and these show that such visits were also a highly formative experience – in her case immersing her in the political issues and violent election battles of 1806. She was also taught about investing in the raw cotton market; that is to say, she provided her cousin Richard Rathbone, then a young trainee, with some of her funds for him to speculate in raw cotton, as part of a business training plan in cotton broking.[54] She also visited 'manufactures', as her mother and grandmother had done, and spent a couple of terms at a finishing school in London.

By then Hannah had come to recognise that Manchester had overtaken Liverpool as a centre for culture and learning, with the early nineteenth-century passion for science being strongly represented there and led by the remarkable Dr Dalton.[55] 'In my youthful days,' Hannah wrote to her son Thomas, 'Liverpool was supereminent but all its luminaries are set & Manchetr ... now supplies better society, tho on the whole perhaps rather scientific than literary.'[56] Many scientific lectures were fashionable and well-attended by women during this period. Bessy attended those given on electricity by Dr Dalton in Manchester in 1807.

With the possible exception of the youngest, Ellen, the horizons of Hannah's other daughters were limited to the familiar surroundings of Quarry Bank. Just as Hannah's mother and Hannah herself saw it as part of their role to help the poor, by introducing the apprentices to reading and to the Bible, Hannah likewise trained her daughters in these skills. They subsequently made a contribution to the education and well-being of generations of apprentice children at Quarry Bank, but seem to have made no further mark.

In the months leading up to the birth of her last daughter Ellen in June 1807, Hannah had been increasingly ill. Bessy's diary entry for 31 May implies that the end was nigh:

> Mama very poorly. told me several things she wished to have done. Her red leather case was to be opened immediately and several memorandums for Papa would be found in it – letter to me in a book.[57]

The manuscript that she called her *Legacy to Elizabeth Greg*, written during illness, seems to have been long conceived but hurriedly written. Started in February 1807, it confirms that Hannah hoped that her eldest daughter would inherit her values and aspirations. It included guidance on the art of household management, a duty that would fall to her upon her mother's death and a talent on which Hannah placed high value. Hannah recovered, but Bessy retained her mother's advice. It covers the attitude and skills needed by the housewife to ensure that everything is provided while she remains unruffled, taking charge of the comforts, the household budgets, the entertaining, the cleaning, the staff, and even:

> it must also be your part to take care in general that the family is well-cloathed … Much female worth and usefulness consists in negatives, never to be inconsiderate, giddy, unneat, awkward, impatient or fretful – never to betray confidence, never to be imprudent, extravagant or foolish, careless or inattentive, unkind, harsh or intemperate … To perform the detail of such a sketch you will have to study the characters of those you serve.[58]

This is a testament to Hannah's own grasp of her role as manager of her households. It shows her mastery of the challenges that she had faced as a new wife, of the efficacy of the advice given by her sister at that time, and her own practicality and capability. All Hannah's daughters would doubtless likewise have seen their mother as a role model and heard her good advice on household management. She added lists of books that were to be recommended as Sunday evening family readings, particularly those that would interest and entertain Samuel.

All Hannah's children were brought up to love their natural surroundings, the landscape and gardens. The girls were encouraged to learn gardening, but it was Robert who became an exceptionally gifted creator of gardens and landscapes, and a noted collector of plants.[59] The cultivation of taste was not overlooked. Hannah made the point that:

> The Eye is too much neglected in the business of Education. I would have a schoolroom, nay a whole house hung with prints of heroic and virtuous actions so that youth could not lift up its eye without receiving a useful and wholesome impression … how important must be the effect of moral scenery on the

1 Miniature of Mrs Elizabeth Lightbody, Hannah's mother. *Reproduced by kind permission of Tim Paine and Jenny Smith*

2 Miniature of Hannah Lightbody as a young girl. *National Trust/Quarry Bank Mill Archive*

3 Miniature of Hannah Lightbody, probably before her marriage in 1789. *National Trust/Quarry Bank Mill Archive*

4 Portrait of Hannah Greg. *National Trust/Quarry Bank Mill Archive*

5 Miniature of Samuel Greg, probably before his marriage in 1789. *National Trust/Quarry Bank Mill Archive*

6 Portrait of Samuel Greg. *National Trust/Quarry Bank Mill Archive*

7 Quarry Bank Mill. *National Trust / Quarry Bank Mill Archive*

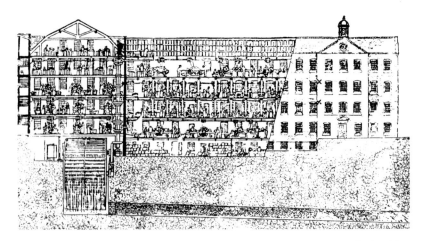

8 Quarry Bank Mill: a cutaway drawing illustrating the scale of the 1817 iron waterwheel and the distribution of power to the machinery on each floor. *National Trust / Quarry Bank Mill Archive*

9 The Apprentice House at Styal. *National Trust/Quarry Bank Mill Archive*

10 The Apprentice House at Styal: a cutaway drawing showing the uses of the separate rooms and floors. *National Trust/Quarry Bank Mill Archive*

11 Quarry Bank House, showing the garden adjacent to the mill. The river is obscured by the shrubbery on the right. *National Trust/Quarry Bank Mill Archive*

12 Oak Cottages in Styal village. *National Trust/Quarry Bank Mill Archive*

youthful mind ... it should look on beautiful conduct, it should breathe an atmosphere of purity, goodness and love.[60]

All the children absorbed their mother's constant search for a moral code to guide them. Typically, reading was the key to unlock these insights and Hannah was an inveterate reader and ever ready to recommend books to her family and friends, including serious philosophy.[61] Reading could become a bone of contention: while Hannah inspired all her children with a love of literature, Samuel often saw it as a dangerous distraction for men about to enter their profession.

Thomas, the eldest boy, was strongly influenced by his mother's passion for literature and especially poetry. He had some ambitions to be a poet and writer, exchanging views on contemporary poets with his mother, but he never achieved success.[62] Hannah was worried about this tendency:

I often blame myself as one cause of your having cultivated a love of poetry &c (so sadly too much my own taste), beyond the more manly studies, living on which ... rather than on the more solid nourishment of the mind that induces strength and power, but I trust it is not too late.[63]

Years later, Tom's youngest brothers, William and Samuel, had a book of their poems privately printed in Paris.[64]

Finally, Hannah saw education as a life-long pursuit:

I have heard many of the cleverest men I have known (and I have been thrown among several) confess that what is called Education, in its usual periods had merely laid the foundations – taught the elements and left all the important and <u>efficient</u> knowledge to be gathered by themselves, when later years and experience had rendered them more fully sensible of the value of it – and so situated as to bring it into immediate application and use.[65]

Training for business

It has often been remarked that Dissenters were singularly effective in business, and the Gregs' correspondence reveals the extent of their worldly aspirations for their children. Although unostentatious and unpretentious, they were ambitious in this particular respect. Samuel saw schooling as a plain matter of acquiring competence and respectability. Hannah, meanwhile, argued for the polish of a rounded education, advocating travel and a liberal culture as accomplishments befitting a man of business. There were many heated debates and much correspondence on this issue, but they both agreed that the children should be capable of winning the respect of their elders and their peers.

The parents wanted the children to make a favourable impression from a very young age; Hannah had written to Bessy when she was staying with her Pares uncle and aunt in 1800 when she was only 9 years old: 'I hope you will consider every opportunity of gaining the esteem of such friends as you are now with as truly valuable – for such esteem you will find the greatest treasure of your life – next to your own.'[66]

In March 1809 she looked forward to going to Ireland with Tom, who was 17 at the time: 'but I hope you will leave all who know you there your friends – it is of great consequence my dear boy that you should do so.' She referred to the:

> development of character as a system of <u>habits</u>, nay a mere collection of <u>actions</u> – and every day even in the life of a humble manufacturer supplies opportunity of habitual practice of the sublime virtues of self-command, self-denial & fortitude & benevolence.[67]

The debate within the family reveals layers of disagreement. While Hannah regarded taste in literature as a civilised accomplishment, Samuel thought that cultivating poetry and literature was a damaging diversion for boys. He had little time for novels, less for poetry:

> To be doating from youth up bespeaks a diseased state of mind
> & indulgence in castle building whilst a man should be fitting
> himself out … cultivate your taste for knowledge – till much of
> this is attained. Read what is useful.

This was Samuel's belief, condemning novels as:

> … prating books & books for prating upon … Your first study
> be a knowledge of man … know your own country, its history,
> commerce and manufacture, for England is indebted to them &
> to her marine for all her consequence. Next the history & polity
> of other countries.

When Tom has acquired this he may have 'the ability to give people confidence in your integrity & of their security'.[68] His experience gave him a clear focus on the way his sons should be trained. Qualities of mind mattered; he wrote to his son Robert in February 1814:

> … one thing I particularly wish that twice a week pursue the
> plan I have frequently spoke of to you as improving the powers
> of attention & memory, to have read to you a subject, which
> afterwards you must write down. This I very particularly wish
> and recommend you do.[69]

Hannah could agree with much of this: in a letter to Tom she refers to her educational aim as providing 'habits of application, attention, the exercise of judgement, good sense and self-command.'[70] She wrote out a long manuscript, entitled *The Art of Happy Living* to guide him as he set off for his new career in London.

Hannah's encouragement that the boys develop wider interests led to serious disagreements with Samuel. In a row over their son John's wish to go to hear Dr Dalton lecturing – and postponing his start in the counting house – Hannah wrote:

> I rather hoped your father had forgotten or relinquished the idea of sending John to Lpool this vacation, but yesterday on his asking leave to have Mr Dalton's instructions this summer, your Father told him he must learn his business. I said nothing of course then, but ventured to remonstrate for this one vacation to allow John to procure Learning while 'the iron is hot' … In short his whole heart seems in it…

But Samuel was adamant: John must learn his business and not go to Dr Dalton's lectures.[71] Samuel put his case for training a man of business in these terms, writing to Robert on 20 February 1814:

> our greatest gratification is to deserve & possess the respect of those among whom we live & who can judge of our merits. We are to distinguish between the pursuits of positive utility and those of amusement & mere recreation. – & between those of intrinsic worth & those of mere ornament – & not to sacrifice to the one the time due to the other.[72]

The problem for the over-educated and academic offspring, then and ever since, may be that the day-to-day routines of business seem trivial compared to the big issues in philosophy or literature. Hannah was anxious that the boys' education should be rounded, rather than narrowly orientated to their eventual careers. She remained anxious to see that the development of character was not overlooked. She was especially worried about Tom in this respect, and wrote him many an encouraging and instructive letter – in addition to her manuscript on *The Art of Happy Living*, which deals at length on the need for a balance. She was also worried about Thomas going off the rails once he was alone in London, guidance that Tom seems to have needed:

For ... all your conduct my dear Friend I must refer to your own conscience, which after such an education ought to be a sure guide and depend upon it, you can never know a moment's peace if you ever offend it. Your heart is formed to kind comfort only in Innocence and Prudence, and the first false step you ever made I should indeed pity you for. Depend upon it you cannot even estimate what it would cost.[73]

At times, Samuel's instructions for their son Robert's education could be very prescriptive. When Robert was sent to Spain on business and for training, with Isaac Hodgson who had just joined Samuel as a partner, Samuel wrote: 'Go in the counting-house of C W & B; you may there acquire much of the manners & language of business & only then go to Cadiz and Mr Beeston. This is my particular wish.'[74] He could be unequivocal in his advice:

I only need to say to you and your Cousin that you cannot, on business, be too minute in your investigations, nor on your communications – deliberate in forming your opinions & laying down your plans, & that it is only by a steady perseverance in well digested lines that success can be ensured.[75]

Robert grasped the point: the boys could work out for themselves where their paths should lie, but Robert's approach was far more confidence-inspiring than Tom's. Robert 'says in his last letter', his mother wrote:

he shall come home disposed to apply 'after stretching his legs & breathing the pure mountain air ... ready to be manufactured into anything, to work at QB, in King St, to be shipped off to Spain, Portugal or Mexico anywhere, everywhere – to do anything everything with more general knowledge perhaps than is absolutely necessary for a Man of Business tho' he should hope with as much <u>common</u> sense as if he had never opened any book but his ledger'.[76]

Duodecimo

In 1811 Hannah embarked on a holiday game for the family. It was simple, literary and obviously much valued, even though it did not last long. She outlined its origins in a letter to her nephew Tom Pares in July 1812:

> a little institution formed over the fireside last winter where a domestic <u>Literary & Philosophical</u> was instituted, officers appointed, rules drawn etc. & all on the spot, in the true spirit of youthful precipitation all in one hour & being 12 little people we christened it the Duodecimo.[77]

Before the members met, each was required to submit a short paper and put it in a lockable box. When all assembled, a paper was drawn out at random and presented by its author. Hannah seems to have learnt this when staying with the Percivals many years earlier.[78] She went on to describe some of her aspirations:

> It may give Robert the opportunity of <u>feeling his way</u> with papers intended for the Manc'r Society – but should it bear no fruit, but merely scatter flowers round the idea of <u>home</u>, it may be salutary to the Youth who may be wandering through the Earth, the Wilds of America, the plains of Mexico, or the City of London.[79]

Hannah's presidential address, a testament of some ambition, survives together with some papers intended for presentation by some of her children.[80] She took trouble over it, showed a draft to Hannah Rathbone and was flattered that the latter copied it out. A page of vivid jottings also survives, revealing her train of thought as she composed a draft statement of her maternal and educational vocation.[81]

The presentation of each paper by its author was to be more than an essay or an exercise in rhetoric – the well-recited paper can and should persuade the listener:

> In reading your paper yourself, you may form some idea how it will be read by others, but you can be no judge how it will be heard till you actually read it <u>aloud</u> before them. & by sympathy with your audience place yourself in their situation, and listen with <u>their</u> ears – … But as we are at present all alike inexperienced in these transactions, we must exercise towards each other the Patience and Candour required by young beginners. To none can it be more difficult thus to speak than to your President, who having been elected as it were by acclamation … she must not decline saying a few words in her new Character …
>
> But, my dear Children!, you to whom it has always been so easy to me to write individually, and at a distance – how strange, how unnatural, and above all how formidable a task is it thus to address you viva voce – in your collective capacity! As a Corporate Body – a <u>Literary and Philosophical Society</u>!

Hannah rose to the challenge with some rhetorical flourishes:

> What can she pretend to write, in whose times <u>Composition</u> formed no branch of female education – where no <u>themes</u> were set, no rhetoric taught, – one whose only Muse has ever been Affection, and whose only Composition, a kind letter – how should she suddenly transform the Mama into the President? The correspondent into the Philosopher? The letter into the essay? The fond tones of maternal familiarity into a grave and ceremonious Address? She, all whose exordiums have hitherto consisted in 'my dear friend' and whose only peroration has been 'I am your loving Mother'.
>
> … I am, however, contented, nay proud, that my letter should prove a foil to your papers – pleased to be seen but in eclipse, and

to shine only thro' my children (the most radiant brilliancy of maternal life! the highest point of true parental glory)!

Hannah then sets out some serious underlying aims, ending with a sermon-like invocation:

Let such meetings remind us … that we are all wayfaring people, scattered in destiny and situation, meeting only occasionally at home <u>here</u>, – but hoping, and let me say endeavouring all to meet at <u>last</u> in our Father's house above. We are crossing the wilderness of this world by different paths … Let us exhort one another never to deviate into the broad way, to abhor the seductions of vice, to despise the allurements if Indolence, to overcome the temptations of folly, to withstand the tyranny of fashion, to aim at brighter objects than worldly ambition can present, and covet nobler rewards than Human power can confer.[82]

The whole address shows Hannah's aspirations as an educator, and also betrays some of the pains she took in expressing this role. She was proving how right William Rathbone had been to see in her a vocation to preach. It suggests too, that however self-deprecating she seemed, she hoped to be seen as an inspiring teacher. This is an obvious echo of the Octonian Society that she so loved in Liverpool, when wise and entertaining figures spoke and debated on issues. Unlike the Manchester Literary and Philosophical Society, women were admitted, and indeed encouraged there. A few outsiders were admitted, including the Rev. J. Tayler, and as he happened to be there on the first evening, the Rathbone's tutor, Dr Houlbrooke, who was at the time the president of the Liverpool Literary and Philosophical Society.

It seems that there were few opportunities for the Duodecimo to reconvene, though it left its mark. Robert became a member of the Manchester Literary and Philosophical Society, and later a Member of Parliament. He and several of his brothers were effective essayists engaged in the national debates about reform and education, Bessy became a persuasive social reformer, Tom Pares an MP, and the Hodgson boys campaigned for the ending of slavery. It may well be that, in the parlour at Quarry Bank House, each learnt the skills of advocacy and confidence in debate, as well as much about the causes that they wished to promote.

The life and work of the apprentices at Quarry Bank Mill

The scale of the early cotton-spinning mills was unlike anything experienced previously, and a key to their success lay in the recruitment and training of the young workforce. Discipline and deftness, concentration and stamina were required in order to operate the cotton-spinning machinery, supply bobbins, attach yarn to spindles. Similar processes would have been familiar in many families and workshops from the mid-eighteenth century, where long hours for young workers were commonplace. What was new was the unrelenting rhythm of the water-powered machinery, and the requirement that the workers keep up a continuous flow of production. Children were regarded as suitable for many such tasks, and all strata of society saw merit in putting children out to work at an early age. A working day of twelve or more hours for children, as well as adults, was normal.

A high proportion of mill workers were women; their skills were needed while their wages were a fraction of men's. Greg's early workforce included a mix of skilled and unskilled adults, and a high proportion of children who worked under contract for a fixed number of years. If they lived outside the area, accommodation was found for them in the village; sometimes they were provided with clothing. They were taught the essential skills and routines, and were expected to be quick learners (which was plausible), reliable and disciplined (which often was not). It soon became clear that young girls were more capable than boys: apart from their manual deftness, as Samuel Greg remarked, they were 'less truculent' than boys.

In addition to the local children employed under contract, Greg soon needed to recruit yet more children. He was able to do so by arrangements with a large number of local parishes who funded the costs of pauper children in workhouses as a charge against the local rates, but which, in some areas, was becoming a heavy cost and administrative burden. In relieving the parishes of the burden of looking after the workhouse children, the mill masters were usually paid a premium of several guineas; they contracted with the parish to provide the children with not only work and food for a fixed term, but also lodgings and the bare essentials of training and education. The children usually started at the age of 9, having been subjected to a medical inspection to ensure that they were fit to work, and were released by the time they were 18. Greg started to employ parish apprentices in the 1780s when the mill was new, and erected the Apprentice House in 1790 (see plates 9 and 10). By 1800 he had about ninety apprentices (sixty girls and thirty boys) living there.

Samuel Greg still lived and worked mainly in Manchester and largely relied upon his mill manager at Quarry Bank, as well as the Apprentice House supervisor. In addition, he engaged teachers to provide lessons for the apprentices, and retained the services of a factory doctor, Peter Holland from Knutsford.

The routines of work in Greg's mill in 1805 were described in well-known testimonies from two truants, Thomas Priestley and Joseph Sefton. These statements were probably the results of some coaching to show their employers in a favourable light, but the descriptions of living and working conditions remain of value. They matched those in other rural mills; it was regularly assumed that hours would be shorter when water levels dropped in the summer, and the lost hours would be recovered by over-time in the winter months when water levels were higher. Priestley recalled:

> ... when we came there, we were, after a day's rest, set to work,
> I was the same as the others to attend 2 machines for spinning

cotton, each of which spun about 50 threads, my business was to supply these machines, to guide the thread occasionally and to twist them when they snapt, and I soon became perfect in these operations, also learned to take the machinery to pieces and apply the oil, a matter that required some care. In this manner I have been employed all the while that I have been in the cotton manufactory of Mr Greg aforesaid.

Our working hours were from 6am in summer and winter until 7 in the evening. There was no night workers. We had only ten minutes allowed for our breakfasts, which were always brought up to the mill for us and we worked that up at night again – 2 days in the week we had an hour allowed us for dinner, while the machines were oiled, for doing this I was paid a halfpenny a time, and other days we were allowed half an hour for dinner, when the boys worked overtime, they were paid 1*d* per hour.

Further information was provided by Joseph Sefton, who was training to become a mill mechanic:

We went to Styal and were employed in the cotton mills of Samuel Greg, which are a short distance. I was first employed to doff bobbins that is, taking a full bobbin off the spindle and putting an empty one on. I then saved straps and put these round the binders (the straps twisted the lists and the lists turned the wheels). I used to oil the machinery every morning. In fact I was employed in the mill work. I did not spin. I like my employment very well. I was obliged to make overtime every night but I did not like this as I wanted to learn my book.

Thomas Priestley told how his accident happened:

… during the time working, and there was a great deal of cotton in the machine, one of the wheels caught my finger and tore it off, it was the forefinger of my left hand. I was attended by the surgeon of the factory Mr Holland and in about 6 weeks I recovered.[83]

As in other early cotton mills, the mill workers worked a six-day week every week of the year, until the 1820s when time off at Christmas and during Wakes Week (late August) was permitted. At Quarry Bank, by 1790 the norm was a twelve-hour working day.[84]

With at least half the workforce being children, discipline in the mill was of paramount importance. In spite of this regular concern, there were serious accidents and a number of fatalities, too. The deaths were sometimes due to negligence or carelessness, as well as to epidemics or diseases such as consumption. Over the years, the mortality rate at Styal was estimated by Robert Greg to be 7 per 1,000, while the rate in Manchester was 33 per 1,000. But death was a familiar occurrence. A sermon of Hannah's to the apprentices gathered on a Sunday evening recalls one of their number who had died during the past year.[85]

There was a different routine for all the mill workers on Sundays. For families who lived locally Sunday was a day of rest, with the devout going to church, and others to gardening, games or sports. But for those in charge of the pauper apprentice children, it was important that their day be filled with positive routines, lest idle hands find mischief. Attendance at the Anglican church in Wilmslow twice each Sunday was a fixed routine (as required in the Health and Morals of Apprentices Act of 1802), but beyond that there was time for gardening and lessons. The procession to church on Sundays was described by a local historian writing in 1886:

> Seventy years ago or more a group of neatly and soberly dressed girls could be seen every Sunday morning, when the weather permitted, filing quietly to their places in the Booth Chapel in order to take their part in the morning service. Their plain, light straw bonnets were bound over the head by a green ribbon. The neat drab dresses were of a stout cotton material – a sort of thinnish fustian, – and the bust was concealed by cross-over buff kerchiefs. Woollen stockings and substantial shoes protected their

feet. Cloaks shielded them from wet or cold. A few lads came with them, but they sat apart. These wore dark corded breeches, woollen stockings, and stout shoes. Their jackets were of strong fustian, and their high crowned hats were doffed on entering the church.[86]

Hannah's roles among the mill apprentices

It is clear that Hannah quickly realised that her vocation to help and educate the apprentice children required more than books. Her motives were shared and possibly discussed with Dr Currie, who had been impressed with David Dale's care of his workforce at New Lanark, and later wrote: 'The labouring poor demand our constant attention. To inform their minds, to repress their vices, to assist their labours, to invigorate their activity, and to improve their comforts – these are the noblest offices of enlightened minds in superior stations.'[87] The potential role of the mill owner and his wife was also grasped by Mrs Elizabeth Evans, the daughter of Jedediah Strutt, one of the pioneers of the factory community at Belper. After reading William Godwin's *Enquiry Concerning Political Justice* in 1793, she well understood the importance of their role, and wrote urging her brother to read it, as 'the grand desideratum in Politics is the diffusion of knowledge and morals among the poor. This the manufacturer has it in his power considerably to promote & is culpable in the neglect of it.'[88]

Hannah, as a manufacturer's wife, would have supported that conclusion, and saw a clear role for herself and her family. In the preface to her first book, Hannah expressed her broad aims, which must have been based on experience of the conditions, needs and potential of the mill-worker families and the young apprentices at Quarry Bank. Hannah had time to reflect on these issues, and had no doubt discussed with Samuel and the factory doctor, Peter Holland, how she could usefully augment the basic education already provided by some teachers hired in to provide a few lessons on weekday evenings. She referred to her 'many opportunities of observing how much the poor suffer from ignorance and prejudice':

> Whoever considers the social state must lament that so many people are brought up in the world without knowing what is required of them, or how to act in the different stations in which they may be placed, and under the vicissitudes of fortune to which they are exposed; they are taught merely to provide for their existence, and left ignorant of the means of rendering their existence respectable and happy.[89]

A remedy, as she saw it, was to remove ignorance by giving advice on: 'the common business of life (Economy made easy)', to include:

> recipes for cheap food and articles of household and personal economy; directions how to manage children, and to treat their common disorders, viz small-pox, measles etc, simple prescriptions for unequivocal diseases, with means of prevention and recovery; advice respecting friendly societies and Sunday Schools … observations on different employments, trades, etc.

It was widely thought that working-class girls should learn only sewing and basic household tasks, fitting them for employment in traditional roles as domestic servants. The mill girls at Quarry Bank were also taught to read and write. (Hannah's eldest daughter, Bessy, confirms that she did teach a number of girls these essential skills.) It seems unlikely that Hannah's first involvement with the mill children should be in the form of an educational book if it was the case that the girls, who were by far the larger proportion of the young workforce, were expected to remain illiterate. It would be consistent with Hannah's open views about women's minds and their right to a good basic education that this basic skill should be offered to all the mill children, girls as well as boys.

So, by 1800, Hannah had become a well-known figure among the mill apprentices, tending not only to their education but also to their spiritual development and, most particularly, to their health and welfare. She addressed them on Sunday afternoons, as well as preparing and dispensing prescriptions in accordance with Dr Holland's directions. She also instituted the practice of getting her sons and daughters to act as tutors to apprentices during their time off work, a routine that all seem to have found valuable. Bessy probably started teaching the apprentice children at an early age, alongside her mother. Each of her brothers and sisters followed in her footsteps.

There is no evidence of Hannah being involved with the managers of the Apprentice House, but there can be little doubt that she took an active interest in their selection, and in the way that the apprentices were housed and fed. Her conversations with Dr Currie and Dr Percival must have provided her with the best possible advice on managing the Apprentice House as an institution that could benefit its occupants as well as their employers. As her experience grew, her role and influence expanded to take in the needs and conditions of the families of mill workers in the growing factory community.

It is hard, however, to escape a distinction made by Hannah, whether consciously or not. On the one hand, her children were brought up – as she and many of her contemporaries had been – to achieve status and acceptance in polite society. Her insistence on the merchant being educated, civilised and cultured is part of this ambition. Her view of the mill workers, on the other hand, was that they not only belonged to the class of 'the poor', but that no amount of effort or self-improvement would be enough to raise them out of that class. It had to remain their station in life. This assumption was, of course, widespread at the time, but seen from another age, suggests a certain myopia. The Gregs were 'upwardly mobile' and, within a generation, many poor workers aspired to be too.

Six

'Tending to the happiness of the human race': Hannah's role in the factory community, 1810–20

New roles for Hannah at Quarry Bank

Christmas Day was the most memorable day of the year in the factory community at Quarry Bank. At the Apprentice House, Alfred Fryer, a local historian noted:

> … all the school work was exhibited to the Quarry Bank family and their friends; prizes were awarded, recitations were given, and the honour of being distinguished as the best girl or boy, steadiest at work, most orderly in conduct, or proficient at school, was greatly coveted by all the young candidates.[1]

The annual party and prize-giving was as much an occasion for the enjoyment of warmth and plenty as for noting progress and rewarding achievements. The beneficiaries were the mill children, and the benefactors the Gregs, who could be satisfied that a proportion of the children had made progress under their care. It was Hannah in particular who set the tone for the education and welfare of the mill children, and who went on to play an influential role in the development of the village, chapel, school and community activities. She became, in effect, the *materfamilias* of the community; its character, if not its creation, was largely her achievement.

Her focus on the mill community was a positive response to those recent incidents in Manchester and further afield that she found abhorrent. She had lived through decades of political unrest there, but between 1810 and 1820 she saw the effects on the local populations of war, industrialisation, mass poverty and malnutrition, and of government oppression imposed by the militia. The first steps were being taken to launch the massive social and political reforms that were needed, but prospects of a better world for her own children were bleak. However, she realised that she could focus her efforts to achieve some worthwhile results in the smaller canvas of the growing community of mill workers at Quarry Bank.

By 1813, at the age of 47, she was a grandmother. Although in frailer health, she was increasingly absorbed in the mill workers' world at Quarry Bank. Her home there was the centre of her family life and the base from which she played a distinctive role in the community. With increasing confidence she turned from writing and applied her talents to the opportunities that lay on her doorstep. She took an active interest in the mill workforce, their health and welfare, their housing, their education and of course their spiritual needs. William Henry recalled her as:

> … captivating and delightful in society, and not less so in the more limited sphere of her own family. I admired … above all the noble enthusiasm and fervent eloquence in favour of everything which she regarded as tending to the happiness of the human race.[2]

These interests had evolved for Hannah over many years, but opportunities arose to achieve more after the end of the Napoleonic wars, when investment and expansion at the mill was matched by investment in housing and institutions for a larger workforce in the village at Styal.

Roles for Robert, Thomas and Bessy

Even as a teenager Robert was being groomed to join the family business and by 1815, following three strenuous terms at Edinburgh University, Samuel looked to him to take on some of the responsibilities in his growing cotton empire. Always concerned for Robert's practical education, Samuel took him along on his trip to Ireland in 1814, then sent him abroad to Portugal and Spain in the company of his older cousin, Isaac Hodgson, who was by then a partner in the business. Hannah anticipated Samuel would soon hand over the reins: 'he will have nothing to do but amuse himself when the Traveller returns and have quite an idle winter next winter ... he shall enjoy himself in the Country & leave all the business to the young men.'[3] This turned out to be far from the truth. Nevertheless, in 1817, Robert was permitted a few months for a Grand Tour of France, Italy and the Ottoman Empire, on the understanding that he would explore commercial opportunities while absorbing the culture.

Robert quickly proved his worth, earning his father's respect and contributing to the expansion of the group of mills and trading enterprises. He was well connected, intelligent and above all industrious, enabling him to combine his commercial responsibilities with ever-increasing involvement in politics and good causes.

Meanwhile, the career of Thomas, the eldest son sent to London to join his uncle's successful insurance-broking firm in the city, was not prospering. In 1811 when Samuel's elder brother, Thomas, offered to give up the business to Samuel, it was making £10–12,000 per year. Samuel wrote to Hannah with his initial thoughts. He spent 'from ½ past 9 till 5 o'clock with Mr Wood' – his brother Thomas's partner:

> during which time he laid before me every book of account, gave me the explanation & insight into everything & had prepared a statement of the profit of the business since my bro entered into it in 1773 … – a business for emolument and security greatly exceeding the ideas I had formed of it …

His brother seems to have offered Samuel the main share – in partnership with two young partners:

> The impression upon my mind at present is that it cannot be rejected without a very material prejudice to the interests of the family – however I will not even in my own mind decide without seeing you and consulting your feelings & inclinations.[4]

A plan was agreed, though later Hannah claims she had forebodings and advised against it. Samuel took on the partnership, and his son Thomas was to be trained with a view to becoming a partner too. In spite of a cascade of letters from his mother advising him about diligence, the company he should keep, and what he should read, Thomas failed to establish good working relations with his uncle and partners. He seems to have devoted his rather limited energies to literary pursuits, but in 1814 he was made a partner, the firm now being called Greg, Lindsay & Co. Like many others businesses, the partnership then incurred substantial losses at the end of the Napoleonic wars and the most experienced partner, George Wood, committed suicide in 1817.[5] Thomas stayed on but the firm never recovered and he eventually retired in 1828 after his mother's death. A disappointment to his parents, he never married.

By contrast, Bessy, the Greg's eldest daughter, was a constant joy to her parents. She was a comfort to her mother and proved to be a valuable source of new ideas. Hannah had placed great confidence in her since she was a child, addressing her first books of maxims to her, and they sustained a close and frank relationship. So it is not surprising that once she was married Bessy asked her mother for advice about her charitable work in Liverpool. The correspondence between mother and daughter shows how Hannah's commitment and skills were passed on. Bessy developed the tact necessary to establish and lead charitable initiatives without threatening men's traditional roles and perceptions. She also learnt how to navigate reforming ideas through committees managed and led by men, encouraging others to take the credit.

Bessy had spent many of her youthful holidays with the Rathbone family at Greenbank, where all the family, and especially Hannah Rathbone, had grown fond of her. Bessy's early impressions there are recorded in her teenage diary, which chronicles the entertaining company of poets, scientists and travellers.[6] Bessy enjoyed the companionship of the young Rathbones, and the children of her mother's Liverpool friends, as they read romantic poetry and novels together, danced, teased each other, and took very seriously William Rathbone IV's political campaigns. All took particular trouble to welcome back William Roscoe, their own Member of Parliament, at the end of the session when he had helped to secure the abolition of the transatlantic slave trade. The children were mortified (and in some cases injured) in the violently hostile reception that he received from the crowds in Liverpool. To Liverpool's most prominent abolitionist this may not have come as a surprise, but it was a lesson in politics for Bessy and her friends.

In her serious moments Bessy was finishing her education, with language tutorials, visits to factories, and lectures on atoms and electricity. She was sent to London for finishing school for a few months and, soon after, became engaged to William Rathbone V. There was some hesitation on her part, probably as she knew that the Quakers would attack him for marrying out.

But after several tantalising weeks of delay, and mounting anxiety shared by her mother and his, they became betrothed and were married on 9 March 1812.

It is easy to imagine the pleasure that this union gave to both Hannah Greg and her dear friend Hannah Rathbone, a joy enhanced with the arrival of their first grandchildren: Elizabeth (Bessy) in 1813, Hannah in 1816 and William in 1819. The young Rathbones lived at Cornhill, over the office in the town centre, while Hannah Rathbone, now a widow, remained at Greenbank. Bessy's role as a sensible and reliable young companion was relished by her new mother-in-law, but missed by her parents at Quarry Bank, though they made occasional visits – 'We have been at Lpool two days – a very sudden flight – Bessy as gay as a lark, looking far better & prettier than ever & fulfilling all the duties of life.'[7]

Bessy used both her mother and mother-in-law as sounding boards, taking their wise advice as she became immersed in charitable works in prisons, education and poor relief in Liverpool. In return, she was making them aware of the vast new challenges in these fields that were facing her generation. Liverpool had been transformed during the twenty years since Hannah had left – its prosperity was much increased, but social conditions for its fast-growing population had deteriorated. There had been severe epidemics exacerbated by the overcrowded and unsanitary living conditions.

With trade recovering, large numbers of poor migrated to Liverpool to look for work, but casual labour was frequently the norm, so major employers seemed to have no sense of responsibility for their employees. During long periods of unemployment, the poor were left to fend for themselves, in ever-increasing numbers. They frequently occupied cellar dwellings or old houses in dense numbers. Meanwhile, many more of the employers' class moved out to live in the more salubrious suburbs. So at the time when Bessy Rathbone came as a young wife to live in town, it was apparent that the town's prosperity came at a price.

The scale of the problems meant that individual visits to the poor, such as those of Bessy's grandmother in the 1790s, were no longer an adequate response.[8] The council was hardly equipped to cope: it made an effort in 1809 establishing a Society for Bettering the Conditions of the Poor, which helped provide relief, but by then much more needed to be done. Ministers of religion had a key role to play in moral reformation and education. They encouraged their congregations to help provide welfare and, from 1815, there was a growth of benevolent societies aiming to encourage 'the labouring classes to accept with fortitude the conditions of urban life, either by moral persuasion or by material relief'.[9] There was a profusion of Bible societies sponsored by various religious groups, and the scale of the problem was met by each district organising relief and education.

These were the issues facing the newly married Rathbones. Their chapel at Renshaw Street was a focus for action and Bessy quickly became a leading participant in schemes for relief. She was energetic, imaginative and capable of leadership at a time when it was generally expected that men would take the lead. Some of her projects and ideas were discussed in correspondence with her mother and mother-in-law. For example, writing to her mother-in-law Hannah Rathbone in 1819, Bessy refers to her new Bible Association: 'Our B association met last Wednesday. I would have given anything you had been there. We have had several most satisfactory instances of amendments in conduct. (3 on leaving off drinking, etc)…'

Then to her Relief Society: 'Our little relief society occupies a good deal of my thoughts and next week most of my time.' And, on the issue of hospital and prison visiting:

> … one of the subjects that interests me most. Mr Lightbody brought me a little book of Mrs Cappe's asking me to read it & circulate it as widely as I could where it wd interest. It is on the importance of Ladies visiting female wards of lunatic hospitals & Infirmaries.

What concerned philanthropists and reformers such as Mrs Fry, Mrs Cappe and their followers was – as Bessy put it: 'the young and innocent mixed with the vicious and <u>without employment</u>, many unable to read.'[10]

Hannah was proud of Bessy. In 1818 she wrote: 'It does me good to hear of your prisons, Bible society etc,' and the following year she asked Bessy: 'Do let me hear about the Matron of the Prison.'[11] Hannah was able to offer her daughter advice on making the Bible accessible and rewarding for people to read, a topic on which she had a lifetime's experience. She suggested:

> You have Browne's Extracts from the Bible I think. Would it not be worth enquiring of some of the Experienced at Newgate what they have found touching, suitable or impressive?
>
> … it seems to me desirable to give either by word of mouth or short abstract … a straight-forward history, story of the Bible, chiefly New Testament, so clear that in hearing a chapter read they may [get] some idea <u>who</u> it was said so & so to whom it was said, when; … Would I could in <u>the least help you</u>.
>
> But the inmates of a prison form a lower material to work upon tho' I believe that they who have committed great crimes are often less hard hearted and more easily awakened than they who fancy a discourse addressed to <u>sinners</u> must not be meant for them.[12]

This was the start of Bessy's long career as a public philanthropist in Liverpool. She listened to several of the leading original thinkers of her day, to see how their ideas could be applied to the issues in Liverpool. Among them was Robert Owen, whose essay *A New View of Society, or Essays on the Principle of the Formation of the Human Character* was published in 1813. Owen had been a successful cotton manufacturer at New Lanark, where he claimed that his new principles worked. He had become increasingly convinced that the 'formation of character' of the manufacturing population could and should be addressed – and he had a plan to achieve this. In *A New View of Society*, Owen argued that the government should provide a national system of education. Hannah Rathbone and Bessy got to know Owen well, but he divided people. In a letter to Bessy following a meeting in Manchester, her mother referred to '<u>*Owenmania*</u>' and '<u>*Owenphobia*</u>', suggesting Samuel (who had probably known Owen as a Manchester manufacturer in the circle of Thomas Percival in the 1790s) was not won over by Owen's imaginative visions.[13]

Hannah, Bessy and Hannah Rathbone were nevertheless impressed. Like Owen, they grasped that the scale of the problem of educating the masses required a universal scheme with state funding. Hannah wrote to Bessy in October 1813 that she was:

> yet well aware that <u>no</u> private fortune whatever could uphold Mr O's excellent schemes (except perhaps Mr Arkwright's who thus would employ his two or three millions), and that his talents are more applicable to some public or National benefit, than to a concern of Business that requires constant attention, faculties & time, mind and anxiety, of its possessors to keep it from ruin, besides a floating capital of 150,000.[14]

Bessy and her mother-in-law kept in touch with Owen, and Bessy went on to inspire others, tackling many of Liverpool's urban problems. As her parents grew older, they became increasingly reliant on her good sense, which was always a source of strength and comfort.

The family was shaken by the sudden death of Hannah's sister, Agnes Pares, on 30 August 1812, aged 51. She left a grieving husband and nine children, two of whom had by then married, while the youngest, Elizabeth, was still only 9. Hannah was grieved and felt:

> now threefold an orphan. The domestic ties had always been peculiarly strong in our family, and those that bound my sister P

and me were more than double-twisted for we had long been all that were left to each other of a family almost unequalled in strong affections – I had also been as a child to her for her age had been so far more advanced than mine.[15]

Hannah took a motherly interest in all the orphaned children of her sisters Agnes and Elizabeth. The following May she wrote of Agnes to her own son Tom:

Formerly when your Father left me I had a sister to go to (who) also listened to all my anxieties, who was parent, sister, friend, who was in short all of my family left to me, all upon who I had a natural contemporary claim. Thinking of her with fondest regret tears my heart.[16]

Five years later, Samuel's radical sister Jane died, and a few weeks later, in September 1817, Hannah's daughter Margaret also died, at the age of 14. Only one letter of Hannah's survives, which tells us little of her feelings in response to these losses. Jane's death was probably anticipated, but we do not know what might have caused Margaret's death. Hannah simply says: 'You could not have remembered my little angel, for a year had much changed her. She was become the tallest of the family except Mama for she improved beyond idea.'[17]

Hannah now spent an increasing amount of her time at Quarry Bank. The house was being modified and enlarged through 1815; Hannah was continuing to devote much of her time to the mill apprentices. In addition, she was able to support Samuel in his vision for a new village for an increased number of families of mill workers.

Investment and expansion

In 1807 Samuel Greg, always alert to opportunities for investing in new machinery, had installed a more powerful waterwheel to replace one of the two older ones. Nevertheless, after having weathered the difficult trading conditions in the Napoleonic wars, he encountered setbacks. Between 1813 and 1815, the trading arm of his business empire, his partnership with Daniel Gardner and Isaac Hodgson, foundered when they were unable to recover massive debts incurred with their agent in Cadiz. In 1815 the partnership had to be dissolved and Samuel had to take the major share of the losses.

Several years of severe economic hardship followed. All the textile areas were affected and the economy only started to pick up in 1817, as Samuel reported to Robert: 'Trade is mending, but much has been the effect of speculation … manufacturing brisker, cotton higher, government strong, money plenty, corn high.'[18] Samuel anticipated this with some foresight, recognising that a dominant position in the industry could only be sustained by further capital spending. He planned major new investments at Quarry Bank, starting with a giant iron waterwheel designed and constructed in 1817–19. In 1819 a new four-storey mill was added, and by 1823 cotton yarn production there had almost doubled (see plates 7 and 8).

The Industrial Revolution continued to transform the economic and social fabric of north-west England. Enlarged towns, bustling with new populations, steam engines, factories, roads, canals and soon railways would dominate the scene. By 1811 raw cotton consumption amounted to about 45,000 tons a year, having almost doubled in ten years. By 1825 there were 104 cotton-spinning mills and 110 steam engines in Manchester alone. But the proliferation of urban mills, as well as the spread of propaganda about the working conditions for mill children, had understandably led to a clamour for further legislation. In 1818 Samuel Greg was appointed by his colleagues to represent them in submitting evidence to Parliament on behalf of the owners of water-powered mills.[19]

Mill owners who thought of themselves as responsible and caring employers now often found themselves being viewed in a hostile light. Samuel's daughter Bessy resented this, as she explained to her mother-in-law:

… much pleased that evidence is to be heard on their side of the cotton business as Isaac says the load of calumny under which they lye is dreadful. 'Ogres' is the cant term in London for all connected with cotton spinning. He is in London now endeavouring not to oppose the Bill but redeem the character of cotton spinners & introduce some clauses which wd put water mills on the same footing as steam. Mama says few mills wd suffer so much as Caton & Quarry Bank. In its present state it wd I suppose do away with <u>country</u> mills & drive all into towns. Town Mills Papa says would be little injured but Country ones very much so.[20]

She was right about the impact on country mills that depended on water power, as they needed a degree of flexibility in working hours. The Act of 1819 in the end prohibited the use of children under the age of 9 in mills, and limited the hours of work to twelve for all who were under the age of 16.

In the 1820s, as a result of the investment at Quarry Bank, there was scope for the workforce to grow, and it increased from 252 to 346. This increase would have been a minor consideration had the mill been located in a town but, in the sparsely populated Cheshire countryside, the mill owner could only secure a workforce if he provided the components of a small community such as a shop, school and chapel, as well as housing. So Samuel Greg built a village. This was the foundation of the factory community at Styal that is still visible today. It was an opportunity for Hannah to exercise her influence.

Hannah's role in the paternalistic factory community at Styal

Spending more time at Quarry Bank, Hannah was able to take a close interest in the housing of the mill workers, their education, health, welfare and their spiritual needs. And she was even more closely involved with the apprentice children, preaching to them on Sundays, and teaching as well as assisting Dr Holland with their medical needs. Hannah's experience among the poor of Liverpool and Manchester enabled her to get to know the families of mill workers as well as several generations of pauper apprentice children at Quarry Bank, and to better understand their hopes, fears and needs.

She summarised her views on the role of a person of wealth and education in response to the needs of the poor:

> To see the poor adequately rewarded, to prevent exertion from exceeding strength or extinguishing spirit, to suppress the deficiencies occasioned by sickness, to procure for the mothers of families the ease necessary for rearing healthy children – to afford hours of pleasure and relaxation to the young, and years of cheerful inactivity to the old. It is, in short, to make man contented with his lot, that the rich should use their fortune and should consider themselves as stewards.[21]

This expression of the role of a paternalist towards the poor may appear arrogant or condescending now, but the nature of such paternalism is worth exploring at the period when Styal was becoming a factory community and Hannah's role in it was being formed. The Greg enterprise at Quarry Bank was seen as an example of paternalistic management, in which the interests of the business were paramount and the constructive treatment of the workforce was a means to that end.

When Quarry Bank Mill expanded at the end of the eighteenth century, the workforce grew to 230. The apprentice children, of which there were about ninety, were a major proportion and their hours of work were long. While urban spinning and weaving mills had to deal with a workforce that was restless, not known for its loyalty, and increasingly argumentative about wages, a settled workforce such as that at Quarry Bank was an asset. Wages were lower there than in the towns, but a lower cost of living and other less tangible benefits appeared to compensate.

These included some security of accommodation and work. Greg's own farm supplied a significant proportion of food to his workers who lived in the nearby houses and cottages – as well as for the apprentice children. The Gregs were well aware of the economic logic of providing some of life's essentials for their workers. A willing workforce could produce more. The same is true of a workforce whose health is maintained.

It would be easy to exaggerate the sense in which the Gregs considered their factory community as an enlightened laboratory for a new society, or as an Owenite experiment.[22] It is possible that Greg's plans were influenced by Owen's later achievements at New Lanark, which he was busy promoting a few years before the main period of expansion at Quarry Bank in 1817–20. Perhaps Samuel was aware through Hannah, and his daughter Bessy, of Owen's vision for villages of unity and mutual cooperation. He remained unconvinced by Owen's idealism, however, and was sceptical of Owen's self-promotion, which he seems to have detected at an early date.

In the early nineteenth century there was a growing contrast between the living and working conditions in overcrowded town centres, compared with the provisions and environment in the better rural mills. While accommodation in Manchester and the mill towns was becoming unhealthy, work unreliable, and starvation a threat, the families of mill workers who had for the past generation been living in the converted barns and farms in the village of Styal already provided a model for the more wholesome domestic life available for rural workers.

The Gregs, like other paternalistic employers, did not merely provide housing. They went further and took an interest in the health, character, education and spiritual well-being of their workers. How was this justified? An obvious analogy was that of the traditional rural landowners, many of whom saw it as their role to employ and house their community. The more enlightened landowners took an interest in the education and welfare of their tenants. From the tenants' perspective, there was the prospect of security of employment, but also the material disadvantage that they probably earned lower wages and risked losing both their home and their job if they fell out of favour.

Since visiting the poor in Liverpool in her youth and seeing the condition of the unemployed in Manchester in earlier decades, Hannah was familiar with the illiterate working classes, their vices, virtues and potential. Her mother had given her the conviction that the Bible was an indispensable guide to help them tolerate their lot and reflect on the responsibilities they had one to another, and on the value in resisting temptation – of which drink and profligacy were the most common and damaging elements. It was evident to Hannah that a fundamental skill for the mill families to learn, therefore, was reading. This enabled them to look into the Bible, with its stories, parables and lessons for life, as well as its Christian message. This was a first step in the 'diffusion of knowledge and morals'.

These themes recur in Hannah's books, her letters and in the fragments that survive of her sermons to the apprentices. To judge by some comments in her youthful diary, her conviction of the potential of the poor was not at the time shared by Samuel. To his credit, he had employed Dr Holland as his factory doctor, also a teacher and a music teacher (presumably to accompany useful group activities such as singing or drills) at Quarry Bank before his marriage to Hannah. Nevertheless, the didactic, religious and paternalistic tenor of provision for the apprentices and families at Quarry Bank is most likely due to Hannah's influence.

The demands for young workers from the textile mills in the north-west was met by transporting children from the workhouses of Liverpool, Chester, Nantwich and further afield, to become 'apprentices' in the cotton mills. The costs of employment were low, but the master was responsible, virtually *in loco parentis*, for the well-being of each child.

The system of engaging pauper apprentices to work to rigid disciplines in remote rural mills was not always a recipe for benevolent paternalism. Many records show a proportion of masters failing in this, with reports of overseers treating their apprentices with cruelty or neglect. Many rural mills were not well managed, the workforce not well supervised, and the evidence of malnutrition, epidemics, injuries and ill-treatment were for a time concealed from the outside world, and indeed from the parish authorities who were glad of schemes to reduce the burden on the parish rate.

In the first generation of rural cotton mills the working week was long; there were initially no annual holidays at all – Christmas Day only became a day off work in 1824.[23] Shocking accounts emerged in the early nineteenth century describing the mistreatment of young employees in some mills: long hours, night shifts, pitiless cruelty at the hands of the foremen, and no sight of justice. Under the 1802 Factory Act, the Poor Law inspectors were required to report on the living and working conditions for the apprentice children who came from their parish, but they sometimes failed to observe the ill-treatment at the hand of the managers.[24] Further factory legislation put to Parliament in 1819 provoked growing public concern, revealing that cruel practices in the employment of children in cotton mills was widespread.

The children from the workhouses were often taken from the dregs of society, physically disadvantaged and perhaps also often psychologically damaged, and possibly abused. The Liverpool workhouse, for example, was notorious for its immorality and abuse. The mill owner was faced with a difficult task of turning these children into a reliable and productive workforce. The inherent difficulty faced by prospective employers of parish apprentices was that, unlike the young children put to work in a family environment, no one was required to take responsibility for their upbringing. If they became aggressive, there was no one to restrain them. Few would have developed any conception of respect for authority, less still of a moral universe of right and wrong; fewer still had been encouraged to learn to read.

At Quarry Bank the apprentices were housed and fed together under the supervision of a superintendent. Discipline was taught, health was valued, and it is probable that the apprentice children encountered for the first time in their lives people who had some faith in their potential, and perhaps even some trust in them. In this environment, there was the asset of stability, of daily and weekly routines. And Hannah Greg and her children took the trouble to get to know the apprentices, encouraging Samuel and the superintendent of the Apprentice House to take a consistent interest in their progress.

Hannah valued the rich natural environment around Quarry Bank Mill and believed this was potentially a blessing for the workforce, notwithstanding that most of them worked a twelve-hour day of physical effort. She made it a high priority that the Quarry Bank children should be able to read the Bible, and develop a sense of morality and respect. They learnt reliability, self-discipline and sociability as well as skills for later life, such as sewing (for girls) and gardening (for boys). They were also taught to respect authority, which was considered to be a key qualification for the working class. This was reinforced by the Bible and by sermons; indeed it was Hannah's view that while each segment of society should strive to reach their potential, the ordained structure of society was immutable, and the lowest classes and the poor should therefore neither complain nor aspire to change their station. She was possibly aware that a well-educated and literate mill worker might become an argumentative and dissident thorn in the side of the manufacturer, challenging this notion that his station in life was immutably fixed, and demanding a greater stake in society.

Peter Gaskell in the 1830s, and later Friedrich Engels in the 1840s, were quick to point out some of the shortcomings of this system. They acknowledged that those country manufacturers who provided housing and charged rent had a more profitable business as a result of a modestly paid and tractable workforce. They were critical of the educated and paternalistic owners such as the Gregs, who made claims for their employment practices. 'The cottage system makes slaves of the operatives', maintained Engels, '... he [the manufacturer] uses the school to train children to subordination ... he dismisses employees if they read chartist or Socialist papers or books.'[25]

The forms of paternalism practised by the Gregs included the provision of rented accommodation. This provided a good rate of return, of course, and was a justification for lower wages than would otherwise be payable in the manufacturing districts. In addition, the family encouraged and initiated several forms of self-help institutions in the growing community.

The Gregs needed and aimed to secure generations of steady, reliable and fit operatives, who were neither feckless nor greedy. In return, they would provide a good degree of security of wages and occupation, in an increasingly cyclical economic climate. The hours of work were expected to be flexible, enabling the hours lost in summer (when the river was low) to be taken up by extra hours worked in the winter months (when water was amply available). This could lead to exceptionally long shifts, a concern that factory inspectors and the Factory Acts were keen to address. Samuel, and later Robert, argued for flexibility and could not understand the concern about the resulting long shifts.

A feature of the Gregs' paternalism was their personal interest in the people who worked for them. The example set by Hannah and followed by her children suggests that they grew to like, understand and respect many of the mill workers, responding to their efforts to educate themselves and to manage their own growing families, and knowing several generations of each family. In an age when many young workers were alone and far from their families, homes and friends, this sense of being cared for was probably significant.

The surviving account books for Quarry Bank show that Greg normally imposed discipline on his workforce not by punishments but by a system of fines. Deductions were made from the wages of the workers either to pay for damage done or for bad conduct. This applied equally to the mill children, who were credited with a variety of amounts for overtime and for doing odd jobs such as clearing out the silt in the pool, carrying wood or lighting lamps.[26] Fines were high for antisocial misdemeanours: such as a 5*s* fine for stealing an apple, and ¼ *d* for breaking a window. The Greg's regime was based along these lines, rather than physical punishment, which appears to have been common in many other mills.

One measure of the effectiveness of the paternalistic management by the Gregs at Quarry Bank could be the retention levels among employees. Among the apprentice boys there were a high proportion of truants who tried and sometime succeeded in absconding, which suggests that the Gregs' regime was unacceptable to them. Inevitably, children who had been uprooted from their homes, friends and neighbourhoods were often desperate to get away from their confined and onerous new routines as mill workers. We know that several apprentice children ran away, as they did at many other mills: there were seven incidents between 1788 and 1790 alone.[27] There is little evidence that the more paternalistic mills had fewer incidents of truancy than those with harsher regimes. In the period 1785–1847, when about 1,000 apprentices passed through the mill, staying for up to ten years, about 100 absconded or attempted to run away, which is not a negligible proportion.

The Gregs were hard-headed in dismissing adult workers (and their families) if they were feckless or unproductive. The implication is that those who remained were loyal and subservient and, from the Gregs' viewpoint, reliable. Samuel Greg once advised his son Robert, whose Lancaster mill was going through a difficult trade cycle, to dismiss any weavers who were unproductive. Although this incident occurred when Samuel was old and a widower – and although it was quite normal for labour turnover to be high in town mills – it reveals Samuel's hard-headed attitude towards inferior workers and suggests that the paternalism at the Styal factory community was linked to clear demands for the workforce to be productive, reliable and competent:

> At Lancaster the positively bad weavers ought to be turned off
> – & they have several – in good times no money can be made by
> them – in such as these, a great deal must be lost by them … Not
> one indifferent hand ought to be retained – they very seldom
> mend – & the turning off will spur the others to their duty.[28]

A good few mill workers at Quarry Bank, however, improved their lot, with the result that a settled community developed, where generation after generation worked for the family firm. Nine apprentices became overlookers, some of them women; one became the school mistress, having married the schoolmaster Mr Schofield. Eleven became mechanics; seventy were spinners. One former apprentice became the mill bookkeeper, 'largely responsible for the sick club', and its treasurer for many years.[29]

Not all the superintendents of the Apprentice House at Styal were models of kindness, however, and there is at least one recorded case of a truant apprentice being punished cruelly, under the directions of Robert Greg.[30] Enlightened self-interest permeated the culture of the Styal factory community, and over time this grated with a number of independent-minded workers. There were obvious disadvantages, as well as advantages, in living in a cottage owned by the master. Discipline and submissive-ness were features of the culture that they were taught, and this cannot have appealed to all. However, the system – in ridding itself of dissident elements – acquired a stability not commonly found among manufacturing businesses at that time.

It remains an achievement of the Greg family to have secured employment and education for so many at a period of convul-sive change, uncertain employment and stress for mill workers. The key ingredient in the reputation of this factory community appears to be the personal interest that many members of the family took in the well-being and welfare of their workforce. It was said many years later that the Gregs manufactured 'out of the poorest and coarsest material the very best set of workmen to be found in the district'.[31]

The Gregs' children saw themselves as 'friends to the poor'. They knew generations of the mill children and were interested in them and cared for their welfare. Bessy Greg ends her diary with a note about her return to the mill: 'After tea we went to Quarry Bank, and the Children were very glad to see us. We went up to the Apprentice House; – all were very glad to see us.'[32]

This relationship was Hannah's doing. She had the skills that make an effective teacher; listening, encouraging and taking a personal interest. Writing to her daughter advising her on her work with the prison inmates in Liverpool, she endorses a comment of Mrs Fry's: 'Mr Smythe asked Mrs Fry how she had so <u>soon</u> worked such change – she replied: "I fancy they have never had a kind word said to them before."' Hannah then underlines this point: 'While under this impression of gratitude & <u>self respect</u> so new to them, nothing, I apprehend, could impress so much as anything said to them or told them – verbal communication is always most interesting – most personal to the feelings.'[33]

Whether this sense of empathy was inherited or acquired, Hannah seems to have had regard for and to have been well regarded by working people from all backgrounds. At a time when social distinctions could cause tangible divisions, the growing consciousness of rank and fortune risked any approach being regarded as patronising. Hannah's respect and affection for her people is apparent in her own account of her care for her groom, William, whose character and spirit she valued. The manner of his death, she felt, had lessons for her. She wrote to her granddaughter Bessy on 11 February 1823:

I am so much in William's room that I can hardly give my mind to any other subject.

I dare say you remember William that drove the carriage, and took care of, and was good to the horses −. He was loved & respected and everybody has been good to him, and taken care of him. It is 12 weeks today since he brought the usual Tuesday party from Manctr home and the next morning he broke a large blood vessel. We thought every hour might be his last for a fortnight − then he was rather better for 3 or 4 weeks − but seldom had any prospect of recovery. The last fortnight has not even been able to have his bed made − and two people sitting up with him every night. His fellow servants think it a privilege to attend upon him. He is now very happy for he says 'he is in sight of home and would not turn back' ... His sufferings have not been great; but have had a blessed influence on his mind. He has always been a good man ... I hope he will be released in a day − or little more, if it pleases God − and that all of us will be better for witnessing 'with how much peace a Christian can die'.[34]

But the last leg of the groom's journey home was probably harrowing for him and his carer, Hannah. He survived another week:

... one week, the last of poor Wm's life, & in which I was not prepared for such encreased suffering, much of what was going on was quite upon me, & I seemed as if I could feel nothing.

Since poor William's removal I can hardly describe how much I miss him − a care and charge 3 months − the last fortnight the care to <u>me</u> chiefly − for he liked my presence and sometimes I shall indulge myself with a history of what passed which I hope I shall never forget & which has made me miss the comfort I enjoyed there even more than the pain etc I felt.[35]

Hannah's caring nature, which is so evident in this narrative, probably pervaded her day-to-day relationships with Quarry Bank employees over several decades. She combined it with an experienced appreciation of the needs of the business.

Village and apprentice housing

As the mill expanded, its viability depended on securing a skilled and loyal workforce, but Styal was still a small, rural and remote village. From the start of his enterprise Greg had rented, adapted and extended many of the available cottages and farm buildings in the surrounding community to house his adult mill workers. Now that many additional adult workers were required, Greg adopted the strategy that other mill owners such as David Dale at New Lanark, and the Strutts at Belper, had done several decades earlier: he invested by building new houses. By 1822, he had forty-two new houses constructed on his land near Oak Farm (see the map of Quarry Bank on p. 118).

They were described by his son in 1846 as follows: 'The cottages have what we call a parlour and a back kitchen and 2 bedrooms and a cistern and a yard; some few have a cellar in addition to that. They also have a good garden attached to each cottage, for which no charge whatever is made.'[36] At a time when housing for mill workers in the industrial towns was often disgracefully shabbily, built with high density and overcrowding, the main hazards to the health of the inhabitants were the unsanitary conditions. Greg's cottages may have had a conventional design and layout but their extensive gardens and rural environment provided a stark contrast to workers' urban dwellings (see plate 12).

The rent books show that over the years the new cottages at Styal were intensively lived in, often with large families sharing the few rooms. But the average occupancy of between six and seven persons per house compared favourably with the density then found in urban housing for workers.

The Apprentice House had to be enlarged too. Its accommodation was described in 1806 by the two runaways, Thomas Priestley and Joseph Sefton, who may have been coached to paint a favourable picture to the magistrates. Priestley reported:

For these apprentices of both sexes there was one house called the 'Prentice House' a short distance from the mill or factory. This house is superintended by Mr Richard Sims and his wife, these persons with their assistants see to all the matters respecting the lodging, washing and the diet of the apprentices. We slept in long rooms, the girls on one side of the house and the boys on the other. There were a good many beds in each room and we had clean sheets oftener than once a month, our blankets and rugs were perfectly clean. The floors of the rooms were kept very clean, the rooms were whitewashed once a year, and were aired every day, we had clean shirts every Sunday, and new clothes when we wanted them.

And Joseph Sefton added:

There were 42 boys and more girl apprentices. The girls all slept in one room, the boys in 3 … There was a door betwixt their apartments, which was locked of a night … We had new clothes for Sunday once in two years. We had working jackets new when these were worn out and when our working trousers were dirty we had them washed. Some had not new jackets last Summer but they were making new ones when I came away.

Health in the factory community

It was far-sighted of Samuel Greg to buy Oak Farm in 1802. It helped him secure fresh meat, grain and vegetables for his growing workforce. Urban mill owners might have thought that they need not worry about provisioning their workforce. However, owing to wartime blockades and a succession of bad harvests, there were years of widespread malnutrition and starvation in the expanding cotton towns. The Oak Farm accounts show a steady provision of fresh butter, butter milk, skimmed and new milk, sour milk and cream as well as flour, meal, potatoes, bacon and cheese.[37] Samuel Greg was very proud of the whole farm and especially of his herd of cattle, and took a detailed interest in the enterprise. The mill workers' diet was further enhanced by fruit and vegetables that they could grow on the extensive plots provided with each cottage.

There had been a modest village shop as early as 1812, but in the 1820s a full-time shop was built as part of the new village, as a profit-sharing enterprise. It sold meat and vegetables from the farm, also commodities such as tea, chicory, coffee and raisins, as well as shoes, clothing and necessities such as bread and flour. As a result, there are no records of starvation or hardship among the Quarry Bank workforce. On the contrary, the evidence of the runaways suggests a reasonably-well balanced regime for the apprentice children. Joseph Sefton recorded:

> On Sunday we had for dinner boiled pork and potatoes. We had also peas, beans, turnips and cabbages in their season
>
> Monday We had for dinner milk and bread and sometimes thick porridge
>
> We had always as much as we could eat
>
> Tuesday We had milk and potatoes
>
> Wednesday Sometimes bacon and potatoes and sometimes milk and bread
>
> Thursday If we had bacon on Wednesday we then had bread and milk
>
> Friday We used to have Lob scouse[38]
>
> Saturday We used to dine on thick porridge

In spite of these advantages, the factory doctor's role remained important. Dr Holland, the doctor appointed by Samuel Greg, was a prominent Dissenter in Knutsford, whose family of Dissenting ministers and teachers had been known to Hannah's family. His work at the mill is of particular interest as it is the first surviving record of a medical service in a factory. His role was initially probably limited to examining each intake of the new apprentices and dealing with cases of sickness. Selection of the fittest was a necessary precaution; between 1811 and 1842 he found only 203 out of 292 children to be healthy on arrival. Of the others, more than half had eye inflammations or were 'delicate'. The remainder were under age, feverish, weak in body or intellect, or scrofulous, and were rejected and returned to their parishes.

The medical records also show the doctor's regular visits, his diagnoses and prescriptions for the mill children. At a time of growing concern about the damaging effects and dangerous conditions in spinning mills, this was a wise precaution of Greg's. But it was also consistent with the common-sense guidance of Thomas Percival, to ensure that the young workforce was able to serve diligently and without unwarranted risk.

Even so, the records do show disease and injury, and several deaths. The cotton dust sometimes caused inflammation; there were pains, stomach disorders and always the risk of a major infection. Treatments regularly included poultices, pills, laxatives and leeches. Holland's system was to examine patients and prescribe treatments during his weekly visits. These are some examples:

March 1 1806: <u>Betty Knight</u>: rheumatic pains in the back and limbs. Chiefly on the right side. Let her sit up to the middle in a tub of water, of new milk warmth, for ten minutes, immediately before going to bed. Let this be repeated each night for four nights; and let her be afterwards well rubbed with a warm cloth, and have her limbs wrapped in a little warm flannel. Let her take two of the pills which will be directed three times a day.

March 12 <u>Mary Crosby</u>: Pain in the bowels. No fever. Has taken a dose of salts. Let her take a dose of salts on Friday, if the pain continues.

<u>Betty Bowen</u>: Pain in the head and side. Let her take a gentle emetic this morning.

<u>Anne Peake</u>: Abscess forming at the top of the foot. Scrofulous hair. Soreness in the seat. Let a poultice be applied at the top of

the foot, composed of alizar and water, boiled up with crumb of white bread. Let her take a teaspoonful of the drops three times a day in a little water.

April 6 <u>James Worden</u>: Bilious fever. Let him take two Table spoonful of the Julep every four or five hours. Let his skin be washed with cold water three times a day.[39]

As we have seen, Hannah Greg had a family interest in medicine; many of her friends were noted physicians. She was keen to promote the importance of sensible precautions such as good air, good hygiene and good diet; at Quarry Bank she quickly became involved with the health precautions and treatments for the apprentice children and in the welfare of the whole workforce. Guided by Dr Holland, she built a responsibility for herself that became important and influential and that matched her temperament and ambitions. Hannah's role was to prepare and dispense pills and medicines according to Dr Holland's instructions, and keep an eye on ill or ailing patients. Her activities and responsibilities were recalled many years later by her daughter Ellen:

> She was most considerate of the feelings of health of all around her, and as the medical man resided at a distance (7 or 8 miles of bad road at Knutsford) she kept notes of all cases requiring attention and made up prescriptions in the house, ready for the doctor's weekly visits.[40]

Between 1813 and 1833, seventeen apprentices died, the main causes being chest ailments, fever or accidents. Hannah's Sunday reading at the Apprentice House would normally refer to recent deaths within their community.[41]

The greatest concern among mill owners was the risk of an outbreak of a contagious fever or an epidemic. These tended to occur where many people were confined together such as in prisons, ships, mills and workhouses. But, as far as we know, both the mill and the Apprentice House at Quarry Bank escaped. Isolation from the diseases and infections of the town, with its poor housing conditions and its fluctuating cohorts of mill workers, surely helped. But precautions at Styal were needed.

An episode illustrates Hannah's sense of initiative and her authority to deal urgently with such risks to the health of the community. When an epidemic threatened the village in January 1818, Hannah took the decision to isolate a possible source of contagion on the Morley side of the river, away from Styal. She had found an ill employee lodging in an overcrowded house in the village, so to isolate this infectious offcomer, she 'laid hold of an empty Cottage, whitewashed it', enabling the stricken woman to occupy it in isolation. She supposed it was a case that:

> [she could] call the 'Lpool fever' in it – she is lately to come from Liverpool. Mr Holland kindly walked up with me yesterday to ascertain her situation – said she was likely to recover – the infection easily averted – left us directions both for this purpose & for the treatment – He made me much easier about it. I need not say we take all precautions. I did not go into the house with Mr H. It is of too extensive improvidence to us on this side the river not to take every care and … I really expect to stop its progress entirely.[42]

Another area of concern for mill owners and their employees was the risk of industrial injury. Accidents often befell an inexperienced workforce in the unfamiliar surroundings of water-powered mills, particularly in the era before factory inspectors, machinery guards and similar precautions. Many masters added to the risk of accidents by insisting on long shifts for young workers.

One domestic accident to a mill worker was recorded by Hannah in August 1819, in a letter to Bessy in which she referred with concern to a woman named Ruth, who fell and badly hurt her knee on the pavement, while saving the child in her arms:

'She will be long confined tho inconvenient to her aunt. To herself I hope it will be a period of improvement, she is very fond of reading – and Sally will teach her to write.'[43]

Injuries to apprentices were dealt with by Dr Holland. One was reported by Thomas Priestley as the understandable (and touching) reason as to why he wanted to run away:

> My business was to supply these [two spinning] machines, to guide the threads occasionally and to twist them when they snapped … during the time working, and there was a great deal of cotton in the machine, one of the wheels caught my finger and tore it off – in about six weeks I recovered … during my illness I thought of my mother and wanted to see her.[44]

Teaching the apprentices

Samuel Greg started by engaging teachers, including music teachers. Aside from his family's direct involvement in teaching the apprentices at weekends, other teachers taught the children in groups on weekday evenings. By 1806 they were teaching groups of boys for five or six nights per week. Joseph Sefton recalled that 'beside Sundays when we all attended', boys could go to classes in the evenings after work: 'we had school every night but we used to attend about once a week.' He complained that he was 'obliged to make overtime every night but I did not like this as I wanted to learn my book'.

In addition, Hannah and her children regularly taught generations of apprentice children throughout the year whenever they were staying at Quarry Bank, particularly on Sundays. This started before the first Factory Act of 1802 made education a legal requirement, ensuring that 'every apprentice shall be instructed in some part of every working day in the usual hours of work in reading writing and arithmetic, by some discreet and proper person … in some room set aside for that purpose.'

Hannah took an interest in the well-being of women and especially mothers in the community. Hers was a pervasive influence. It did not seek recognition but it seems to have been appreciated. At that time, the apprentice girls mainly learnt sewing; they made their own clothes, plus shirts for the boys, and had little additional time to learn to read and write beyond the instruction given by the Gregs' daughters. It might have been supposed that Hannah would have thought it a fundamental aim that girls, no less than boys, should be able to read and write, so it is perhaps surprising that, according to some accounts, the weekday lessons for girls did not include reading and, to judge by their signatures, some girls remained illiterate. On the other hand, the Gregs' daughters seem to have had some success on their Sunday visits at teaching both boys and girls reading. Hannah Mary's contribution to the 1808 collection of family verse when she was herself only 8 years old confirms: 'The Mill girls go on very well / I've taught 3 of them to spell.'

Fryer, the local historian, recalled in his deferential style that the tradition was maintained after Hannah's death:

After dinner (that is the Sunday midday meal) the school was held, and then all the Misses Greg came up from Quarry Bank and taught the young people. Instruction was given in reading, writing, and arithmetic; and whilst paper and pens were employed by the more advanced scholars, the younger ones (in those days of quill pens and paper duty) commenced their education by tracing figures on a sanded board. The kindness and gentleness of the young ladies is still sweetly remembered by aged persons whose course is now nearly run … and even now when referred to they are mentioned by their Christian names with evident affection.[45]

By the time that Bessy was married, her three younger sisters – Mary Anne, Agnes and Sally – were living at Quarry Bank continuously and devoted much of their time on Sundays to the education of the apprentice girls. As they remained unmarried, this became their fixed routine for several decades. The attention paid to the education of apprentice children was noted by the parents of local families, and in due course Hannah contributed to a school for all the children in the community.

Each year ended with a festive prize-giving day. This often coincided with the end of the fixed term of some apprenticeships and seems to have been a happy and memorable occasion. It closely resembled the annual Christmas prize-givings at Hannah's London school, which suggests that the whole occasion was initiated by her. It was strongly supported by Samuel, who (a daughter later recalled) would travel back from appointments miles away to be present. Hannah and her daughters also worked hard to prepare for it. Samuel himself presided, asking the questions; later on, his sons conducted the tests.[46] In the 1820s the viva voce was accompanied by an exhibition of the children's work.[47]

The Rathbones joined in at one party and William later wrote to Hannah: 'We all envied you and your children the distribution of the prizes among your Scholars. I have no doubt it wd improve the virtuous principles in the minds of our young Friends, without inducing vanity.'[48] The best part, no doubt, was that the party finished with seasonal treats of food, drink and presents. Even the Greg children were thrilled at the sight: 'We boys sat on top of boxes to be given to the departing apprentices – the table with rows of prizes, the coffee cans and the buns and Mrs Shawcross's private pantry.'[49] In a world where such treats were scarce, the children's excitement can easily be imagined, and with it the Greg family's pride in the progress of many of the children who had come to them as outcasts.

From the start Hannah had been concerned about the religious education of the mill children. Readings from the Bible were to be a fundamental part of the curriculum, since she saw the Bible as a compendium of lessons in charity, communal living and in understanding others, as well as a source for inspiring ideas such as endurance, meekness and faith in the afterlife.

At an early stage Hannah took on a regular Sunday evening reading or sermon for all the apprentices. It mattered greatly to her, and she made herself walk up to the Apprentice House to do it even when feeling unwell. William Rathbone's prediction that Hannah might become a preacher turned out to be prescient, for in a few notes that survive, entitled *Sermons for the Children of the Apprentice House* (1819), there are glimpses of her approach and the tenor of her short addresses. She took this role very seriously, reminding apprentices of her role in their welfare: 'I bring you food … and medicine.'

These drafts contain an unusual mixture of encouraging ideas and inspiring quotations from the Bible, interspersed with instructions and encouragements for mental and moral improvement. The children were encouraged to accept that their place in the world was likely to remain lowly.

So, for example, on 21 September 1819, she takes a text from Luke 19, 'he that humbleth himself shall be exalted', and starts by looking back on the blessings of the past year – the wants supplied, health preserved, and all other comforts and blessings. 'The past year cannot return,' she reminded them, and encouraged them 'to seize every opportunity of improvement and wisdom with goodness and kind actions. Give pleasure to fellow creatures,' she exhorts them, 'love truth, detest falsehood, delight in assisting others, be neat and clean, respectful in manners, bear reproof with submission and in determination to do better, so that this time next year, all can look back on improvement.'

In April 1820 her theme is comradeship and mutual cooperation, with a text from St John 13, 34: 'As I have loved … that ye also love one another.' Hannah reminded her young audience how Jesus loved his disciples, referring to them all as 'his brethren'. She commended them to look at bees which work 'building their cells and filling them with honey, without disagreement.'

On the text 'I will praise thee,' Psalm 139, Hannah makes an appeal to the imagination of the younger apprentices, pointing out the miracle of their God-given attributes – describing how we are all 'fearfully and wonderfully made. There are I believe 6000 joints in this room yet perhaps scarcely any out of order.' She reminds everyone there – perhaps encouraging some audience participation, that we all have amazing faculties – hearing, talking, breathing: 'You can also pronounce different words and letters, to shout, to sing, to whisper, to cry. Remember He who gave you all these blessings.'[50]

Even before the influx of new families, the Gregs had heard that children living locally and working at the mill as free labour, as well as the working children of local families, had expressed the desire to share in the sort of basic education that the apprentice children were being given. Within a few years, it became a legal requirement that all mill children should be given several hours' education per week in suitable premises. Thus, in 1823, the village school was built. It is reported that Hannah paid out of her own pocket for the building and equipping of the infant school.[51] The school premises at Styal were also frequently used in the evening for adult education classes, and Hannah's two youngest boys were regular teachers there. John James Audubon, who visited the Gregs at Styal in September 1826, left us this account:[52]

> I accompanied the 2 brothers [William and Samuel] present … to a discussion Club instituted on their premises for the advancement of their workmen; – going there we passed the chapel – and a long line of cottages for the work people, and at last entered the school-room where about 20 men had assembled … The question presented consisted of ascertaining the superior advantage between the discoveries of the compass or the art of printing.

He went on to give a talk on 'birds, alligators, beavers and Indians'. Samuel Greg junior became an enthusiastic and popular lecturer, who gave talks on geography in 1826 and in 1831 on other scientific subjects. But the evening classes were at this time for men only. His younger brother William also worked hard to enlighten his local audience on his youthful passion for animal magnetism, writing on 3 September 1830:

> I am now very busy reading and arranging and meditating for my lectures on history, which will be ten times the labour of my last; also collecting from all history and all science every fact, or principle, or opinion, or admission, or event, which can in any way bear upon magnetism, or suggest any argument for its correctness, whereby I have amassed a profusion of ancient and modern learning, which I think will astonish the natives when I bring it forward.[53]

Hannah's role in the village

From an early date, the development of village organisations and facilities appears to have been delegated by Samuel Greg to his wife and daughters. Hannah referred to 'Mr G having lately referred anything in the village to be done or undone to "the ladies".'[54] They had a major influence on the religious complexion of the new chapel.

Hannah was probably a supporter if not the originator of a sick club (1817), a women's club (1816) and a female society that started in 1827. Practical answers were also provided for the mill workers when they needed cash. This was a recognised problem, particularly in a community where wages were received after deductions for such things as rent and shop purchases. The Gregs acted as bankers, providing formal facilities for their workers to borrow money from them – on interest – for particular needs. In addition, Hannah from time to time privately lent small sums to those in urgent need.[55] She also responded to the idea of an insurance scheme enabling women to set money aside to provide for themselves and their families in the event of illness, funeral expenses or maternity. Hannah claimed some credit for the creation of a mutual improvement society: 'I pleaded for an institution for securing and paying interest for what could be saved from wages, suggested to me by one of our own workers at the Mill.'[56]

Membership of the 'sick club' was compulsory: it cost a farthing per person per week and would pay out up to twelve weeks' half pay for illness as well as funeral expenses. Although no specific evidence of Hannah's involvement has been found, it is likely that she knew about such mutual support organisations in other paternalistic factory communities around Manchester. Nothing is now known of the women's club or the female society but they were probably providential organisations that addressed problems of women working, such as the need for payment and support in the weeks after childbirth. Hannah saw the strains and problems caused when mothers of young families were breadwinners, and the need, as she put it, 'to procure for the mothers of families the ease necessary for rearing healthy children': this may have been the purpose of the women's club. In addition, some planning and organisation would be needed to provide a rudimentary crèche for groups of infants too young to be left alone while their mothers were at work, and Hannah's funding of an infant school may have been a response to this need. It must have been clear to her that with so many mothers returning to work often soon after childbirth, the upbringing of their children, let alone their own health, would be at risk unless a few helpful steps were taken. Hannah probably understood how important it was to provide some solutions, and grasped the opportunity to help make them happen.

It would not be correct to claim that all the village institutions introduced at Styal were equally pioneering. Many other rural factory communities had been established well before the Greg factory community. In the 1780s Arkwright had been the initiator of the rural cotton-factory community with houses, inns, a truck shop, chapels and a church. Arkwright, had organised prize-givings, dances and occasional feasts for his workers. At Belper and Milford, Jedediah Strutt built scores of houses from 1793–94, all with gardens (and some workers rented allotments as well). Workers were supplied with coal, milk, meat and vegetables. The women of the family built a Dissenting chapel for the workers and a Sunday school in 1784. By 1812 William Strutt started a Lancasterian school. Hannah's friend Richard Reynolds was renowned for his philanthropy at Coalbrookdale, where he had laid out rural walks for his iron workers; at New Lanark, as Dr Currie had told Hannah, David Dale provided for the schooling of his mill children on a large scale, and later Robert Owen had given his workforce there unprecedented facilities, care, and above all, education.

So perhaps the distinguishing feature of the Gregs' factory community from the outset was the commitment exhibited by the family. They provided scope and encouragement for the mill-worker families to live respectable lives, no doubt exercising forms of criticism or deterrence where standards lapsed. They continued to take an interest, providing improvements and additional facilities over the decades, and they also encouraged successive ministers, teachers and members of the community to arrange additional activities and resources. Robert Greg, for example, discussed the merits of converting the shop into a cooperative venture, consulting one of the Strutts as well as opinion on the ground. He also provided a barn for the Methodists to convert into their chapel.

The minister speaking at the funeral of Hannah's youngest daughter Ellen referred to the complexion of the community as being distinguished by a sense of duty, respect and affection.[57] These qualities were probably a reflection of Hannah's role: she set the standards of care as well as the tone and pattern of relationships. Critics of this paternalism could observe that the loyal and steady complexion of the Quarry Bank workforce over several generations might not have suited individual workers who aspired to better themselves, or those who might find this form of pervasive paternalism unacceptable. The universe of Styal and Quarry Bank Mill may indeed have developed into a homogenous rural factory community, but there is evidence that the workforce was unusually efficient, with a high level of productivity.

Social upheavals and Hannah's response

While the factory community at Styal was evolving in the years after the Battle of Waterloo (1815), the fabric of society across Britain was also experiencing change. In spite of straitened economic conditions and trade restrictions, the country's industries had developed and many of its business leaders had flourished. Even during the long period of the Napoleonic wars, many of the middle classes prospered and there had been technological progress and consumer spending. This had given the chance for barely educated entrepreneurs to leap on the bandwagon of the new manufacturing and service industries and to grow rich.

Meanwhile, agrarian England offered poor rewards for those who stayed on the land; hundreds of thousands were tempted to find work in the towns and cities, many in the new urban industries. This created intolerable pressure on the housing and health of the towns. The biggest change of all was the unprecedented pace of industrialisation. It is now considered a fact that technical innovations take a generation or two to gather pace and realise their full economic potential, reaping rewards and generating major social change. This was true of the spinning and weaving inventions of the Industrial Revolution, as well as all the other developments in steam power, and in the chemistry of bleaching and dyeing. By the first decades of the nineteenth century, these transformations were widely experienced as major upheavals, particularly among the thousands of hand-knitters and handloom weavers, whose livelihood was now mortally threatened by mechanised production.

While Manchester, the second largest town in Britain, led the rest of the world in its investment in manufacturing, like many parts of the country, it continued to suffer social disorder.

After Waterloo and twenty years of war, the demand for reform in British society was rekindled there, with unprecedented protests, marches and demonstrations by the unemployed masses, and sometimes fights for the right to work, to obtain food, and for a new form of government to address these issues at a time when parliamentary representation failed to do so. Radical political agitation, now often adopted by large numbers of the working population, was perceived as a threat to law and order; it provoked years of repression. Municipal leadership was still in the hands of conservative landowners and loyalists. Backed by the militias, they contained with tough measures any threat of insurrection or reform.

For Hannah, this oppressive climate presented a mental and moral challenge to many of the confident, optimistic certainties with which she had been brought up. She strongly believed in the value of all classes being literate, and was confident that access to the Bible would help provide workers with a moral compass. But in the early decades of the century, the literate mill workers of north-west England were reading and discussing radical and inflammatory literature as well as the Bible. The moral leadership of prominent Dissenters in Manchester had been increasingly challenged by loyalists: now it was also being challenged by radicals.

Hannah was profoundly affected by these trends. She observed with dismay a changed world; one in which her optimism and faith in society, education and reason were severely tested. The government's inability to address the needs of vastly increased numbers of poor workers appalled her. Its repression of their justifiable anger, she feared, would spark a revolution like that in France. And, meanwhile, there was no reform of the franchise. Hannah had experienced previous threats to public order and social stability in Manchester in the 1790s, and then in the period of the Irish Rebellion, with the conspiracies and food rioting of 1798–1801. But worse was to follow in 1812, and in the decade that followed. The plight of the handloom weavers was the most tragic. Tens of thousands fell victim to industrialisation and had nothing to fall back on. Manufacturers could hardly sympathise with Luddites, but alongside the machinery breakers were crowds of starving workers, for whom there was great public sympathy. Samuel Greg was not a manufacturer who had invested in power looms – his son Robert, who did, later claimed that his father was slow to realise their potential. Nevertheless, as a prominent figure in the industry, Samuel probably felt threatened by the new mood of militancy and anger among the populace, which was often directed against capitalist employers. Hannah, once again, had come to feel deep anxiety for his safety.

Hannah's younger contemporaries began to address these issues, starting fresh debates about education, culture, political economy and science. There was much common ground in their idea of the 'march of mind', the notion that progress could be achieved through an increase in knowledge and in its effective diffusion. New worlds were opening up, furnishing Hannah's mind with fresh ideas and often new hope. British explorers were telling her about their recent discoveries of remote continents, and scientists (as they were now called) of the discoveries that were being made in geology, botany and medicine. Europe was again open to British travellers, and there were new thoughts emerging from Germany about philosophy, the Bible and children's education. Hannah also absorbed new ideas about social reform from Mrs Fry and from Robert Owen.

One of Hannah's main concerns remained parliamentary reform, which entailed changes to the franchise and to representation; she was one of those who kept the torch of reform alive but, like many Dissenters, she could not sympathise with radical movements that demanded a complete revolution, with land and housing distributed equally. She judged the ultra-radical working population of the northern mill towns to be 'savages' – and indeed she may have seen at first hand how threateningly they behaved when marching to demonstrate in Manchester.

In 1818 Hannah's daughter Bessy looked to her mother and mother-in-law for advice about her husband William Rathbone's idea of voluntarily banning bribery in the forthcoming Liverpool elections. Hannah wrote of her strong support for both electoral and parliamentary reform:

> Now seems to me to be the time for the firm stand to be made in favour of the true patriotic principle, the germ of freedom of Election & parity of Representation which tho it be now as the Mustard seed, may grow into the overshadowing tree, whose branches shall in time … prove the resort of the virtuous on all future occasions …[58]

Hannah strongly supported campaigning for fair elections:

> feeling it quite important in my personal view … – to address rational beings to give an <u>unbribed,</u> <u>sober</u> Vote – for the sake of Freedom of Election and Personal Independence – to seize the opportunity of introducing into the nation the purity of Political Principle. – of treading back our steps to the path of political honour – of bringing back the true spirit of the English Constitution – of producing reform in the representation …[59]

A new generation of Dissenters in north-west England had become a group to be reckoned with. Pressing for reforms and mounting campaigns, they had their own chapels, schools, institutions and academies and were influential elements in the movement for constitutional reform. Within a generation, members of these bodies who shared a new vision and ambition for local and national reform had made Manchester a hotbed of pressure for new municipal organisation, for free trade and for parliamentary reform.

The Gregs were closely associated with this great movement: in fact Samuel Greg was one of the very few men of the older generation of Whigs and reformers to join it. The Gregs were also immersed in the unfolding battles of opinion when reformers and petitioners clashed with the authorities, often witnessing at first hand the suffering of the local population. Hannah's response to two major episodes in 1812 and 1819 reveals her strong political convictions. Rather than risk exposure to the hostility of the civic leaders and the atmosphere of intolerance in Manchester (as did Samuel, Robert and Bessy), Hannah remained on the periphery at Quarry Bank, where she was able to observe and comment on developments while safeguarding her fragile health.

The government machinery for maintaining law and order was clumsy and provocative, with citizens' rights by no means guaranteed; *habeas corpus* was suspended three times in the decade following 1810. While normal rights such as the right to meet or demonstrate were curtailed, especially during periods of alarm, government spies and agent-provocateurs infiltrated the manufacturing regions, which were regarded as potentially the most likely to be seditious. In February 1812, machine-breaking was made a capital crime. Worst of all, the industrial areas, now regarded as under threat, were 'protected' by 12,000 troops. But as wheat prices climbed and workers found it virtually impossible to feed their families, there were food riots in towns through the north-west and, on 20 March 1812, the cotton industry had its first taste of Luddism when William Radcliffe's Stockport power-loom sheds were attacked. The Manchester Exchange Riots followed.

Hannah heard in detail about these riots from her young friend, Benjamin Heywood Bright.[60] He described what he heard and saw that morning in April 1812 in Manchester when the crowd surrounded the Exchange and broke in. He paints a picture of the aggrieved mob, and how insidiously their opposition grew to violence. And he predicted more violence leading to the overthrow of the prime minister, Spencer Perceval, and the foreign secretary, Lord Castlereagh – and their 'sordid principles' too. Later that month, Bright gave Hannah a further description of riots at Middleton, where he identifies 'the great cause of contention & complaint, as weaving by machinery', and is concerned at the high casualties among the rioters – eleven killed and twenty-one wounded.[61]

Hannah's sympathies are clear from the letter she wrote the following month to her son Tom:

> At present it is most serious and alarming – if Ministers are not prompt at meeting the distress of the country with some measures of relief – the condescension of government may come too late. One cannot but suppose they and London in general are ignorant of the condition and of the formidable numbers of the great manufacturing districts. Whether the level of discontent and of the <u>revolutionary</u> spirit, so long allowed to fourment in a mass of unemployed population, will evaporate in the sunshine of returning plenty and reviving trade, if <u>long delayed</u> is the awful question.– the unread history –. At present 10,000 Military keep and probably will keep us quiet … I believe your dear Father as little unpopular as any master spinner yet you will not be surprised that when he is in the dark or much past his hour, I am afraid with terror I dare not utter – but he has promised never to stay out late …
>
> Manchester looked very miserable – there are many beggars about – but they now no longer go about in bodies – and subscriptions are everywhere made for their relief, but money will not make potatoes or flour … The next assizes will be dreadful …[62]

The government's overreaction to these disturbances horrified all liberals. Secret committees of Parliament heard evidence, much of it fabricated, suggesting a scale of sedition sufficient for a general insurrection. The government's response was a period of 'alarm', which lasted from June to December 1812.

Hannah wrote to Tom in August as trade picked up further and threats subsided: 'The American war makes all gloomy again but no fear of tumults. Gen Ludd waits to see what comes next in this upside down world – but he is not formidable. It is not politics but starvation that ever occupies the populace.'[63] The truth was that the liberal and Dissenting elite were in danger of losing the leadership of reform, while the mobs – motivated at first by anger and hunger – were soon to be mobilised as a political force.

After decades of anxiety, blessed relief emerged in April 1814, with news of Napoleon's abdication. Hannah wrote at once to Tom:

> … to talk about the very affecting news that has poured upon us and kept the world in agitation for so many days. The news fills us with … virtuous emotion & exultation. After 20 years of indignation and disgust at Human nature and political life and men, how refreshing it is to contemplate the sublime and beautiful (prospect) of Public virtue, of Magnanimity & the wisdom in the <u>dignified moderation</u> of the conqueror …

The King Street house was magnificently lit up: 'Your Father has sent out for 1000 lamps for the Illumination on Monday … making The word Peace over the pediment over the door. The emblem seems appropriate and simple,'[64] an occasion of young Ellen's childhood that she later recalled.[65]

Peace brought the prospect of a resumption in trade, but even after Waterloo, hardship and hunger brought out militant mobs in the manufacturing districts. The government was again repressive, introducing another period of alarm from February 1817 to January 1818, with habeas corpus suspended for twelve months.

Then came the tragedy of Peterloo. Hannah was at Quarry Bank in the summer of 1819, but both Samuel and Robert were present at St Peter's Fields in Manchester and saw the clash from close quarters. Their intended role, as active but moderate reformers, was probably to be observers, as were some other prominent citizens and manufacturers. Samuel, along with a majority of manufacturers but a minority of merchants, signed a petition critical of the magistrates' actions on the day.[66]

The background to the Peterloo massacre is well known, but Hannah's reaction is vivid and telling.[67] The important thing for her was to get to the truth. Bessy anxiously wrote to her mother from Liverpool, hoping to learn what had really happened, and why and what the repercussions might be. Hannah's responses give a vivid picture from the perspective of a committed onlooker. She clearly conveyed her doubts about the newspaper accounts, but had an immediate grasp of the historical significance of this event and the risk that it could become a catalyst for a mass revolt. Her greatest fear was that if emotion and anger got the better of the participants, a bloodbath could engulf the country, as it had in France.[68] Hannah blamed the government for its indifference to the suffering of the labouring classes of Lancashire:

> The <u>wants</u> ought to have been relieved & the minds conciliated before they were ripened into despair and desperation – at least they should have been attended to and not disregarded and disbelieved. But the Rubicon is passed & I fear more readiness for insurrection than was imagined.

The whole event quickly acquired a symbolic or mythic status. Hannah told how her granddaughter (also called Bessy) was staying at Quarry Bank at the time and, obviously impressed by all the discussion and concern about Hunt, the leading radical orator who was arrested that day in Manchester:

> in going to see the sunset with us last night she ran wild, gathering flowers & bringing me a large nosegay of flowers squeezed together (no leaves) large daisies all alike one a little higher in the middle 'for Grandmama see this is Mr Hunt with the crowd pressing round him'.

Hannah added a melancholy postscript:

Society was destroyed after the French Revolution at Mancr and wholly so after the Irish Rebellion and now the very frame of Society in all its institutions. I think one may reasonably complain that parliament – after fatiguing itself with comparative trifles … anything, something might have been done to soften, to assist, to cheer or to pacify.[69]

The government congratulated the Manchester magistrates, and the enquiries that followed risked producing a whitewash. The evidence of the Gregs' neighbour, the Rev. Edward Stanley, the respected rector of Alderley, was important; it confirmed that the violence was unprovoked.[70] Samuel forwarded a copy of the rector's carefully written statement to his son-in-law Tom Pares, who had been elected Member for Parliament for Leicester in 1818, with a covering note asking him to take into consideration the evidence of the rector who:

… was present in Manchester on 16 August – saw it – was a correct observer … The testimony of an eyewitness so respectable a character of an ancient family, & a true churchman – would probably have considerable weight. Consider the object & use your entire discretion but on no account let it transpire whence the suggestion comes.[71]

The aftermath of Peterloo, as predicted by Hannah, was more repression, with the government introducing the illiberal Six Acts. The government also imposed more surveillance during another period of alarm, which lasted from August 1819 until March 1820.

Hannah Greg was right in judging this episode as pivotal, but her fears of insurrection were too pessimistic. The Peterloo Massacre had also strengthened the resolve of the 'Band', that group of young Manchester reformers who through persistence and talent transformed the political landscape and led the reform movement that swept the country in the 1830s. Their origins lay in a group that began to meet in 1815 in secret at the warehouse of the Dissenting textile merchants, the Potter brothers. They were joined from the start by the few remaining seasoned campaigners of the older generation, all of whom opposed the Corn Laws. Samuel Greg was among them, as well as Robert Philips and Samuel Jackson.[72] Potter soon brought in a fresh generation, journalists such as John Edward Taylor, and younger manufacturers and merchants. In due course, Robert Greg would be conspicuous among these. It is rewarding to reflect that Samuel, battle-scarred from twenty years of opposition, was participating in the start of a new campaign in which the younger generation were taking a determined lead, and to suppose that he was getting ready to pass on the baton to his son Robert. It is also likely that both Samuel and Robert were given every encouragement by Hannah, whose ardent views on reform remained undimmed.[73]

Although a committed reformer and educationalist, Hannah seems not to have been concerned by the spreading opinion among reformers and agitators that it was wrong for young children to work long hours in cotton mills. They could probably demonstrate that at Quarry Bank, where the workforce was well supervised, the risk to their health was effectively managed, while in other mills children might be exposed to harm. But perceptions of the rights of children were changing, and the Gregs' regime at Quarry Bank was soon to be questioned.

Hannah's health

Hannah's last child, William, was born in 1809, eighteen months after her daughter Ellen, a pregnancy that had been life threatening. In the following decade, Hannah's health remained fragile. A preoccupation about her health and that of her friends and family was understandable, but even from the time of her diary, Hannah seems to have been inclined to draw attention to her own ailments. She was often ill in the first years of her marriage when she was living in Manchester, and she claims that her work on her first book of maxims was undertaken as she was getting over a period of illness; she had then planned a holiday in the Lake District in 1803 for the sake of her health. The symptoms were hard to diagnose and treat. Her children were well aware of her frailty, writing of her as: 'Experienced well in every worldly ill / Also expert in swallowing a pill.'[74]

Treatments at that period were based mainly on hope and faith, with the addition of opiates to relieve painful symptoms. When Hannah was ill in 1806, she complained that, 'so totally are my own intellects weakened by my illness (and the nature of it), that I not only dare not exert strong attention (which absolutely threatens my life).'[75] The symptoms – severe stomach pains and associated with these a concern about eating many foods – seem to have been linked to the gall bladder. The frequent headaches are unexplained, but the difficulties Hannah often found in concentrating her mind may be ascribed to the effects of laudanum, which was most likely prescribed to numb the pain.[76]

Over the next twenty years Hannah was often the victim of this complaint and this affected her spirit and confidence and worried her family. Samuel wrote occasionally to his daughter Bessy with news of it. For example: 'Your mother is but so-so – her stomach plagues her greatly.'[77] There was another crisis in 1817 when Isaac Hodgson informed her son Robert abroad in Italy: 'For sometime past yr mother's health has been in a very precarious and indeed alarming state. She is at present something better.'[78] A few years later, Samuel wrote: 'All well except your mother who is ever hungry yet will not allow herself to eat, her stomach is very weak.'[79] The following year, he reported: 'Your Mother is not stout & certainly does not gain either much flesh nor strength – she wants someone about her who will take some pains to dispel low spirits.'[80]

Samuel Greg also suffered bouts of illness. In 1817 the couple decided to try a few weeks in Bath and by December Hannah was reported to be in better health, but her mental energy had been affected.[81] Her later letters, while still full of reflections, admonitions and enthusiasms, reveal a more fragile mind and some physical frailty. Nervous anxiety often seemed to be caused by dwelling on forebodings, and her family tried to prevent her from suffering after bouts of introspection.

While a cause of anxiety to her family and friends, Hannah's health hardly diminished her interest in their activities and concerns. It may have prevented her from joining in a busy social life in Manchester, but she created a sphere of civilisation around her at Quarry Bank, bringing together a succession of interesting personalities, whose company the whole family enjoyed.

Seven

'The lady of the valley':
cosmopolitan and convivial hospitality
at Quarry Bank, 1820–28

And is she there and cheerful still
The Lady of the Valley kind
The trembling frame borne down by ill
Sustained by the 'Immortal Mind'?

The Master of the Valley too
By busy life not worn away
There smiles he still? Kind, friendly, true,
And gay or ready to be gay?

And swarms there still the lawn, the Road,
With all the varying Population?
Books – drawings – oe'r the table strewed
And guests of every sect and nation.

This poem, entitled *Quarry Bank*, written by Hannah's old friend
Professor William Smyth, hints at something of the spell felt by
visitors there. A neighbour and contemporary of Hannah's when

a youth in Liverpool, he was a noted conversationalist, a confirmed bachelor, convivial (or as he puts it, 'gay'), and a popular and frequent visitor to the Gregs at Quarry Bank. He appreciated the combination of a family home and a cosmopolitan *salon* in which men and women of learning, science and culture met to converse, casting over it all 'a web of social love'.[1]

This was Hannah's vision and creation, an unusual achievement. She did not aspire to emulate the style and ostentation of the country estate of a traditional landowner or some newly rich manufacturer or merchant (such as Samuel Greg's elder brother Thomas at Coles in Hertfordshire). The most frequent visitors were probably numerous children and cousins for whom Quarry Bank was a haven of seclusion in the countryside. Hannah was not ambitious socially and, unlike her brother-in-law John Pares, did not mix much with the local gentry. It was the intelligentsia who attracted her.

Hannah, who had always enjoyed spirited and ardent conversation, used her newly enlarged home to bring together bright minds from different worlds. There they appreciated a wide range of topics that could be openly discussed. There too, one of Hannah's aims could be fulfilled: she was ambitious for her children, and took a great deal of trouble to introduce them to people of distinction and influence. Here the children could meet, hear and get to know some of the more influential and able people in the worlds of learning, literature, the arts, science, politics and commerce.

So home life at Quarry Bank became known for its intelligent and open discussions, where learning and culture as well as social change and politics were ready topics. Hannah had realised a vision of her home as a place where civilised values were to be cultivated and discussed.

Refinements to Quarry Bank House and its landscape setting

In 1808, when Hannah's children wrote: 'deep in a vale their mansion stood', their mother changed the description of their home to 'their *cottage*'. This gives a clue to the way Hannah saw her life at Quarry Bank at this period: rural and unpretentious. A cottage implied for them a place for the holidays, for family and close friends, fashionably informal, perhaps, but not conceived of as their permanent home. However, a few years later, towards the end of the Napoleonic wars, the Gregs were adding to Quarry Bank House. Their scheme was to demolish the old service wing and rebuild an enlarged version from basement level, with accommodation on two floors above. Having previously had eighteen windows, the enlarged house was then taxed on thirty-three; from then on it could realistically be described as a mansion rather than a cottage (see plate 11).[2]

Building started as the Napoleonic wars were ending in 1814. Account books show the work charged by plasterers for stucco ceilings, for brickwork and joinery. Hannah wrote to Robert expecting all to be finished by the following summer. 'I rejoice to hear that Quarry Bank will be inhabitable in June or the beginning of July.'[3] But completion was delayed.[4] Hannah feared that Robert would not be impressed by the end result of the enlargement:

> … you will find us at least if you come in the next 3 months not only rough and unfinished at QB but 5 or 6 coughing. One anxiety that you should not think Q bank much disfigured for which I fear you will in proportion to the cost see very little additions of convenience attained.[5]

Why did they extend the house, at a time when the two eldest children had left home? Until about 1812 the family's routine was to spend some of the summer, weekends and part of

December, Christmas and New Year at Quarry Bank, as well as long weekends in April, May and October. The family probably reckoned that with increased space they could spend the whole year there in some comfort. Indeed, Hannah sent no letters from the Manchester address after May 1815.

One explanation seems to be that the parents were giving up King Street as their main base. When Samuel was young, King Street had been the most fashionable place to live, but it had evolved into a commercial rather than a residential area, a street of offices and banks. Merchants and manufacturers had moved to more salubrious houses in the country. It is unlikely that Hannah appreciated living in the town centre, for apart from the volatile public demonstrations in the streets, central Manchester was increasingly dirty, crowded and unpleasant. Samuel too was persuaded by Hannah that central Manchester was no place for home life.

Quarry Bank, once enlarged, could then also be used for more entertaining and the convivial house parties enjoyed by children, grandchildren, cousins and visitors. To accommodate these changes, the new plans included a large modern iron kitchen range, a wine cellar, wet and dry larders, a salting room and a pantry for storing table linen, glass, cutlery and tableware. Hannah saw the need for a pivotal figure to preside over the family home, providing a still calm centre:

Home was always the theatre of my exploits and the boundary of my views and prospects … [my] paramount dread [was] of home being a dull place to either husband or children … When I am desponding … dispirited and discouraged … thinking perhaps my family might perhaps do better without me, I have tried to tell myself that a loving mother of a very large family can never be wholly useless while she sits in the parlour, ready to answer questions – to supply wants, to fill up deficiencies, to do anything others happen to leave undone – to be always found, always listening, always watching – a rallying point for the dispersed household.[6]

John Morley, describing the interior, suggests that it was decorated in a restrained Regency taste:

> The house over which this excellent woman presided offered an ideal picture of domestic felicity and worth. The grave simplicity of the household, their intellectual ways, the absence of display, and even of knick-knacks, the pale blue walls, the unadorned furniture, the well-filled bookcases, the portrait of George Washington over the chimney-piece ...[7]

Apart from the piano, there was a harp that Hannah played; in addition to the portrait of Washington, the house contained portraits – probably prints – of other contemporaries such as Mrs Barbauld, William Roscoe, Samuel Romilly, William Smyth, Rev. William Shepherd, Benjamin Franklin and General Lafayette.[8]

The family seems to have taken a greater interest in their garden once they had decided that Quarry Bank should be their main residence. It may be a coincidence that some lists of plant purchases survive from the same period as the enlargement of the kitchen and house. Garden improvements and investments were increasingly fashionable – and frequently competitive – activities. Some of their friends such as the Woods and the Lloyds were knowledgeable gardeners, showing off exotic specimens grown in the glass houses of their country homes in the countryside around Manchester.[9]

Samuel was probably as interested as Hannah in this enterprise, and the seed orders were in his name. In a letter from Ireland, he interrupts his flow to ask her to keep an eye on the glass house: 'The less heat in the hot house the better, & the most air that can be given – a cart of dung from the Farm wd do the vines a great deal of good.'[10] Hannah was involved with any difficult staffing matters such as in 1811, when 'the poor Gardener (whom we have long kept from charity) going suddenly mad has made it a day of such agitation.'[11]

The main rooms of the house still overlooked the lawns slop-
ing down to the river. Flower beds flanked the river walk, and
paths led up the valley, but the most distinctive aspect of the
garden was still the sandstone rock face, with dramatic paths
leading up to the woods and orchards, and the new focus of
interest – the walled fruit garden with its ambitious glass vine
house – on the plateau above. Family and friends would regularly ascend to the top to see the sun set over the valley, its
colours reflected in the river and mill pool. The upper garden
became a civilised haven of treasured horticulture to contrast
with the wider dramatic landscape, the woods and the small area
of parkland that sheltered a herd of deer. Visitors such as John
James Audubon recorded a succession of impressions:

> We turned quickly to the right and moved slowly down a decliv-
> ity when I saw Quarry Bank, a most enchanting spot, situated
> on the edge of the same river we had crossed; the grounds truly
> picturesque and improved as much as improvements can be.[12]

In July 1810 Tom wrote affectionately of the whole place and
its atmosphere in a valedictory poem as he set off for the life of
a man of business in London. Allowing for the old-fashioned
conventions of Tom's style, these verses conjure up a garden and
landscape in which the natural features are enhanced with shady
walks, shrubs and dells, in contrast to the areas devoted to flowers. This is all reminiscent of Shenstone, and a good description
of the gardening style cultivated and overseen by Hannah:

> Ye twilight walks, and woody dells.
> Ye rocks, and every shrubby glen …

> This Lake, where swallows dip their wing;
> These woods that wave with rustling sound;
> Those bowers, the favourites of the spring,
> Diffuse sweet inspiration round …

Mild Flora too, here spreads her reign,
And crowns with Joy the gardeners' care;
Here herbs and flowers throng the plain
And scent unseen the balmy air.[13]

Learned friends

As her health became more fragile, Hannah invested more effort in helping her children to a position where they could be torch-bearers for her ideals, and could address the issues and ills in society that had concerned her for so long.

Sensitive to changes in the cultural climate, she recognised that the world of learning had moved on since she was an impressionable young woman in London and Liverpool, absorbing Enlightenment thinking in the company of Dr Price, William Rathbone and Dr Currie. While reform of Parliament, of the franchise and of the penalties faced by Dissenters remained unresolved, there was a sense of progress as scientific and industrial inventions and their application were transforming lives and fortunes. Hannah was well aware that Manchester and the cotton industry had become a crucible and exemplar of social and industrial revolutions, generating progress and new wealth. But she also saw how exploitation brought in its wake unforeseen pressures on housing, health and welfare, and new opportunities for the education of the working class.

The younger generation confronted these issues with a degree of confidence, convinced that scientific endeavour could conquer numerous ills. Hannah had not studied natural philosophy (as science was then called) at school, but she understood the growing importance of science and technology. An avid reader and keen listener, she was aware of new worlds unfolding to industrialists, intrepid mariners, botanists and explorers. She read books on travel and science and listed among her favourites Erasmus Darwin's *Zoonomia*, St Pierre's *Studies of Nature* and

Thomas Beddoes' *Popular Essays*. She encouraged Bessy and John to attend the lectures of Dr John Dalton, and Robert engaged him as his private tutor. Robert was introduced to geology by Dr Corrie and then, in Edinburgh, was taught by Dr Playfair, one of the leading scholars in this field. Later, William and Sam were taught by Dr Traill in Liverpool, and by Dr Combe, the exponent of animal magnetism in Edinburgh, and became fervent collectors of specimens, facts and statistics on all manner of subjects.[14]

The Manchester Literary and Philosophical Society, under Dr Percival's successor Dr Roget, the lively and literate man of medicine and science, became less political and rather more academic and scientific.[15] This gave Hannah fresh opportunities to meet and to entertain the leading lights in the scientific and academic community.[16] Not many women in the provinces excelled at this, but Hannah knew several models. One was Hannah Rathbone, who frequently entertained visiting literary figures, politicians and reformers in 'the delicious and elegant comfort of Greenbank'. The setting and the approach could almost be a description of Hannah Greg's later world at Quarry Bank:

> Plenty without coarseness; exquisiteness without that super-delicacy which oppresses by its extravagance. It was a house to which the sick went to be nursed, and the benevolent to have their plans carried out. It was anything but a Puritanical house; the library was copious, novels and poems were read aloud in the parlours, … There was a capital garden, … there was a piano, and there was water and a boat.[17]

Another Dissenting woman in this period who used her home as a centre for cultured and intelligent discussion was Mrs Eliza Fletcher of Edinburgh.[18] She was unashamedly radical in her political views, and had brought together the founders of the Edinburgh Review. A friend of Robert Owen and Elizabeth Fry, she was at this time one of the few women in Edinburgh, or indeed in any provincial British city, who created a social circle of academics, literary, professional and business leaders, and encouraged the next generation to learn from them. Hannah, informed of all these attributes and introduced no doubt with enthusiasm by Robert, who had met her when at university in Edinburgh, twice entertained the Fletcher family at Quarry Bank.[19] And an earlier model whose work would have been known to Hannah was Ann Jebb, who actively and publicly supported the work of her husband, a Dissenting minister, by providing a welcome and engaging forum with his learned friends.[20]

Samuel Greg, though no intellectual, was a convivial host and supported Hannah in her role as a hostess at Quarry Bank, but it was still rare to find Dissenting men among the manufacturing class who were prepared to devote themselves to promoting cultural and educational improvement from their homes. The Unitarian Ashtons and Fieldens, and the Quaker Ashworths each managed large rural factory communities that were often models of their kind, but there is barely any evidence that shows them, or their wives, cultivating the arts and sciences in their drawing rooms. Among the Gregs' contemporaries, perhaps the outstanding intellectual was William Strutt jr. While his father, the founder of the dynasty, was single-minded and ascetic, his eldest son, William, had great mechanical ingenuity and a wide interest in science and culture.[21] However, it seems that the Gregs knew the Strutts only distantly, and were probably not influenced by them.

Convivial times at Quarry Bank

After a gruelling apprenticeship in the first years of Hannah's marriage, when her domestic responsibilities almost defeated her, Hannah had become an accomplished mistress of her Manchester household. Her aim was to ensure its smooth running, with attention to detail, fluent routines and a refined level of entertainment that pleased Samuel. At Quarry Bank she made her home a haven that was informal yet civilised, where serious conversation had a place; books and journals were not kept in a library (a man's sphere) but in the salon, where guests could come to relax. At times a salon for the liberal intelligentsia, Quarry Bank was always an elegant and tasteful home for the whole family. Friends commented on the lively mixture of young and old, Britons and foreigners, and the wide range of religious convictions that could be encountered there.

It seems that Hannah shone in this bright company, as William Henry recalled many years later with admiration: 'the delicacy of her taste, her lively relish of everything beautiful or sublime in nature and in art ... and her warmth of fancy and command over the imaginations of others.'[22] J.J. Tayler wrote of his 'vivid impression of hours of pleasing & instructive conversation'.[23]

This achievement was the outcome of good organisation, planning and sheer hard work, as Hannah explained to her daughter Bessy when desperately ill in 1807. Anticipating that Bessy might soon have to take over her duties as head of the household, she wrote her advice in a set of notes. The household was a stage, as she saw it, with her role as that of a 'Manager of a Theatre' − a subtle and self-effacing impresario, whose aim was to bring out the best in others:

> ... you must in short see that all is done without taking a share in any particular work as the Manager of a Theatre, who casts the characters of each performer without being sufficiently at leisure or abstracted to take part himself. Your work must be to turn the work of everyone else to advantage, and to make of it a sum of comfort, accommodation, welfare and happiness in the use of all ...

Hannah included some advice that probably reflects her own hard-won experience in adapting to the demands of household management:

> There must be no bustle over your work even when it is the hardest, but you must appear after it when called to meals or company,

composed, cheerful, neat, remembering that manner, temper, self-denial, are the great virtues that you are called to exercise – that to be agreeable must be your accomplishment 'par excellence', your forte, to spread an atmosphere of comfort and domestic affections around you – and that to do this it is not brilliant attainments that are necessary – ... (for the Mistress of a family is in effect its Servant).[24]

All this work created an informal and relaxing atmosphere, as noted by Catherine Stanley, a neighbour:

Have you ever been to Quarry Bank? It is such a picture of rational, happy life. Mr. Greg is quite a gentleman; his daughters have the delightful simplicity of people who are perfectly satisfied in their place, and never trying to get out of it. He is rich, and he spends just as people do not generally spend their money, keeping a sort of open house, without pretension. If he has more guests than the old butler can manage, he has his maid-servants in to wait. He seldom goes out, except on journeys, so that with the almost certainty of finding a family party at home, a large circle of connections, and literary people, and foreigners, and Scotch and Irish, are constantly dropping in ... You may imagine how this sort of life makes the whole family sit loose to all the incumbrances and hindrances of society. They actually do not know what it is to be formal or dull: each with their separate pursuits and tastes, intelligent and well-informed.[25]

Though not socially ambitious, Hannah (and probably Samuel) cultivated connections that could prove to be of value to the business or to the children. As Hannah put it in one of her maxims, 'Good company is the best supplement to education'.[26] Their daughter Ellen much later recalled these aspirations:

she was indefatigable in her endeavours to make all happy and comfortable, cultivating their friends or those who might advantage them, for she had a great opinion of the educational value of good society, and her ambition was that wherever their lot in life might be cast, they might be sure to find some friend who had known her kindness.[27]

Hannah's letters are full of plans to bring children and nephews together with distinguished house guests: 'one of the greatest pleasures of my life has been bringing congenial minds within the sphere of attraction,' she wrote to Tom Pares, while arranging for him to meet both Professor Smyth and another favourite guest, Dr Roget.[28] Thomas Pares and Professor Smyth got on well, to Hannah's delight; a useful introduction as Thomas was about to start as an undergraduate at Cambridge.

In 1808 Mrs Eliza Fletcher wrote:

> We stayed a week with them, and admired the cultivation of mind and refinement of manners which Mrs Greg preserved in the midst of a money-making and some what unpolished community of merchants and manufacturers. Mr Greg, too, was most gentlemanly and hospitable.[29]

In a 'list of company' at Quarry Bank dated 1810, a few years before the kitchen and accommodation were enlarged, many guests came to stay but there is a shorter list of those who simply came to dine.[30] Eighty-seven people are listed in total, the largest proportion being family: nephews, in-laws, and Samuel's sisters' families from Ireland: the Warres, Lyles and Batts. In addition, there are old family friends from Liverpool, a selection of widows of old family friends, and a new generation of outstanding men of medicine such as Dr Henry Holland, Dr William Henry (a former pupil of Thomas Percival and now one of Manchester's most prominent physicians and chemists), and Dr Holme (the physician to Manchester Infirmary, Dispensary, Lunatic Hospital and Asylum, and the House of Recovery).

The children's teachers were also invited and Professor Smyth, one of the most popular and regular of Hannah's guests, stayed twice. The Gregs also entertained some of their younger contemporaries such as B.H. Bright, the young antiquary, as well as some powerful business figures, among them many people of distinction and wealth, committed to their chapels, to municipal and electoral reform and, above all, to learning and progress. They include one of the Heywood brothers, who were by that time prominent Manchester bankers; Samuel Oldknow, a veteran cotton manufacturer and landowner who transformed Mellor and Marple; George Wood, the merchant who was an active Whig and campaigner against the Test Acts; several guests were Warrington Academy-educated, such as Thomas Robinson. There were cotton merchants, supporters of the Moseley Street Chapel, as well as founder trustees of the Portico Library; another guest was George Duckworth, an attorney and the Public Notary for Manchester, who had founded the Manchester Constitutional Society in the previous decade with Samuel and a few other prominent Whigs.

A later guest was Professor Playfair, the outstanding geologist, man of science, astronomer and a leading figure in cultural and social circles in Edinburgh, who in 1812 published the first of the volumes of his *Outlines of Natural Philosophy*. He came with 'his pupil', who was presumably Hannah's son Robert.[31] If they were lucky, guests were given a plate of turtle, one of the Gregs' favourite dishes.

The horizons of the Gregs were wide and ever expanding, as the exploits of guests were described and their ideas discussed in the parlour at Quarry Bank. One instance is the sequence of visits made by John James Audubon, whom Hannah entertained at Quarry Bank on 26 September 1826 on the recommendation of the Rathbones. His first visit to England to find patrons for his books of illustrations of the birds of America had started well, in Liverpool, where the Rathbones had opened many doors for him. While staying with the Gregs he had visited a debate in the school room; he had also dined with Samuel Greg in Manchester. Hannah then wrote to invite him at very short notice to Quarry Bank to stay and dine with Professor Smyth. This was a success: Audubon enjoyed the hospitality and his meeting with Smyth, a 'tall, fresh, ruddy, complete gentleman. One evening spent with him and the fair, kind circle at the Quarry Bank is worth a hundred such … as I had last evening.'[32]

Audubon was invited back to stay for a long weekend. He formed a favourable impression of his hosts, describing them to his wife:

> Mrs Greg is one of those rare examples of the superior powers of thy sex over ours when education and circumstances are combined – She is most amiable, smart, quick, witty, positively learned, with an incomparable memory and as benevolent as Woman can be – her and her husband form the finest picture of devoted, tender and faithful attachment I ever met with.[33]

Though Audubon refused the ministrations of Hannah, who worried about his health, he was rapturous in describing the family sitting together in the library, which they used as a sitting room. The daughters were drawing or working 'at light things'; another guest was an Italian lady, the wife of a Leghorn business associate. The conversation, as he described it, flitted:

> … from Green Bank to Quarry Bank, from one pleasure to another, not like the butterfly that skips from flower to flower & merely sees their beauties, but more I hope, as a bee, gathering honeyed knowledge. The next evening Mr Greg was in high spirits, so was his lady … Much entertaining poetry was read and repeated, we had a little music and a great deal of interesting conversation, much of it about his home country.[34]

Audubon returned for a final visit the following week. He had walked from Manchester and lost his way: he drew the whole day and 'in the afternoon I began a sketch of Mr Greg: quite satisfied'; but faults were found, and amusing suggestions made, especially by an Irish nephew. He was also taken to weavers' cottages, one of which had a collection of stuffed birds.[35]

Hannah derived much vicarious pleasure from accounts of foreign journeys, receiving sparkling letters in particular from her cousin Samuel Rogers, the poet, describing his travels;[36] and likewise from Henry Holland who, at the age of 22 was already qualified as a physician and was gaining a reputation as an explorer, with a published account of his travels in Iceland. In April 1813 he was travelling in Portugal, Gibraltar, Sardinia, Sicily, the Ionian Isles and Greece.[37] 'The travels that have tantalized me I confess [to] either of you,' Hannah wrote to her son Tom, 'are those of Dr Holland … To have been his companion on his present tour would have been an education in itself.'[38] Robert, meanwhile, in a note to Tom a few weeks later, provides a little local colour:

> On Saturday we read two letters from Henry Holland one from Joanina the capital of alti Pasha. The Pasha offered him 40,000 piatsres to stay with him one year as physician which he refused seeing some heads newly cut off hung up before the seraglio.[39]

Then in 1817, after peace had settled over Europe at last, Robert was allowed to go on his Grand Tour to France, Italy and the Ottoman Empire.[40] He wrote home frequently with his impressions. Hannah was especially moved when he wrote about Athens: 'Your personal companions can scarcely have accompanied you more closely than I have done for I have read perpetually treading your step.'[41]

In 1823, Hannah's younger sons Samuel and William were being taught by Dr Traill, Liverpool's successor to Dr Currie as a literary physician, and also by William Scoresby, the arctic explorer. They were introduced to Hannah and became regular guests at Quarry Bank. Even in her declining years, Hannah maintained an interest in Traill. This brilliant Liverpool physician and explorer was a founder member and first secretary of the Liverpool Literary and Philosophical Society and also a prime mover in the founding of the Liverpool Royal Institution, where he lectured as Professor of Chemistry and became one of the institute's first presidents.[42] In 1827, Hannah wrote to Bessy full of interest in their discoveries and specimens, which they seem to have lent to William: 'You will believe that I shall keep an anxious eye to Dr Traill's and Mr Scoresby's Curiosities.'[43]

The exploits of the arctic explorer Captain Parry were also followed with close interest. In 1826 he had married the daughter of the Gregs' neighbour Lord Stanley, and seems to have been a friend of the Gregs. Hannah mentions him in the last letter she wrote.

Literary life at Quarry Bank

In addition to organising stimulating company, Hannah presided over a literary life at Quarry Bank. Books were read aloud, discussed, recommended and analysed. Hannah's critical mind and wide range of reading made her an informal authority, almost a tutor in literature, among her circle of family and friends.

Choosing books with some care, she led the family's Sunday evening readings, which had become an important ritual. The books must be of interest to the children, but suitable – with no hint of immorality:

> This <u>perpetual observation by older persons</u> is particularly necessary in reading <u>novels</u> to young people. All (my Girls) have hitherto read I believe are Miss Edgeworth's, who is so inimitable in telling a story, or drawing a character, but I question whether I should have read 'Leonora' to them had I not found that they had picked it up at Lpool last winter – It is rather too <u>French</u> I think.

The story of a coquette in France was probably judged too racy. Hannah also admitted to her daughter Bessy that she had become skilled at impromptu bowdlerising:

> The Duchess's letters are almost superior to anything I ever read and indeed I had read the book to myself without perceiving a

few objections which struck me when I came to read it aloud, and which made me find my skill in <u>unperceived skipping</u> very convenient.[44]

Hannah's choice of readings also had to keep Samuel interested and, above all, entertained. He mainly wanted straightforward stories: nothing too philosophical or sentimental. Fiction was an area of contention. As Hannah put it, 'my husband nor anybody I believe in Manchester approving novels, from the habit of classing all sorts together.'[45] When Hannah was growing up, reading novels was still widely regarded as a potentially corrupting, wicked and idle pastime. Writing to William Rathbone, she could later justify it:

> There certainly are some very good novels now published calculated to teach a sufficient knowledge of the world without or before, mingling in its scenes – of excellent moral effect and truly philosophical ... Reading novels has all the good effects of going into the countryside without the restraint and trouble of it – they dissipate thought and exhilarate the spirit.[46]

In her 1807 draft testament, Hannah set out lists of titles that she thought suitable for Sunday readings. These show how her taste and choice evolved as her family grew up. The list included a few texts that meant much to her in her youth, but also covered a wider range of history, science and politics. In the early decades of the nineteenth century there was a wide market for fiction, including stories of sentiment and virtue. Hannah listed dozens of them, as well as novels and plays that she believed to be cheerful, innocent and harmless, such as Sheridan's *The Rivals* and *School for Scandal*.[47]

Mrs Inchbald's novels should be avoided, as being 'very dismal and too affecting for Mr G'. Hannah added some devout books, 'to read to your Father if he will permit', including Priestley's sermons, and the lives of Howard, the penal reformer, Franklin and Washington. She was a very discriminating critic, and the writer Maria Edgeworth received rare praise: '... so inimitable in telling a story, or drawing a character.'

In April 1813 Hannah met Maria Edgeworth and her father, whose joint work *Practical Education* had been recommended to her by William Rathbone some twenty years previously. Henry Holland, who had met the Edgeworths in Ireland in 1809, organised the introduction. Hannah wrote to Tom in April 1813 of her meeting with the author whom she had long admired:

> ... invited to meet the Edgeworth's at Mr Hollands at Knutsford and stayed till 2 o'clock the next day, no one else was there. Saw more of them than in a week of mixed company. They all seem amiable, attached and most happy in each other, but Mr E talks so incessantly & in such a boastfully egotistical manner that we could scarce hear Miss E speak. She is nice ... but all she says bespeaks the very gesture of <u>good sense</u> that pervades her writings. Mrs E is a very agreeable sensible lively woman 15 years younger than Miss E but they seem as quite equal friends ... Our interview was pleasant and indeed most flattering.[48]

Did they discuss the education of children, the future of Ireland, or the responsibility of landlords in village communities (all interests that the two women shared)? We do not know, but the encounter perhaps underlines the distinction between Maria, the dedicated, imaginative, professional writer, and Hannah, who lacked the imagination for fiction but was more of an observant social critic and commentator.

Chapel politics

In the 1820s Hannah and her daughters found themselves caught up in local and chapel politics. This is partly the cause – or maybe the result – of Samuel leaving such matters in their hands: 'Mr G having lately referred anything in the village to be done or undone, to the "Ladies".'[49]

It seems that in about 1820, a growing number of Congregationalists and Independents among Greg's workforce wanted to build a chapel of their own. The Congregational church was active locally and from 1806 had itinerant preachers in the area, generating support for their faith. The fast-growing workforce at Quarry Bank, and the declining state of the Anglican Church at Wilmslow also attracted the attention of Methodist preachers, who also went so far as to ask for land on which to build a chapel. These were the factors that persuaded Samuel Greg to take the initiative, and fund the building of a chapel. It would be a high priority for the Gregs that whoever was appointed should embrace the many shades of Dissenting belief within the local community, and Samuel wished to retain the vital role of appointing the minister, given the authority and influence a minister could have over his congregation of village tenants.

By the summer of 1822, the chapel being built near the school and the new village houses were nearly complete. The family was called to the 'topping out' ceremony, as Hannah described it in a letter to Hannah Rathbone:

> After breakfast this morning a sudden cry was heard from Mr G. and John that the workmen waited, and the whole family sallied up to the Oak Chapel. Bessy was your deputy and every one of the family had a hand in it, everyone laying their brick … May a blessing go with it. Every one who chuses will follow as the day advances to lay their brick, and the workmen have a little treat at night to drink 'the Ladies' health.[50]

Meanwhile, the selection of a suitable minister was discussed. 'The Ladies' – that is, Hannah and her unmarried daughters – took an active part in this. Their discussions resembled a scene from Mrs Gaskell's *Cranford*. First, the Methodists offered to supply volunteer lay preachers, but the family could not agree to this. As Mary

Anne explained: 'The Methodists offered to supply it gratis, but we wished something superior to the general run of Methodist ministers … and we object to their discipline.'[51]

In the spring of 1822, however, Hannah's four eldest daughters heard an eligible minister preach at Leicester. On leaving the chapel they agreed 'that if ever we built a chapel this was the person we should like for minister … We thought he appeared to have uncommon simplicity, liberality and devotion.'[52] He was the Rev. Halford Jones of Tamworth, a Baptist. They liked Baptists, so Jones was approached. He visited the new chapel, preached and met all concerned, but failed to make a favourable initial impression.

A rival contender preached the following Sunday. This was a Mr Metcalfe and 'we were all very pleased with his great mildness and simplicity'. A few weeks later the Rev. Jones was given another chance, but again failed to impress; considerable family discussions ensued on the merits of the rival candidates. Factors considered included their ability to relate to the workforce, to help in the village community, and their social graces. There were also theological issues: Mr Metcalfe was Calvinist, and if he held to their 'exclusive tenets, might not' provide a welcome to Methodists. On the other hand, Samuel did not want a minister who would be 'so great a favourite' of his daughters: ladies being always supposed to be very subject to ministerial influences. Hannah was interested in ensuring that the minister's approach to doctrine would be comprehensive, and she liked what she saw of Mr Jones's faith:

> … he avowed no doctrine that did not appear to me that of <u>Friends</u> – they the Baptists never mention the word Trinity – hold the Bible as everything & paramount … The Baptists are the most nice about the education of their Ministers of any sect.[53]

With the family divided, Hannah wrote to her daughter Bessy, describing how long it took Samuel to make up his mind between the candidates:

— though as is usual [he] kept us in mortal suspense from viewing the subject in different lights from day to day — almost from hour to hour — and reminded me of the 4 months suspense between Mr Shepherd's and Mr Tayler's school which almost cost me my life and others of the same nature still written in wrinkles on my brow and mind.[54]

In the end, Mr Metcalfe was invited to preach again. This was a disaster: he had a nose bleed during the service and could not preach. He then withdrew, leaving the vacancy for Mr Jones, which he accepted with good grace. Although Mr Jones's preaching may at times have been over the heads of the congregation, he remained a popular and successful minister until moving to Manchester in 1833.[55] An ecumenical welcome seems to have been provided for the different sects and denominations prevalent in the Styal community. Hannah was glad of the resolution, and pleased that the family could air and settle their differences and maintain mutual respect.

Oak Chapel at Styal did not adopt Unitarianism until Robert Greg appointed the second minister, the Rev. John Colston, in 1833. As might have been anticipated, the choice of this specific denomination seems to have provoked local Methodists to press for a chapel of their own in 1837.

Hannah's own faith

Unitarianism as a separate and defined branch of Dissenting faith only became a distinctive sect after 1791, when Theophilus Lindsey founded the Unitarian Society for promoting Christian Knowledge at Essex Street Chapel in London. Unitarianism then gradually became a denomination with its own institutions. (These distinctions, which may seem pedantic to modern readers, were of much significance in Hannah's time and in her circles.) From 1806 Unitarians set out to gain support and build congregations

throughout Britain and, following the legalisation of the denomination in 1813, support grew. Manchester's Cross Street Chapel
became an influential centre. It was in the very nature of Hannah's
Dissenting faith that new circumstances and new ideas should
inform and enrich her beliefs, and this raises the question whether
she embraced this emerging Unitarian movement.

It seems clear that she did not become a Unitarian. She
adhered to Mosley Street Chapel, which retained a select cross-
section of prosperous Dissenting merchants and manufacturers.
She had her children christened there, and she was close to the
congregation and to the minister, even while spending more of
her time at Quarry Bank. While Cross Street Chapel adopted
the progressive and proselytising mode of the new breed of
Unitarians, reaching out to a wider social range, Mosley Street
continued to maintain Priestley's mode of Dissenting belief, and
Hannah seems to have taken pains to satisfy herself that its new
minister, J.J. Tayler, would be comprehensive, rather than narrowly doctrinaire, in his approach. The congregation remained
non-denominational, welcomed a wide variety of views, and
did not aspire to convert or take over other denominations. In
a new age of missionary 'outreach', however, it was sometimes
regarded as elitist and somewhat out of touch with the pressing
social issues of the wider population.

While the new Unitarians made converts among all classes,
Mosley Street Chapel and its congregation remained aloof, and
indeed differentiated itself from Unitarians. Hannah's remarks
about Unitarians and Unitarianism were often disparaging, and
the Rev. J.J. Tayler could also be critical.[56]

Hannah's congregation was content to remain a small tight-
knit group. The religious complexion of Mosley Street Chapel
kept intact the characteristics of Rational Dissent, and in many
doctrinal respects – and in its small but rather elite congregation
– was able to distinguish itself from the Cross Street chapel and
the other Unitarian chapels being formed in many of the growing towns of north-west England.

There is a further aspect of Hannah's religious faith that J.J.Tayler very likely understood and supported: she set a high value on the spiritual value of the sublime and the beautiful, whether in art, nature or in human inspiration. J.J.Tayler was sympathetic to this aspect of his religion and, in the decades following Hannah's death, was one of the leading Dissenters to articulate and develop it.

By the time Hannah was in discussion with Tayler, Unitarianism had become widely recognised as a tolerant, questioning and evolving faith, embracing Rational Dissenters. Hannah doubtless shared the embracing nature of this faith; so her contemporaries might have described her in broad terms as a Unitarian, although she herself would probably have rejected that label. Religious life for Hannah was normally a more personal and less public matter. Hannah left this summary of her faith:

> Let me but try to believe what is true, and to do what is right that this world may leave me as the next should find me – prepared to pursue the improvement of intellect, that attainment of unbounded knowledge, that satisfaction of intense curiosity in a world where, neither care nor business will distract and overwhelm.[57]

Hannah and Samuel's final years

By the 1820s Hannah had experienced several bouts of severe illness and was increasingly frail. In his poem quoted at the start of this chapter Professor Smyth referred to the 'trembling frame'. She was prone to anxiety, which also affected her health, and Samuel came to rely increasingly on her friends such as B.H. Bright, the Taylers, or their married daughter Bessy to cheer her. The three unmarried daughters who still lived at home – Mary Anne, Agnes and Sally – seemed not to be able to cheer her as effectively. But, through willpower, Hannah could rise above such setbacks, as Samuel observed:

> Wm R, his wife & little one I left at QB. They have since left &

yr mother apprehends infected with the measles … which lays all
the family under apprehensions. She is however in unusual good
strength which indeed seldom fails when others stand in need of
her assistance.[58]

With her range of interests, her understanding of the sufferings and
needs of the poor in society and her compassion, it may seem surprising that in her later life Hannah's horizons were largely confined
to the home, but this is probably explained by her increasing debil-
ity. Excursions were arranged often with the aim of improving her
health: as well as being with grandchildren at the seaside in Wales
and, of course, to Hannah Rathbone at Greenbank in Liverpool.

In 1817, when Hannah was 50, and possibly again a few years
later, she went to Bath, no doubt for her health, She also stayed
in Liverpool, Caton, Leicester and, in 1823, went with Samuel to
London to arrange his withdrawal from the shipping insurance
partnership.

Her last book, *Practical suggestions towards alleviating the sufferings of the sick*, seems to have been conceived after this visit
to Bath, where she probably realised that there was a need for
such a book.[59] But the book, written in partnership with Mary
Hodgson and her sister-in-law Emily Hodgson, took several
years to assemble and Hannah did not live to see its success.
Her spells of illness became more frequent and laid her low for
weeks. Arthur Stanley, the Dean of Westminster, writing a preface to the memoirs of Hannah's son Samuel, recalled:

> being told how the aged mother of the family was carried in the
> evenings by her sons, up the steep hills that surrounded the deep
> hollow in which the house was situated, in order that she might
> witness from time to time, the sunset which, in the close seclu-
> sion of Quarry Bank itself, she could never have seen.[60]

Hannah's husband and family worried. Her daughter-in-law
Mary wrote to her husband Robert in 1827:

I have not heard of your Mother since Saturday when the
account was that of tediously slow amendment, Meat was, then,
entirely prohibited, & in its place Mr Holland had recommended
fine flour boiled hard to be taken with a minute portion of
brandy. So far as this has been tried, was with success ...[61]

After several lengthy spells of illness and confinement to her
sickroom, Hannah died at Quarry Bank on 4 February 1828 at
the age of 61. Her daughter Ellen recalled her last days:

She had been ill some time having had an attack of Gallstones
from which she had suffered seriously on a previous occasion,
and we had hoped recovering when she had a slight apoplectic
fit – & Mr Holland who had attended her for years said it was
quite hopeless, as her frame was worn out. – Younger doctors
were called in who hoped to save her. She only survived I think
a fortnight & the food and stimulants administered seemed to
cause discomfort.[62]

Samuel outlived Hannah by six years, dying in 1834 at the ven-
erable age of 76.

Lost without her, he was comforted by Bessy, his eldest
daughter, and looked after by the other, unmarried daughters at
Quarry Bank, and as a guest of his brother at Coles. He travelled
to Scarborough, to London, and to see his sisters in Ireland.
He looked to Bessy to help with the drafting of letters to
accompany mourning rings, and admitted to an unaccustomed
feeling of helplessness – recognising the support of strong
women in his life.[63]

He reluctantly handed over control of his business to his son
Robert, who had found him increasingly stubborn and reluctant
to let go. Robert had by then married and asked for his father's
approval of his plan for a new house for himself and his growing
family at Styal, near Quarry Bank. Samuel's reaction was critical:
he thought it risky and extravagant.

He wrote occasionally to Robert with gleanings of business or political news, or with advice on some mill issues, but by 1833 he was urging Robert to be more prudent in investing in the business. By now Samuel was no longer feeling capable of offering advice that was of any value: 'I feel decay of my powers both body & mind. I am unequal to any conflict with men or things. I think I had better retire from the concern at once.'[64]

Samuel's death on 4 June 1834 followed an incident when one of the deer in his park charged him and knocked him over. He was buried alongside Hannah in Wilmslow parish church.

How should Hannah Greg be remembered?

Did Hannah's children fulfil her hopes of social change?

Hannah shared the hopes of the Rational Dissenters whose company she enjoyed in her youth, and throughout her life supported the role of reason in the quest for truth. She encouraged toleration, and promoted education as a liberal force. She must have been glad when penalties for denying the Trinity were removed and Unitarianism was finally legalised in 1813, but the Test and Corporation Acts, with their limitations on Dissenters' rights to hold public office, were not repealed until a few months after Hannah's death in 1828.

As we have seen, Hannah was outraged by the brutality and bribery in elections. With Rational Dissenters and other reformers, Hannah continued to argue for fairer elections and more equitable representation. With her faith in gradual improvement and progress, she entrusted these causes to her children. How successful, then, were the children in fulfilling her dreams and aspirations?

After suffering thirty years of frustration during her lifetime, the arguments for the widening of the franchise, for parliamentary and municipal reform, were won in the decade after Hannah's death, enabling a new generation of Whigs to reform local government and represent the major industrial cities in Parliament for the first time. One of the main catalysts was the 'small but determined band' of reformers who first met in 1815 and who included Samuel and, later, Robert. Hannah's own enthusiasm for this cause doubtless helped them sustain it.

Many of Hannah's children inherited recognisable aspects of her personality. Thomas had her sensitivity to literature; Robert, her liberal and reforming mind; Bessy, her empathy with the working classes and her determination to win recognition for the roles and potential of women. Samuel had her commitment to education and her optimistic, idealistic vision; John, a sharp business mind; William, her ability to reflect and write. But none combined the full range of attributes that distinguished both their parents.

Although they grew up in a world that had greatly changed, Hannah would have been proud of a number of their achievements, especially those of her ablest daughter Bessy, who made her mark as a leading social reformer in Liverpool. She was small, attractive, quiet, winning and efficient. Audubon was captivated when he met her in 1826: 'never was a woman better able to please & more disposed to do so.' He was impressed with her beauty, good sense and candour.[1]

Hannah passed on to Bessy her own liberal views about the role and potential of women in society, and she adapted them to be in tune with the more conservative times. Bessy adopted a strategy that became a feature among later generations of able women: of working through committees and letting the menfolk take much of the public recognition. A notable example is her contribution during the Liverpool cholera epidemic, where she worked alongside Kitty Wilkinson, the protégée of her grandmother. This was the same woman who, as a child, had been taught to read the Bible by Bessy's grandmother Elizabeth Lightbody and who had visited the poor with her in the 1790s. Kitty was a tough survivor. Mrs Lightbody had found her a place as an apprentice at the

Hodgson's mill at Caton, and after she had worked for her term there, she returned as a young woman to Liverpool where she married a cotton porter in the Rathbone's warehouse. Kitty said she had never forgotten Mrs Lightbody, and while she and her husband were energetic in supporting those in need in their community, she became Bessy's 'right-hand' in her District Provident Society work in the Frederick Street area. Kitty loved being associated with the granddaughter of her benefactor: it was recorded that 'after the lapse of more than thirty years, she never sees one of the grandchildren of the old lady (who also strongly resemble her) without shedding tears.'[2]

Although Kitty Wilkinson has gone down in history as the heroine who established washhouses for the poor, much of the credit should go to Bessy. It was with Bessy's support and assistance that Kitty established a pioneering washhouse in her own cellar, to disinfect contaminated washing from the surrounding area. During the 1832 cholera epidemic, 'with these humble means aided partly by assistance from the District Provident Society and from some benevolent ladies', the washing of eighty-five families per week was made possible, with a one penny per week per family contribution. Kitty was indefatigable and very brave. Eventually, on William Rathbone's advice, the council invested in washhouses and Kitty Wilkinson was put in charge.[3] It was Bessy who wanted Kitty to receive the recognition. Bessy visited her weekly, making notes that were turned into a *Memoir*, which helped immortalise Kitty but in which Bessy's own role is hardly mentioned.

This initiative shows how the Rathbones worked together, with Bessy handling the practical work, and William writing the persuasive letters, providing the essential data. It was an important partnership, where Bessy was the indispensable organiser while never claiming a leading role. She did not explicitly set out to further the role of women in society, but by championing Kitty Wilkinson she enabled Liverpool to recognise one of the town's first working-class heroines. Enlightened idealist she may have been, but she was also a remarkably hard worker. She led and guided numerous committees and had a 'great natural aptitude for administration and organisation'. When she was 81, she gave her son William, then an MP, her ideas for Forster's Education Bill, the first legislation in Britain on compulsory elementary education. Forster told William: 'the most valuable suggestions I received during the passage of the Bill were those from your mother.'[4] The dedicatee of three of Hannah's books, Bessy lived up to her mother's hopes and expectations, making her mark as a hard-working philanthropist supporting generations of those in need in one of the most demanding of conurbations.

Bessy's brother Robert Hyde Greg (1795–1875) was a model of talent, diligence and robust character: no wonder that his parents looked to him rather than his older brother Thomas to carry on the family business. A polymath, he excelled in every field that he turned his mind to. These included art, agriculture, architecture, mineralogy, gardening, geology, science, mechanics, mathematics, economics and adult education.

He became one of the leading promoters of free trade, of the repeal of the Corn Laws, and of the Reform Bill, an issue dear to his mother's heart from her own youth. He was close to the band of Manchester Whigs and Dissenters who started to plan these reforms with his father, and was one of a circle of north-western Unitarians elected to Parliament, so he should be remembered as one of the men who established the international reputation of Manchester as the home of free trade.

But he had blind spots: he lacked emotional intelligence. For example, he was insensitive to the significant change in the public's appreciation of the vulnerability of child factory workers. The terms of employment of factory apprentices were being increasingly questioned, and most manufacturers had abandoned the system by the 1830s. Some critics compared it with the plight of slaves. Yet Robert Greg persevered with his apprentices at Quarry Bank and was rigorous in his application of punishments to those who escaped.[5]

He had little sympathy for the rights of unions and others who could impose restrictions on the way he conducted his business. The strain of Unitarian faith that he adopted was both conservative and elitist; so, like his younger brothers Samuel and William, who started out with brilliant prospects and prodigious energy to improve the lot of workers and remedy the ills in society, they each became conservative, opposing extensions to the franchise and fearing the demands of the increasingly vociferous and organised working classes. The concept that they inherited from their mother, that the station of the poor must remain immutable, was by now well out of step with the aspirations of the masses.

Samuel's case is particularly tragic: providing his workforce at Bollington with enviable facilities and a wide range of opportunities for education, he promoted an idyllic factory community – an elaboration of the community he knew as a boy at Styal – as a model of a future industrial society. He was mortified when the workers turned on him a few years later in 1846 in a dispute about wages; he withdrew from the firm, a broken man.[6] The episode also illustrates the limitations of paternalism in an industrial society where workers had become better educated, more articulate and more conscious of their rights.

Hannah's positive influence can be seen in the career of her nephew, Adam Hodgson (1789–1862), who combined mercurial energy and drive with a social conscience. Adam deserves to be remembered, and indeed publicly commemorated, as one of Liverpool's outstanding social reformers, particularly for his leadership and commitment in the campaign for the emancipation of slaves.[7]

How then should Hannah be remembered now?

Looking back on Hannah's life, we can see that she faced and overcame a number of trials and challenges. It was of little practical benefit to her that at a young age she became an heiress; it was a fact about which she never spoke. She had to learn to cope without a father and, while cultivating and enlarging her unusually sharp intellect, to temper it to the society around her. She belonged to a sect that was often marginalised and unfairly treated, but as the descendant of a pioneering Dissenter, she was prepared to face these conflicts. Living in Manchester, she had to endure being vilified and ostracised, but she was resilient in the face of threats and intimidation and sustained her faith in reform.

Her desire to educate herself and others led her to share her knowledge and ideas among family, friends, and a wider circle, though never stridently. Reticent at first to compile a book, she grew in confidence and ability, and hoped to be remembered for what she wrote. Aphorisms have long been out of fashion, and it is unlikely that her books will be revived, but they reveal an exceptionally well-furnished mind.

Resilience and determination were needed when she rescued herself from a crisis in the early days of her marriage, and went on to establish a subtle relationship with her husband. She usually got her way, and this enabled her to flourish, establishing an informal *salon* at Quarry Bank; planning the education of her children; improving the house, garden and landscape; and above all, in her care and concern for the Quarry Bank workforce and the community of mill workers. Samuel entrusted to her a leading role in the welfare and medical supervision of the mill apprentices, a role for which she was unusually well qualified; he went further, enabling her over decades to supervise their education. Hannah was also a strong source of practical support among the mill women and the worker families in the Styal community.

However philosophical she became, there were a number of disappointments she had to bear. Her eldest son Tom, on whom she placed her greatest hopes, and for whom she wrote reams of letters and advice on his role as a merchant, turned out to be a failure. He may have been charming – he tried perhaps to become a poet – but he seems to have been idle, and resistant to the demands of his father and the entreaties of his mother.

She seems to have tempered her radical vision of a world when women's capabilities would be recognised and welcomed. She had sacrificed some of her convictions and suffered as a consequence, but saw the virtue in resilience rather than inflexibility. She taught her daughters an overriding lesson that she had learnt: 'in many of the silent walks of life, especially of female life, we are called to exercises of patience, of self-denial, of self-command.'[8] It took her some time to accept that, being married, her views on women's rights as well as on politics should not intrude. She found other ways to assert and recognise the roles and potential of women, sharing her views with her daughter Bessy, with her closest friend Hannah Rathbone, and with a range of female correspondents.

It is, however, hard to see how she could ever reconcile herself to the Greg family's slave plantations in Dominica, or to the practice of enslavement. It is most likely that her marriage prevented her from publicly dissociating herself from her husband's views on this. No one can tell how much pain is concealed by her silence on this matter.

Not least of the trials Hannah faced was her own physical health. Bearing thirteen children over twenty years, the last after she was more than forty years old, could be considered heroic, even in the context of that period and especially taking into consideration the other demands that were made on her during those years.

After Hannah's death, family and friends sent Bessy epitaphs and eulogies together with their condolences; even discounting the euphemistic nature of this genre, they portray some of the positive character and personality of Hannah that her contemporaries wished to remember. B.H. Bright and the Rev. J.J. Tayler were among her admirers of a younger generation. Tayler (who as a boy came to stay at Quarry Bank to recuperate from illness) wrote as: '... one who cherishes with more devotion the memory of those thousand little nameless acts of goodness and delicate attention to the happiness of her friends, which made her life a continuous stream of benevolence.' And Bright spoke of 'the finest example of steady and unaffected uprightness. I have never been privileged to know any human being gifted with such kind attractive feeling so habitual, so refined …'

The Rev. John Corrie recognised the combination of a fine mind with a virtuous heart: 'The refinement of her taste, the high cultivation of her understanding, her warmth and generosity of feeling.' He also wrote of 'the true benevolence of her heart and her active and unvaried discharge of all the great domestic virtues'. William Henry wrote:

> At this moment I can picture to myself what she was nearly thirty years ago. Captivating and delightful in society, and not less so in the more limited sphere of her own family … True it is, that her judgements of motives and conduct in others were then sometimes much too favourable – that her views of what is practicable in the improved constitution of society were frequently too sanguine, and required the correction of sober reason and cold experience; but they took their colouring from sensibilities … which … prompted her to active beneficence and most generous charities.[9]

These reflections confirm that Hannah combined a cultured mind with strong moral principles, while her engaging personality was stimulating company. A daughter-in-law later recalled: 'She was a woman of unusual mental power and cultivation, and of a purity and elevation of character still more remarkable.'[10]

Hannah's judgement of her own worth was much more modest: in a note to Bessy she wrote:

> They will have lost a friend who, tho' not ostensible in caresses or of much indulgence, was uniformly kind and useful to them, ready always to administer to their comfort and enjoyment but

perhaps still more remarkable for her negative care, her constant vigilance in guarding and withholding them from evil of every kind – a sort of negative care and true affection.[11]

The opinions of Hannah's contemporaries are rightly more comprehensive and amplify the judgement that the Styal factory community as it stands today can be seen as a reminder of her life's work, and a place where, as her descendant Mrs Jacks said, she made an impact that was worth remembering.

Notes and Abbreviations

Preface and acknowledgements, pp. 7–10

1. When quoting from manuscript material I have retained, wherever practicable, the original spelling and punctuation.
2. www.davidsekers.com.
3. W.R. Greg, *Enigmas of Life* (London, 1891), Memoir xi. He added of his mother that she put 'duty first, then self-culture'.

Chapter 1, pp. 15–29

1. Elizabeth Lightbody (jnr) to Robert Lightbody, 4 April 1788, QBM GLB 1.170.
2. Her grandfather, also called Adam (1677–1731), was the first to have prospered. He lived at Conheath, Caerlaverock, and followed in his father's footsteps as a merchant. After his first wife's death he married Agnes Nicholson, from the neighbouring village of Blackshaw in Dumfriesshire. In addition to the three children from his first wife, Adam Lightbody had five more: in order of seniority, William, Adam, James, Thomas and Robert. But most of them were still young when their father died in 1731, leaving Agnes with eight children to support. One of Agnes's brothers, John Nicholson (c.1692–1754) offered his sister a lifeline, undertaking to support three of her five Lightbody boys in Liverpool and set them up in the linen trade. By the time their mother Agnes died in 1748, these Lightbody boys, like the Nicholsons, had become prominent and successful Liverpool merchants, part of a powerful and successful group of émigré Scots based in Liverpool. When their uncle, John Nicholson, died

childless in 1754, he provided for his three Liverpool nephews William, Adam and Robert Lightbody to inherit his considerable estate.

Robert, William and Adam Lightbody are listed as trading from Dale Street in 1766. Hannah's uncle William (1715–83), the eldest of this generation of the Lightbodys, seems to have been the first to have made his own fortune. His marriage to Anna Brooks (1723–77), the daughter and heiress of one of the leading merchants and citizens of the town, bolstered his fortune further. Adam's career and fortune were more modest. By 1774 Adam was living at 1 Paradise Street, next to his brother Robert who inherited No 2 from Robert Nicholson.

3. Hannah's great-great-grandfather was Philip Henry (1631–96). His stoical tenacity, stirring sermons and care of his flock were legendary. His son Matthew Henry (1662–1714), wrote about him and published a famous commentary on the Bible.

4. Letter in Paine collection, dated 20 November. 1686.

5. Anna Laetitia Aikin (1743–1825), daughter of John Aikin, moved to Warrington in 1758, where she published her first book of *Poems* which was admired by Elizabeth Lightbody. She married the Rev. Rochemont Barbauld in 1774.

6. The Academy founded at Warrington in 1757 was among the most successful and influential of the institutions founded to educate Dissenters. Several of Hannah's Liverpool friends and cousins had been educated there and several of the leading tutors were friends of her mother's. After it closed down in 1786, Manchester New College was founded to take its place.

7. *Diary of a journey to Scotland*, Elizabeth Lightbody, *c.*1760, Paine collection.

8. Paine collection. See Chapter 5 for further reference to Kitty Wilkinson (*née* Seaward) and her later achievements. See also Herbert R. Rathbone, (ed.), *Memoir of Kitty Wilkinson* (Liverpool, 1927) and Winifred R. Rathbone *The Life of Kitty Wilkinson* (Liverpool, 1910).

9. Thomas Hodgson (1737–1817), with his brother John (1735–1813), had left home at Caton near Lancaster in the 1750s to make a career at sea under Miles Barber, the noted local Africa merchant. They probably moved to Liverpool with Barber after 1765. Thomas was stationed off the Gambia as Barber's agent, returning in 1773 suffering from ill health, when he established an independent partnership with his brother. Their first ships were aptly named *Two Brothers* and *Caton*. When he married Elizabeth, he was involved in the Africa trade as a merchant and investor, owning the station on the Isle de Los as late as 1793. Between 1771 and his retirement in 1796, he had been involved in more than fifty slaving ventures. A number of his ships

were lost, and he seems not to have made his fortune in this business. In 1784 he established the Caton cotton-spinning mill with Thomas Gardom and his brothers-in-law John Pares and Isaac Capstick. He died in his retirement at Caton a respected figure.

10. Thomas Pares senior (1716–1805) was among the most prominent lawyers, merchants, manufacturers and financiers of the East Midlands hosiery trade, investing in land and grand houses and estates (his wife was a second cousin of the Earls of Stamford). Like Thomas Hodgson, John Pares (1749–1833) was an Anglican. He had leased a site at Calver as early as 1778 with John Gardom to build a spinning mill there, subscribing to and then challenging Arkwright's restrictive patents on the new cotton-spinning machinery. In 1784, he was a major backer of the Caton Mill, which his brother-in-law Thomas Hodgson was to manage. This able and dynamic businessman was also a regular visitor to Liverpool in the 1780s and 1790s, where he was a director of the Liverpool Assurance Office. He was a director of Heygate and Pares, hosiers in the City of London, and went on to found Pares Bank in Leicester.

11. Martha Rogers was then 17, Maria 21 and Sarah 20. Since the death of their mother a decade earlier they and their brothers Daniel, Thomas and Samuel were all looked after with great skill and dedication by another loyal cousin, Mary Mitchell. See P.W. Clayden, *The Early Life of Samuel Rogers* (London, 1887).

12. London Borough of Hackney Archive, D/F/ SHI/19.

13. HG to granddaughter Bessy Rathbone, 11 February. 1823, LU RP XII. 2, and HG to daughter Bessy Rathbone, 19 February. 1823, LU RPVI. 1.13.

14. HG to Mrs Lightbody; QBM GLB 1.495.

15. Thomas Rogers (1734/35–93). He was a Dissenting Deputy, that is, a representative of his area, and a member of the Society of Constitutional Information. Later, at the end of the 1780s, he would be active on the London Committee for the Repeal of the Test and Corporation Acts, and become the chairman and a leading player in the New College, Hackney.

16. In its short life, Hackney New College became the most advanced of all the Dissenting academies, a hive of intellectual enquiry and radical thinking. Staff and pupils later had close links to the radical movements developing in the 1790s such as The Society of the Friends of the People and The Society for Constitutional Information, and with leading politicians of revolutionary France.

17. The epithet comes from J.G.A. Pocock, *Radical criticisms of the Whig order in the age of revolution*, in Margaret and James Jacob (eds), *The Origins of*

Anglo-American Radicalism (New York, 1991), 48. Richard Price (1723-95), philosopher, theologian, mathematician, actuary and pamphleteer, was a founder member of the Society for Constitutional Reform (1780) and when the Society for Commemorating the Revolution in Great Britain (known as the Revolution Society) revived its activities, Price played a prominent part in its proceedings. He was well known to Hannah and her mother.

18. Mary Wollstonecraft (1759–97) gave up her school in 1785. Hannah probably knew her later writing, but it is not known whether or not they met.

Chapter 2, pp. 30–6

1. Samuel Curwen, *Journal and letters of Samuel Curwen*, 1 and 2 June 1780, (1842, reprinted 1959 Bedford Mass), 281.

2. Hannah Lightbody, *Diary*, 17 February 1787 (Quarry Bank Mill archive, Janes collection).

3. Following their own practice, we refer to these groups, often derived from Presbyterians, as Dissenters. The term 'non-conformist' was not applied to them until the nineteenth century, and by the same token it is misleading to refer to them as Unitarians before 1813 when their legal status was confirmed.

4. Dissenters were excluded from holding public office, discrimination that they resented and fought by seeking the repeal of the Test and Combination Acts. Thomas Rogers, Dr Kippis, Dr Price and Mrs Barbauld, the leading campaigners in London, were in close touch with radicals such as Dr James Currie, Thomas Percival and other allies well known to Hannah in the north-west. 'To exclude us from jobs is no more reasonable than to exclude all those above five feet high or those whose birthdays are before the summer solstice. These are arbitrary and whimsical distinctions … We want civil offices. And why should citizens not aspire to civil offices? Why should not the fair field of generous competition be freely opened to every one.' (Mrs Barbauld, *Address to Opposers of the Repeal of the Corporation and Test Acts*, 17–18.)

Chapter 3, pp. 37–75

1. This manuscript surfaced among other family papers at Quarry Bank Mill in the late 1970s. It is referred to by courtesy of Emily Janes and quoted also by kind permission of the editors of the *Journal of Enlightenment and*

Dissent who published David Sekers (ed.), *The Diary of Hannah Lightbody 1786–1790* in full (No 24, 2008). In subsequent citations it is referred to simply as Diary. Now also available online: http://www.english.qmul.ac.uk/drwilliams/journal/issues/24(2008)Sup.pdf

2. Diary, 3 August 1788, *Ibid*. 23 January 1788.

3. *Ibid*. 16 and 17 September 1789; *Ibid*. 25 December 1787.

4. *Ibid*. 3 December 1787.

5. *Ibid*. 13 October 1787; *Ibid*. 30 December 1788.

6. *Ibid*. 10 November 1787.

7. John Aikin, *An address to the Dissidents of England on their late defeat* (London, 1790), 18.

8. Diary, 11 February 1788. Bold Street leads from Church Street out towards Toxteth Park. The Lightbodys took No 7.

9. Jonathan Binns's diary, LRO, Binns Collection. Dr Binns, a Quaker and member of the Liverpool Committee for the Abolition of the Slave Trade, was one of the few to make a public stand in this city.
He suffered harassment as a result, but his son Jonathan remained a vocal anti-slavery campaigner.

10. Diary, 3 January 1789.

11. Diary, 3 July 1787; Diary, 15 January 1787. In September 1788, her sister Elizabeth's fifth child was due: 'Sat up all night with my poor Sister. 16: My Sister delivered of a dead Child. 17: Thankful to see my Sister easier.'

12. *Ibid*. 8/9 May 1788.

13. *Ibid*. 10 and 11 June 1788.

14. Paine collection. This is copied out in the hand of Anna Lister.

15. Benjamin Arthur Heywood (B.A.H) and Nathaniel, sons of the Liverpool merchant and banker Arthur Heywood, were educated at the Warrington Academy, and set up their bank in Manchester in 1788.

16. Gore's *General Advertiser*, quoted in Brooke, *Liverpool as it was during the last quarter of the eighteenth century 1775–1800* (Liverpool, 1853), 278-82.

17. Diary, 10 December 1787. Among these were Samuel Thornton, the MP, and Benjamin Boddington, both members of the Committee for the Repeal of the Test and Corporation Acts; Joseph Denison, the London agent and eventual partner of the Heywood banking business; Andrew Kippis, who was a pivotal figure as professor of Belles Lettres at New College, Hackney.

18. Diary, 6 December 1787.

19. Billson, *Leicester memoirs* (Leicester, 1924); a ground plan is also illustrated.

20. 'Went to Caton and was transported with the scene', Diary, 27 July 1787.

21. Diary, 8 April 1787.
22. For an extended discussion of the contribution of each of these men to Hannah's formation, see www.davidsekers.com.
23. Dr James Currie (1756–1805) had been a medical student at Edinburgh University where he was a member of the Speculative Society, and had acquired a hatred of all forms of bigotry and a lasting interest in the work of the Scottish philosophers, from Hume to Dugald Stewart. By the time he had settled in Liverpool in 1780 he had developed progressive Dissenting views and a readiness to argue for social change. In 1783 he married Lucy Wallace, the daughter of a leading linen merchant, and in 1786 after a few years as physician to the Liverpool Dispensary he was appointed as physician to the Infirmary. Though by then already suffering from consumption, he was highly regarded for his medical research as well as for his zeal for social and political reform. The Liverpool Literary Society, which he founded with William Roscoe, was a beacon of penetrating debate on current issues. Currie was an energetic campaigner, writer, reformer and debater engaged in the campaign for the repeal of the Test and Corporation Acts, in the development of effective treatments for epidemics and fevers, the care of the insane, and the abolition of the slave trade. According to his son: 'He also favoured universal religious toleration, supported the United Irishmen, and sympathized with the French revolutionaries; he considered Pitt a traitor to the values he had once championed. His views were well known in Liverpool.' See Thornton, *James Currie, the Entire Stranger and Robert Burns* (Edinburgh, 1963).
24. Diary, 10 May 1787; *Ibid.* 12 May 1787.
25. *Ibid.* 29 June 1787.
26. William Currie, *Memoir of James Currie of Liverpool* (London, 1831), I, 405; James Currie to HMR, 15 June 1801, LU RP II.75.
27. William Cockin (1736–1801), a Kendal-born teacher and writer, friend of the painter George Romney. Diary, 11 July 1787.
28. Diary, 14 August 1788. At least one passage from Reid is in Hannah's 1799 book of *Maxims*.
29. Thomas Percival (1740–1804) had married Elizabeth Bassnett in 1766, whose family was connected to both Anna Cropper and to Kaye Street Chapel. Percival had been the first student at the Warrington Academy and became one of the youngest ever Fellows of the Royal Society. While his career as a physician in Manchester took off, he found time to contribute papers to medical journals, and published his *Essays Medical and Experimental* (1773). A prime mover behind the foundation of the

Manchester Literary and Philosophical Society in 1781, he helped make it the leading institution of its kind in the country, remaining president from 1782 until his death. He harnessed support on a large scale to ensure the opening of Manchester New College in 1786, following the demise of the Warrington Academy. His children's development was a matter of constant interest to him, and Percival published *A Father's Instructions* (1775), *Moral Tales, Fables and Reflections* (1777) and a private edition of *A Socratic Discourse on Truth and Faithfulness*. His final work and the one for which he is best known is his *Medical Ethics*, a topic on which he is still considered to be the founding father. See E. Percival, *Memoirs of the life and writings of Thomas Percival MD* (London, 1807).

30. William Rathbone IV (1757–1809) was probably the first to see the potential for importing raw cotton from the southern states of America, the earliest shipments taking place in 1784. William Rathbone IV's father handed the responsibility for his established transatlantic shipping business to him that year, when he was 27. Although leaving school at 16, he had an exceptional appetite for knowledge, teaching himself French, Latin and Greek, and reading widely among contemporary thinkers such as Dugald Stewart and William Godwin. In 1792 Rathbone was prominent in efforts to avert the war with France, and in that year, and again in 1809, led a campaign against the monopoly of the East India Company. He also advocated freedom of trade, and rejoiced with William Roscoe in the abolition of the transatlantic slave trade in 1807.

31. As intense reading was such a key part of Hannah's character, a more extensive survey of the evidence in the diary and at later periods, is provided at www.davidsekers.com.

32. Diary, 1 March 1788; *Ibid.* 31 March 1787; *Ibid.* 3 May 1788; *Ibid.*; 9 April 1789, *Ibid.* 22 May 1788.

33. *Ibid.* 1 September 1787; *Ibid.* 8 August 1787. Rev. Joseph Smith (1755–1815); a Cheshire man, he studied for the ministry at the Warrington Academy from 1769–74, and succeeded Dr Clayton as minister at Benn's Garden Chapel in Liverpool in 1781. It was very likely at Warrington that he developed his wide interest in aesthetics, contemporary poetry and literature.

34. *Ibid.* 1 June 1788

35. *Ibid.* 25 March 1787.

36. *Ibid.* 1 June 1788.

37. *Ibid.* 21 February 1787.

38. Alexander Gerard, *An Essay on Taste* (London, 1759), 86.

39. William Roscoe (1753–1831), poet, botanist, historian, collector, abolition-

ist and radical, was the leading cultural figure in Liverpool for several decades. He was also an early supporter of Mary Wollstonecraft.

40. William Shenstone (1714–63), poet and landscape gardener, noted for his original garden at The Leasowes in Halesowen, historically in the county of Shropshire.

41. 'It was a highly liberal and intellectual association. A topic previously agreed was made the subject of conversation and sometimes a paper relative to it was read'. Among the topics were: *The division of legislative powers; Physiognomy*; and *The Effects of the different branches of cultivation of mind on the individual*. Obituary of Dr Yates, *Monthly Repository*, 1827, 68.

42. John Aikin, *Letters from a father to his son* (London, 1796), 341, Quoted in Ruth Watts, *Gender, power and the Unitarians in England 1760–1860* (London, 1998), 77.

43. Hannah Greg, *A collection of maxims, observations &c* (Liverpool, 1799), 44.

44. See for example, Diary, 11 March 1787.

45. Hannah Greg, *A collection of maxims*, 43.

46. He was not related to the nineteenth-century slavery emancipation campaigner James Cropper.

47. Ernest Axon, *Memorials of the family of Nicholson* (Liverpool, 1928), 59.

48. This and the following excerpts are from Diary, 19 May 1787.

49. Joseph Priestley (1733–1804), the discoverer of oxygen, and formerly tutor at Warrington Academy, was a leading Dissenting minister and radical. In his evolving form of Rational Dissent, Priestley preferred the minimum of liturgy, and did not believe in miracles, transubstantiation, the Holy Spirit or in the doctrine of atonement.

50. Hannah Greg, *The Moralist; or a collection of maxims, observations &c* (Liverpool, 1800), 140; *The works theological, medical, political, and miscellaneous, of John Jebb, MDFRS* (London, 1787), 2. 105. I am grateful to Martin Fitzpatrick for identifying the source of this quotation.

51. (Hannah Greg), *The Monitor* (Liverpool, 1804), 71. Social Affections, xxvi.

52. Thomas Clarkson's history of the abolition campaigns pointed to the thin brigade of Liverpool abolitionists who opposed slavery in the 1780s. See Thomas Clarkson, *The history of the abolition of the African Slave Trade* (London, 1808); also Brian Howman's PhD thesis, *An analysis of slave abolitionists in the North West of England*, ch 1.

53. Yates's sermon was a landmark in Liverpool, being one of the very few public attacks on the slave trade there in this period. He 'gave great offence to many influential members of his congregation'. (S.A.T.Yates, *Memorials of the family of the Rev John Yates* (London, 1890).) Hannah's account may be the only surviving summary of its contents.

54. Currie, *Memoir*, 111

55. Currie, *Memoir*, 1, 135.

56. William Rathbone IV, for example, wrote to Hannah referring to 'impossible slavery' in the West Indies. W R IV to HG, July 1798: LU RP II. 1.42.

57. HG to WR IV, April 1798, LU RP II. 1.65.

58. Jonathan Huddleston, *And the children's teeth are set on edge: Adam Hodgson and the razing of Caton Chapel*, www. tioli.co.uk. Ch 7, 19–20. n 22. Clarkson opposed this notion, but the fact remains that abolition and emancipation took decades to complete,

59. The Horsley quotation and reference to the source is on a scrap of paper, QBM BLS 82.

Chapter 4, pp. 76–118

1. Diary, 6 February 1788.

2. *Ibid.*, 19 May 1787.

3. George Philips (1766–1847) was a member of the Manchester Literary & Philosophical Society, a Trustee of the Infirmary; a radical, he advocated female suffrage.

4. SG to HL, 26 June 1789, QBM GLB 1.168.

5. Diary, 17 July 1789.

6. HL to SG, QBM BLS 10 (no date but possibly 20 June 1789).

7. These provided for Hannah to retain in trust her inherited wealth made up of her share of the house in Paradise Street, and of land at Garston and Wavertree, and to derive an income from a bond of £7,000 'at the disposal of Mr Greg'. Undated note of Samuel Greg, QBM GLB 1.34, and Abstract of the will & codicils of Samuel Greg, LU RPVI. 2. 40.

8. Thomas Truxes, *Letterbook of Greg & Cunningham 1756-57* (Oxford, 2001), 29ff.

9. John Greg's account, QBM GLB 1.294.

10. R.H. Greg: Mill Memoranda in MRO, Greg collection, C5/3/1 Memoranda book.

11. John Greg, QBM GLB 1.294.

12. John Morley, *W R Greg, a Sketch* in *Critical Miscellanies*, III, 14; W.R. Greg, *Enigmas of Life* (1891 edition), Memoir, x.

13. Daniel Patterson (ed.), *John James Audubon's Journal of 1826, the voyage to the Birds of America* (Nebraska, 2011), 7 October 1826, 226; *Ibid.*, 187.

14. John Greg in QBM GLB 1.294; From HG's Collected letters in Peter Spencer, *A portrait of Samuel Greg* (Styal, 1982) 24.

15. SG to Bessy. May 1828, LU RPVI.1.153.

16. HG's collected letters in Spencer, *Samuel Greg* (Styal, 1982). QBM GLB 1.168.

17. V.A.C. Gattrell, 'Incorporation and the pursuit of Liberal hegemony in Manchester 1790-1839', in Derek Fraser (ed.), *Municipal Reform and the Industrial City* (Leicester, 1982), 57, n 57.

18. Archibald Prentice, *Historical sketches and personal recollections* (Manchester, 1851).

19. Audubon, *1826 Journal*, 20 October, 254.

20. QBM BLS 25.

21. John Greg in GLB 1.294.

22. They were travelling with Hannah's cousin Mary, the daughter of her uncle. Robert Lightbody, and with Samuel's youngest brother Cunningham, who had been his best man.

23. Jane Kennedy and Fanny, the daughter of Thomas Percival.

24. Benjamin Arthur Heywood.

25. Ellen Melly, *Reminiscences*, October 1889, QBM F 110.

26. Mrs Cole's book *The Lady's Complete Guide; or Cookery in all its branches* was published in London in 1788, with a section of family prescriptions. It also contains advice on budgeting and household accounts.

27. QBM GLB 1.479 (undated, but probably in the early spring of 1790).

28. *Diary of Anna Walker*, 30 March 1789, quoted in W.H. Thomson, *History of Manchester to 1852* (Altrincham 1967), 237.

29. This and the preceding quotations are from HL's diary for 1790 pp 113–19, where the entries are undated.

30. Currie, *Memoir*, I, 68-9.

31. Katrina Navickas, *Loyalism and Radicalism in Lancashire, 1798–1815* (Oxford, 2009), 35; 41–2.

32. M.J. Turner, *Reform and Respectability: The Making of a Middle-Class Liberalism in Early Nineteenth-Century Manchester* (Manchester, 1995), 45.

33. Meanwhile in 1791 Samuel Greg again put his head above the parapet by involving himself in the issue of the reform of the East India trade, and as a leader of a peace initiative. Currie was a leading peace campaigner in Liverpool and, under the pseudonym of Jasper Wilson, wrote his famous attack on Pitt in 1793 soon after Napoleon had declared war on Britain.

34. Gatrell, 33.

35. HG to William Rathbone, 29 July 1794, LU RP II.1.62.

36. The radical Thomas Walker accused them of failing to take the initiative as reformers in the 1790s: 'They have as a body, constantly fallen short of their own principles; they have excited opposition which they have never

completely supported; and through fear, or some other motive, they have been so strongly the advocates of an overstrained moderation, that they have been rather the enemies than the friends of those who have ventured the most for the rights of the people.' Quoted in John Seed, 'A set of powerful men in many things', in K. Haakonssen (ed.), *Enlightenment & Religion*, 167.

37. From Hannah Greg's collected letters, in Spencer, *Samuel Greg*, 25.

38. Dated 1794, from Hannah Greg's collected letters, in Spencer, *Hannah Greg*, 8.

39. From Hannah Greg's collected letters, in Spencer, *Hannah Greg*, 8.

40. JC to HG, 14 November 1797; and Currie, *Memoir*, II, 183.

41. HG to HMR, April 1798, LU RP II. 1.65. Grey's role at this time is discussed in Albert Goodwin, *The Friends of Liberty* (London, 1979), 438-42.

42. HG to HMR, 1 September 1819, LU VI.1.131.

43. Catriona Kennedy: "Womanish Epistles?' Martha McTier, Female Epistolarity and Late Eighteenth-Century Irish Radicalism', *Women's History Review*, Volume 13, Number 4, 2004, 660.

44. 'Do not be surprised if you hear of an Information being laid against a certain republican Countess "more sinned against than sinning"', QBM BLS 75. Two undated mss in the Greg archives at Quarry Bank Mill (BLS 69 and BLS 75) appear to be transcriptions or excerpts of letters from Lady Londonderry, probably to Jane. Her husband and stepson, as the most senior servants of the crown in Ireland, could only have regarded this evidence as seditious.

45. Ellen Melly, *Reminiscences*, QBM F 110.

46. HG to HMR, 1 September 1819, reflecting on the Peterloo massacre, LU RP VI.1.131.

47. HG to WR IV 31 July 1798. LU RP II.I.64. 'Enthusiasm', a key word in Enlightenment discourse, probably implies here a lively commitment to a wide range of social reforms.

48. Letter from Ellen Melly to Edward Greg, 1 July 1886(?), QBM GLB 2. Ellen Melly, *Reminiscences*, QBM F 110.

49. SG to HG, 29 June 1813; QBM BLS 14.

50. HG to HMR, 18 December 1792, LU RP II.1.60.

51. Paine collection.

52. Hannah Greg's addition to letter from Agnes Pares to Mrs Lightbody, 23 November. (?) 1795, Paine collection.

53. Letter dated simply Thursday 26 November (1795?), QBM BLS 13C.

54. Note of family chronology by Anna Hodgson, Paine collection.

55. HG to HMR, Tuesday 1 September 1819, LU RP VI. I. 131.

56. This portrait belonged to Alec Greg and was destroyed in a fire in the 1980s.

57. Spencer, *Hannah Greg*, 3; HG to WR, 31 July 1798, LU RP II. 1.64.

58. HG to Bessy, 23 August 1819, LU VI. 1. 129

59. Spencer, *Samuel Greg*, 13.

60. Spencer, *Samuel Greg*, 12.

61. Diary, 21 February 1787.

62. HG to HMR, 31 July 1798, LU RP II. 1.64.

63. 'we shall rejoice when Quarry Bank is made convenient for all your family', WR to HG. 5 August 1798, LU RP II. I.44; 22 October 1798. LU RP II. I. 45.

64. Spencer, *Hannah Greg*, 3.

65. WR to HG, July 1795(?), LU RP II. 1.42.

66. Spencer, *Hannah Greg*, 3.

67. WR IV to HG, 3 October 1799(?), LU RP II. 1. 56.

68. WR IV to HG, (1788?), *Records of Rathbone family*, 354-6.

69. HG to WR IV, 1797, from her collected letters, Spencer, *Hannah Greg*, 4.

Chapter 5, pp. 119–59

1. From Eliza Hodgson to brother Isaac, from Quarry Bank (where she was staying with sister Anna); 2 September 1801, QBM GLB 1.221.

2. HG to HMR, January 1806, LU RP II. 1.68.

3. HG to Bessy Greg, 17 July 1809, LU RP VI. 1.165.

4. The Mouldsworth estate was inherited by Hannah's mother in her old age; the Gregs could have taken it on after her death in 1801, but declined to do so.

5. HG and SG to Bessy in Leicester, 1 June 1800, QBM archive.

6. HG to Tom, 10 June 1810, Spencer, *Hannah Greg*, 15.

7. HG to Hannah Mary Rathbone jr, 24 March 1808, LU RP II. 1.70. These lines were written by Margaret and Samuel, and possibly later amended by Mary Anne and Thomas Greg.

8. *Ibid.*

9. Learned or explanatory footnotes to poems were becoming fashionable, following the examples of Erasmus Darwin's *Botanic Garden* and later Coleridge's *Rhyme of the Ancient Mariner.*

10. Crambo is a game in which one player gave a word or line of verse to be matched in rhyme by other players.

11. Maria Edgeworth, Old Poz, a play for children, 1795.

12. From Bessy Greg (aged 11) plus overwritten text by HG to Miss Mary Hodgson at Mrs Wilson's in Newcastle upon Tyne, November 1801, QBM GLB 1.497.
13. RHG to Bessy, 21 June 1802, QBM GLB 1.259.
14. Undated ms, Paine collection; probably *c*.1804 when Thomas was 11.
15. Emily Greg (ed.), *Reynolds – Rathbone Diaries* (London, 1905)
16. 'Sorry to find that you had not derived… the health we had hoped from your Cumberland tour', HMR to HG, 27 August 1803, LU RP II. I. 49.
17. HMR to HG, 11 April 1806, LU RP II. 1. 52; HMR had lost Joseph (1793-94) and Theophilus (1795-98).
18. HG to HMR, January 1805, LU RP II. 1.67.
19. The money went to support the Manchester and Salford volunteers. Gatrell 33/4.
20. HG to WR IV, January 1805, LU RP II. 1.67.
21. HG to Miss ? Rathbone, 24 March 1808, LU RP II. 1.70.
22. 'It is in the scheme of Providence that Revolution accompanied with War and Civil Tumult shall proceed …'. *Ibid*. Her views probably echoed those of many Whigs, and Roscoe in particular who in 1808 published his pamphlet *Considerations of the Causes, Objects and Consequences of the Present War*, in which he was critical of the economic and foreign policy of the government.
23. HG to RHG at Corrie's school in Birmingham, 5 December 1807, QBM Edward/Gore collection.
24. HG to Tom at Corrie' school, 5 April 1808, QBM Edward/Gore collection.
25. HG to Tom, 1 March 1809, QBM Edward/Gore collection.
26. HG to WR IV, 31 July 1798, LU RP II. 1.64.
27. HG to HMR, January 1806, LU RP II. 1.68.
28. He gave Hannah a copy of a French edition of *A Father's Instructions – Consisting of … A Socratic Discourse on Truth and Faithfulness*, which was first published in 1781. Diary, 17 June 1788.
29. Thornton, *James Currie*, 144.
30. 21 June 1791. Currie, *Memoir*, ii.
31. HG to WR IV, 29 July 1794, RP II. 1. 62.
32. Having discussed Rousseau's *Eloise* with the Rev. Joseph Smith, *Diary*, 11 February. 1787. When advising on the upbringing of a grandchild, for example, she read and discussed with Bessy, the original distinction between education and instruction made by von Fellenberg, HG to Mrs Bessy Rathbone, November 1821, LU RP VI. 1.133.
33. Cliona O'Gallchoir, *Maria Edgeworth: Women, Enlightenment and Nation* (Dublin, 2005) 25.

34. WR IV to HG, 1 July 1798 (?) LU RP II. 1.42. Maria Edgeworth (1768–1849) published *Practical Education* in 1798, with her father Richard Lovell Edgeworth as co-author. Edgeworth assimilated views from Thomas Reid.

35. Hannah Greg, *A collection of maxims, observations etc* (Liverpool, 1799), Preface.

36. The books that Hannah had privately and anonymously published were: *Virtue Made Easy* (Liverpool, 1799), *A collection of maxims, observations, etc* (Liverpool, 1799), *The Moralist* (Liverpool, 1800), *The Monitor,* (Liverpool 1804), *Practical suggestions towards alleviating the sufferings of the sick* (London, 1828). She listed ten other titles of manuscript essays and collections that she thought worth editing and preserving. For a wider discussion of Hannah's writings see www.davidsekers.com.

37. Spencer, *Hannah Greg*, 11.

38. Hannah Greg, *Maxims and Observations*, <u>Social affections</u>, III XXX 43.

39. *Ibid*. XXXII p 45.

40. Ellen Melly, *Reminiscences*, QBM F 110.

41. Poem by Greg children transcribed by HG writing to Miss Rathbone, 24 March 1808, LU RP II. 1.70.

42. TG to his sister Elizabeth, 21 June 1802, QBM GLB 1.259.

43. Hannah Greg, *Catechisms of Safety and Health 1800*, MS in Quarry Bank Mill archives.

44. Adam Hodgson to Thomas Greg, 25 November 1808, QBM GLB 1.222. Corrie had been educated for a time at New College Hackney under Dr Price and Dr Kippis, and later became President of the Birmingham Philosophical Society.

45. HG to Bessy, 18 February 1823, LU RP VI. 1.13.

46. QBM GLB 1.03.

47. WR IV to HL, 11 January 1805, LU RP II.1.51. Carpenter's schools, first at Exeter, then in Bristol, proved to be very successful, educating some of the most prominent Unitarians of the period.

48. John Playfair was then at the height of his fame as a geologist, physicist and mathematician. RHG to Thomas, 19 December 1813, QBM GLB 1.232.

49. Ellen Melly, *Reminiscences*; also HG to Thomas Pares jr, 22 January 1816, DRO Pares collection, D5336/3/214/12

50. HG to HMR, 31 July 1798, LU RP II. 1.64.

51. HG to WR IV, January 1805, LU RP II. 1.67.

52. Spencer, *Hannah Greg* 2.

53. HG to Bessy, 1 June 1800, QBM archive.

54. He was mortified to tell her in January 1809 of his losses: 'I have not been very comfortable about your cotton spec., but hope from the news just

received it may yet turn out well'; enclosed in a letter from Hannah Rathbone to Bessy Greg quoted in the *Diary of Hannah Mary Rathbone*, appendix III, LU RP III.3.

55. Dr John Dalton (1766–1844), inventor of the atomic theory.

56. HG to Thomas, 17 April 1810, QBM Edward \Gore collection.

57. Diary of Elizabeth Greg in Emily A. Rathbone (ed.), *Records of the Rathbone Family* (Edinburgh, 1913), 302.

58. *Legacy to Elizabeth Greg*, 3 February 1807, quoted in Spencer, *Hannah Greg*, 8. For a discussion of Hannah's role as a hostess, See Chapter 7.

59. HG to Thomas, 5 April 1808, QBM, Edward/Gore collection.

60. Hannah Greg, collected letters, undated, Spencer, *Hannah Greg* 10/11.

61. For a discussion about Hannah's reading, see www.davidsekers.com.

62. There are manuscript fragments of poems and a history of poetry attributable to Thomas, for example QBM BLS 2, BLS 58, BLS 60.

63. HG to Tom, 1 March 1814, Quarry Bank Mill archive, STQBM 2002-7092.

64. *Poems*. Paris, printed by Crapelet, 1833. Cover is signed, 'Robert Hyde Greg.' Beneath the half title is written, 'by W.R. Greg and Samuel Greg'. MRO C5/9/3.

65. HG to Tom, 1 March 1814, Quarry Bank Mill archive, STQBM 2002-7092.

66. HG and SG to Bessy Greg, 1 June 1800, QBM archive.

67. HG to Tom, 15 April 1810, QBM GLB 1.61.

68. SG to Tom, 27 February 1814, QBM Edward /Gore collection.

69. SG to HG from London (no date), QBM GLB 1.178

70 HG to Tom, 15 April 1810, QBM, GLB 1.51.

71. HG to HMR, 21 May 1816 or 1817, LU RP VI. 1.114.

72. SG to RHG, 26 February 1814, BLS 25. The Six Acts was a body of unusually repressive legislation aiming to prevent civilians from practicing military training , to muzzle the radical press, and to outlaw large meetings.

73. HG to Tom, 25 May 1809, QBM GLB 1.176.

74. SG to RHG; 2 December 1814 QBM Edward /Gore collection.

75. SG to RHG, 5 February 1817, QBM GLB 1.180.

76. HG to Tom, 1 April 1811, QBM Edward /Gore collection.

77. HG to Tom Pares jnr, 10 July 1812, DRO Pares Collection Dss 336/3/214/6.

78. The entertainment was probably derived from John Aikin's and Anna Barbauld's idea of 'the Budget Box' in their *Evenings at Home*; or, *the juvenile budget opened* (London, 1792-96).

79. HG to Tom Pares jnr, 10 July 1812, DRO Pares Collection DS 336/3/214/6.

80. QBM BLS 81. Among the latter are a short handwritten but anonymous two-page essay entitled 'Habit is a second nature', BLS 49; a single page invocation addressed 'To the Comet', BLS 60; a copy of an essay by Adam Hodgson dated 26 June 1812 on the advantages that result from combining commercial and literary pursuits, BLS 3.

81. 'Our future gathering in our Father's House above; Corresponding members… Many necessary circumstances – unsurpassed prosperity – good home – good schools, health, plenty, love & harmony; and a thousand minor blessings … Enjoy with consciousness, for few families have so much to enjoy … shine through my children (crossed out) … Let me [be] seen only in Eclipse and shine only through my Children, pleased to receive light by their progressive acquirements, and happy in the … sunshine. Proud to receive light from their knowledge and to be kept warm in the sunshine of their filial love.' QBM BLS 77.

82. QBM BLS 81 and BLS 84 (last page).

83. *Transcript of the Examination of Joseph Sefton*, MRO, C5/1/8 (1806), and of *Thomas Priestley* C5/8/9/5.

84. Sarah Peers, 'Negotiating Work, absenteeism at Quarry Bank Mill in 1790'. *THSLC* 158 (2009).

85. Isaac Hodgson reported another death of a child at the Caton Mill: 'I am just returned from the deathbed of one of our Apprentice Boys. He was (alive – crossed out) at work this day last week, & has been rapidly carried off by an inflammation on his lungs. He died while I was standing by him.' IH to Tom Greg, 25 November 1808, QBM GLB 1.222.

86. Alfred Fryer, *Wilmslow Graves* (1886).

87. Quoted in Roy Porter, *English Society in the Eighteenth Century* (London, 1982), 310.

88. Elizabeth Evans to William Evans at Darley Abbey, 24 October. 1793, quoted in R.S. Fitton and A.P. Wadsworth, *The Strutts and the Arkwrights, 1758–1830* (Manchester, 1958), 166-7. Elizabeth Evans and her father Jedediah Strutt, the developer of the early factory community at Belper, were Dissenters.

89. (Hannah Greg), *Virtue Made Easy*, preface.

Chapter 6, pp. 160–207

1. Fryer, *Wilmslow Graves*.

2. Memorials assembled by Bessy Rathbone; LU RPVI. 2.31.

3. HG to RHG in Madrid, 22 May 1815, QBM GLB 1.163.

4. SG to HG, 1811, QBM GLB 1.178.

5. Hannah wrote to her daughter Bessy and later her son Robert of her dismay. HG to Bessy, 21 May 1818, LU VI. 1. 114; 'Poor Tom is much fastened since Mr Wood's death.' HG to RHG, 19 August 1817, QBM GLB.

6. Extracts from the Journal of Elizabeth Greg, April 1 to 24 July 1807, in Emily Rathbone (ed.), *Records of the Rathbone Family*, 284–313.

7. HG to Tom, 13 April 1814, QBM, Edward/Gore collection.

8. Margaret Simey, *Charity Rediscovered* (Liverpool, 1992), 21.

9. *Ibid.*, 24.

10. Bessy to her mother-in-law HMR, 5 June 1818, LU RPVI. 1.189.

11. HG to Bessy, 6 August 1819, LU RPVI. 1.127–131.

12. HG to Bessy, 6 December 1818, LU RPVI. 1.124.

13. Hannah referred to Samuel's 'free expression of his prejudice against Mr O … which had arisen from the impression of his <u>early</u> character'. HG to Bessy, 2 October 1813, LU RPVI. 1.109.

14. HG to Bessy, 2 October 1813, LU RPVI.1.109.

15. Hannah Greg, collected letters August 1812 (?), in Spencer, *Samuel Greg*, 2.

16. HG to Tom, 13 May 1813, QBM Edward/Gore collection.

17. HG to Mrs Philips, 18 September 1817, QBM GLB 49.

18. SG in London to RHG at Milan, 5 February 1817, QBM GLB 1.180

19. He wrote to Hannah: 'I may be delayed in consequence of Sir Robert Peel's Bill to regulate mills … Isaac Hodgson this day informs me of my being appointed a delegate from the trade. It is fortunate that I can leave matters in your hands.' Hannah Greg collected letters (no date), Spencer, *Samuel Greg*, 23.

20. Bessy to HMR, 20 May 1818, LU RPVI. 1.188.

21. (Hannah Greg), *The Monitor*, Social Affections, VII. 64-5.

22. There were earlier examples that the Gregs would have known, such as the villages built by the Strutts, Ashworths and Arkwrights, whose mills also employed pauper apprentices, unlike Owen's. For other factory communities, see Sidney Pollard, 'The Factory Village in the Industrial Revolution' in *English Historical Review*, 79, 1974.

23. See Sarah Peers, 'Negotiating work': in *THSLC*, 158.

24. Katrina Honeyman, *Child workers in England, 1780–1820* (Aldershot, 2007), 253-6.

25. Friedrich Engels, *The Condition of the Working Class in England* (1844), 186.

26. Walter Lazenby, *Social and Economic History of Styal, 1750–1850*, MA thesis (University of Manchester, 1949).

27. Lazenby, 155, provides details of the costs of recovering them.

28. SG to RHG, 3 April 1829, QBM archive 1820–30.

29. Robinson, *What Became of the Quarry Bank Mill Apprentices* (Styal, 1996), 16.

30. See www.davidsekers.com for a discussion of Robert Greg as a mill owner.

31. W.R. Greg, *Enigmas of Life*, prefatory memoir, 1889.

32. Journal of Elizabeth Greg, 24 July 1807, from Emily Rathbone (ed.), *Records of the Rathbone Family*, 312.

33. HG to Bessy, 6 December 1818, LU RP VI. 1.124.

34. HG to Bessy, 11 February 1823, LU RP XII. 1.2.

35. HG to Bessy, 19 February 1823, LU RP VI. 1.13.

36. Report from the Select Committee of the House of Lords on the Burdens affecting Real Property 1846.

37. Frances Collier, *Family economy of the Working Classes in the Cotton Industry* (Manchester, 1964), 39.

38. Lob scouse: a beef and potato stew.

39. *Physician's notebooks*, MRO, Greg collection, C5/1/4/-21.

40. Ellen Melly, *Reminiscences*, QBM archive, F 110.

41. 'Many who have seen the year begin may not live to see it end. It could be you or me. Let us be ready.' Hannah Greg, *Sermons for the Children of the Apprentice House* (1819), QBM archive.

42. HG to Bessy, January (?) 1818, LU RP.VI. 119.

43. HG to Bessy, 20 August 1819, LU RP VI. 1.125.

44. Examination of Joseph Sefton and Thomas Priestley before magistrates in Middlesex 1806, MRO, Greg collection C5/8/9/4.

45. Fryer, *Wilmslow Graves*.

46. Lazenby, 330.

46. Lazenby, *Ibid.*, quoting diary of Mary Anne Greg, 194.

48. WR IV to HG, 11 January 1805, LU RP II. 1. 51.

49. Letter from Henry Russell Greg to George Melly, QBM Archive.

50. Hannah Greg, *Sermons for the Children of the Apprentice House* (1819), QBM archive.

51. Spencer, *Hannah Greg*, 6-7.

52. Audubon, *Journal of 1826*, 181. John James Audubon (1790–1851), the American naturalist. He came to Liverpool and Manchester in 1826 to find subscribers for his book *Birds of America*.

53. Morley, *Critical miscellanies*, Vol 3, 1886.

54. Hannah Greg to H.M. Rathbone, 22 August 1822, quoted in Lazenby, 218, with 'Norcliffe Chapel MSS' as the source for the original.

55. 'A small cash book gives the details of the amounts borrowed and the weekly repayments, and also several of the forms of agreement have survived. This assistance tided over many an awkward moment when a family was stranded on some temporary embarrassment, and was thus of great assistance in stabilising the community and helping it to reach a fair degree of social integration.' Lazenby, 120.

56. Spencer, *Hannah Greg*, 7.

57. P.M. Higginson, 'Sermon on the death of Mrs Ellen Melly, 1894', quoted in Mary Rose, *Gregs of Quarry Bank Mill*, 116.

58. Hannah goes on to say she sees it as her role to promote this cause in Manchester. HG to HMR, 12 June 1818. LU RPVI.1.122.

59. HG to Bessy, June 1818, LU RPVI. 1.123.

60. B.H. Bright (1787–1843) had been a contemporary of Robert Hyde Greg at Carpenter's school in Exeter. His mother had been a friend of Hannah's in her youth in Liverpool and his father was a distinguished Bristol Dissenter and merchant. He became a noted antiquary.

61. B.H. Bright to HG at Leicester, 4 April 1812, QBM BLS 32 and 23; also April 1812, QBM BLS 24.

62. HG to Tom, 13 May 1812, QBM Edward/Gore collection.

63. HG to Tom, 4 August 1812, QBM GLB.

64. HG to Tom, 13 April 1814, QBM Edward/Gore collection.

65. 'I can just remember the peace illuminations, and our house in King Street being festooned with coloured lamps which Robert had arranged as a rainbow.' Ellen Melly, *Reminiscences*.

66. Archibald Prentice, *Historical Sketches and Personal Recollections* (Manchester, 1851), quoted in Gattrell, 57 n. 57.

67. A large public meeting planned at St Peter's Fields in Manchester for 16 August 1819 was called to 'consider the propriety of adopting the most legal and affectual means of obtaining reform of the Commons House of Parliament.' 'Orator' Hunt was to be in the chair. This gathering was on a scale that alarmed the authorities, and the local yeomanry were backed up by large numbers of professional troops. Sixty thousand assembled peacefully on the day, but as the meeting was about to start, the yeomanry were sent in on horseback to arrest Hunt and others on the platform. They lost control, or so it appeared to the magistrates, who called in the professional soldiers. In the ensuing panic, many in the crowd were injured and several lives were lost.

68. HG to Bessy, August 1819 (Thursday Morning), LU RPVI. 1.126, 127, 128.

69. HG to Bessy, 23 August 1819, LU RPVI.1.129.

70. This account was published in F.A. Burton (ed.), *Three Accounts of Peterloo* (Manchester, 1921).

71. From SG at Quarry Bank to TP at Leics, 10 March 1820, DRO, Pares collection, 3/214/26.

72. In 1822 Robert went to give evidence in the trial brought by Thomas Redford accusing the leader of the Manchester Yeomanry, Hugh Birley, of assault. Robert was one of many witnesses confirming that the attack on the crowd was unprovoked.

73. Gattrell, 35.

74. HG to Miss Rathbone, 24 March 1808, LU RP II.1.70.

75. HG to WR IV, 1 October 1806, LU RP II.1.69.

76. 'My head is confused by Laudanum (which has however relieved the illness that overpowered me yesterday),' June 1818, LU RP VI. 1.123.

77. SG to Bessy, (undated) 1814, LU RP VI. 1.115.

78. IH to RHG, 18 August 1817, Paine collection.

79. SG to Bessy, 11 November 1824, LU RP VI. 1.137.

80. SG to RHG, 22 May 1815, QBM GLB 1.163.

81. HG to Mrs Philips, 18 September 1817, GLB 49 QBM GLB 1.125.

Chapter 7, pp. 208–33

1. Manuscript in Quarry Bank Mill archive; watermarked 1818. William Smyth (1765–1849), scholar and poet; although no radical he was a friend of prominent Whigs in London. Thanks to this connection he was appointed Regius Professor of History at Cambridge in 1807.

2. Peter Brears, Report on the historic development of Quarry Bank House (2007) for the National Trust. QBM.

3. Robert Greg to his mother, 2 May 1815, QBM GLB 1.272.

4. HG to HMR, 20 May 1815, LU RP VI. 1.112.

5. HG to Robert, 22 May 1815, QBM GLB 1.163.

6. Hannah Greg, *Collected letters* (undated), in Peter Spencer, *Hannah Greg*, 9.

7. Morley, *Critical Miscellanies III*, 219.

8. Undated list, probably of portraits hung at Quarry Bank in the later nineteenth century. QBM BLS 35.

9. The plants ordered by the Gregs in 1817 included red cedars, laurels and rhododendrons as well as garden flowers such as primula, lilies and campanula. Vegetable seeds ordered in 1819 included six varieties of onion and five

varieties of pea. Two beehives were ordered, plus many brooms and several watering cans, which suggests that there was a new era of activity.

10. SG in Cork to HG, 29 June 1813, QBM BLS 14.

11. HG to J Pares, 6 August 1811, DRO Pares Collection, D5336/3/214/2.

12. Aububon, *Journal of 1826*, 19 September, 181.

13. Tom Greg (attr) *Quarry Bank*, inscribed: 'written July 1810'. LU RPVI.2.36.

14. Thomas Traill (1781–1862), from 1804 a leading physician in Liverpool and friend of Roscoe. In 1832 he became Regius Professor of medical jurisprudence at the University of Edinburgh.

15. Dr Peter Mark Roget (1779–1869). A nephew and protégé of the Whig politician and lawyer Sir Samuel Romilly, Roget had studied with several of the leading physicians, chemists and economists of his day. Though well liked in Manchester, where he became the first secretary of the Portico Library and a vice president of the Lit & Phil, he returned to London in 1808. He wrote his *Thesaurus* there.

16. Hannah Rathbone's home at Greenbank may have been a model, where Dr Dalton described the routine thus: 'the etiquette in Liverpool is to sit down to dinner at a little after three, as soon as the cloth is drawn in winter and candles are brought in; when the bottle has gone round about half an hour, the ladies retire, the gentlemen remain till a servant informs them tea is ready. When all meet together again in the tearoom, where they remain till they are informed supper is on the table.' Emily Rathbone, *Records of the Rathbone Family*, 112–14.

17. Henry G. Hewlett (ed.), *Autobiography, Memoir, and Letters of Henry F. Chorley* (London, 1873).

18. Kathryn Gleadle, 'British Women and Radical Politics' in Amanda Vickery (ed.), *Women, Privilege and Power* (Stanford 2001), 1,335.

19. Eliza Fletcher's roles and importance are discussed in Jane Rendall, 'Women that would plague me with rational conversation: aspiring women and Scottish Whigs, *c.* 1790–1830', in Sarah Knott and Barbara Taylor (eds), *Women Gender and Enlightenment*, (New York, 2005).
    In another provincial centre, Norwich, Susanna Taylor was also a hostess who held intellectual and literary gatherings, bringing together local women, Dissenters and national figures such as Brougham and Southey, while darning her children's stockings.

20. See Anthony Page: 'No effort can be lost: the Unitarianism and republicanism of Ann Jebb' (1735–1812) in *Intellectual Exchanges, Women and Rational Dissent, Enlightenment & Dissent*, 26, 136.

21. He became an FRS and was a founder of the Derby Philosophical Society.

Erasmus Darwin and many of the leading scientists of the day were his friends.

22. Memorials assembled by Bessy Rathbone, LU RPVI. 2.31.

23. *Ibid.*

24. *Legacy to Elizabeth Greg*, 3 February 1807, quoted in Spencer, Hannah Greg, 8.

25. Quoted in Morley, *Critical Miscellanies III*, 217.

26. Hannah Greg, *The Moralist*, 79.

27. Ellen Melly, *Reminiscences*.

28. HG to her nephew Tom Pares jr, 1 September 1811, DRO Pares Collection, D5336/2/214/3.

29. *Autobiography of Mrs Fletcher: with letters and other family memorials, edited by the survivor of her family* (Edinburgh, 1875), 97. See footnotes 18, 19.

30. 'List of company' at Quarry Bank, QBM BLS 36.

31. HG to J. Pares, 1 September 1811, DRO, Pares Collection, D5336/3/214/3.

32. Audubon, *Journal of 1826*, 26 September, 194. The Gregs followed with interest Audubon's journeys to London and Edinburgh, and later subscribed to two copies of his *Birds of America*.

33. *Ibid.*, 7 October 1826, 225.

34. *Ibid.*, 9 October 1826, 229.

35. *Ibid.* 26 September–9 October.

36. For example, a letter written 1814/15 from Venice, QBM BLS 5.

37. In 1814 Holland published an account of the eastern part of this journey, *Travels in the Ionian Isles, Albania, Thessaly, Macedonia etc.* The son of Dr Peter Holland, he became Queen Victoria's doctor.

38. HG in Manchester to Tom in London, 15 April 1813, QBM Edward/ Gore collection.

39. RHG to Tom, 1 May 1813, QBM GLB 1.229.

40. Beryl & Alan Freer (eds), *The Travel Journals of Robert Greg* (Donington, 2007).

41. HG to RHG, 19 August 1817, QBM GLB 49.

42. Traill had been invited to accompany Scoresby on the latter's voyage from Liverpool to map the coast of Greenland in the Liverpool-built whaler, the *Baffin*, in 1821.

43. HG to Bessy, 4 December 1827, LU RPVI. 1.147.

44. HG to Bessy, January 1815, LU RPVI 1.111.

45. HG to WR IV, 1 October 1806, LU RP II. 1.69.

46. *Ibid.*

47. The selection is discussed on the website www.davidsekers.com.

48. HG to Tom: 15 April 1813, QBM Edward/ Gore collection. Maria's father was Richard Lovell Edgeworth, the inveterate inventor and writer. His fourth wife, Frances, was a year younger than his eldest daughter Maria (not fifteen years younger as reported by Hannah).

49. HG to Mrs Hannah Rathbone, 22 August 1822, copy in QBM F 122.

50. *Ibid.*

51. Mary Anne Greg: excerpt from 1823 *Diary*, QBM archive.

52. *Ibid.*

53. HG to Bessy, 19 February 1823, LU RPVI. 1.13.

54. *Ibid.*

55. He was later honorary secretary of the Manchester Literary and Philosophical Society and became a Fellow of the Royal Astronomical Society.

56. J.J.Tayler to HG, 17 October 1820, QBM, Edward/Gore collection. From 1803, however, Hannah was a member of the Unitarian Society for Promoting Christian Knowledge.

57. HG collected letters, Peter Spencer, *Hannah Greg*, 10.

58. SG in London to RHG in Milan, 5 February 1817, QBM GLB 1.180.

59. SG to Bessy, 13 January 1824, LU, RPVI.1.150. For a discussion of *Practical suggestions towards alleviating the sufferings of the sick*, see www.davidsekers.com.

60. S. Greg, *A Layman's Legacy*, preface by A. Stanley, Dean of Westminster (London, 1877), v.

61. Mary Greg to RHG, (?19 January) 1827, QBM GLB (?1.270).

62. Ellen Melly to her niece Louisa Gair, 3 April 1879; QBM GLB 2.

63. SG to Bessy, May 1828, LU RPVI.1.153.

64. SG to RHG, August 1833, QBM, Edward/ Gore collection.

Epilogue, pp. 234–42

1. Audubon, *Journal of 1826*, 4 October 1786. The impressionable artist admitted that women's beauty frequently captivated him.

2. Herbert Rathbone, *Memoir of Kitty Wilkinson of Liverpool 1786–1860* (1927).

3. 'Though credit is always given (to Kitty) for originating the scheme of establishing in her own cellar a wash house … there is reason to suppose that Mrs Rathbone played an equal though less conspicuous part in originating the idea.' (Simey, *Charity Rediscovered*, 27).

4. William Rathbone VI, *Sketch of Family History* (1894), 56. 57

5. Robert Hyde Greg, *The Factory Question*, 1837. *Account of the Circumstances*

Connected with the Punishment of Esther Price and Lucy Garner, MRO, Greg Collection, C5/8/22 (1843).

6. Samuel Greg, *Two Letters to Leonard Horner, Inspector of Factories* (1838 and 1840). For an extended discussion on Hannah's children and their careers, see davidsekers.com.

7. (Hannah Greg), *Maxims*, Fortune, avarice, ambition etc., xvi, 89.

8. The author is indebted to Jonathan Huddleston for information on Adam Hodgson. See *And the children's teeth are set on edge*, at http://www.tioli.co.uk/.

9. Memorials and recollections of Hannah Greg, LU RPVI.2.31.

10. (Mrs Samuel Greg), *A Layman's Legacy* (London 1877), preface.

11. *Legacy to Elizabeth Greg*, 3 February 1807, quoted in Spencer, *Hannah Greg*, 8. Hannah Greg, collected letters in Spencer, *Hannah Greg*, passim. For a discussion of Hannah's role as a hostess, see Chapter 6.

Abbreviations

BL	The British Library
DRO	Derbyshire Record Office
E & D	*Journal of Enlightenment & Dissent*
HG	Hannah Greg
HMR	Hannah Mary Rathbone
LRO	Liverpool Record Office
LU	University of Liverpool, Special Collections & Archives, Sydney Jones Library
MRO	Greater Manchester County Record Office
ODNB	Oxford Dictionary of National Biography
QBM	Quarry Bank Mill Archive
RHG	Robert Hyde Greg
SG	Samuel Greg (senior)
THSLC	*Transactions of the Historic Society for Lancashire & Cheshire*
WR	William Rathbone (IV)
WRG	William Rathbone Greg

Bibliography

Manuscript material

Derbyshire Record Office – Pares Collection:
Liverpool Record Office – Binns Collection; James Currie papers;
    Nicholson papers; Kaye Street Chapel papers; Liverpool Library papers
Liverpool University, Sidney Jones Library – Rathbone Collection
London Borough of Hackney Archives
Greater Manchester County Record Office – Greg collection;
    Manchester Mercury; Manchester Directories
Quarry Bank Mill – Greg collection; Edward/ Gore loan; Emily and
    Michael Janes collection
Family papers and portraits – Nick Lightbody, (including the type-
    script by William Lightbody, *Lightbody history and records*, 1922); Dr Tim
    Paine and Jenny Smith.

Hannah Greg's traced published works

Virtue Made Easy (Liverpool, 1799) © British Library Board, 8405.b.45;
    also on ECCO.
Observations; A collection of maxims, observations, etc. (Liverpool, 1799)
    © British Library Board.
The Moralist (Liverpool 1800) © British Library Board.

The Monitor, or a Collection of Precepts, Observations, etc. (Liverpool, 1804)
  © British Library Board (1388.c.12.).
Practical suggestions towards alleviating the sufferings of the sick (London, 1828)
  © British Library Board.

Publications by members of Hannah Greg's family

Greg, Elizabeth, Extracts from the Journal of Elizabeth Greg, April 1–24
  July 1807, in Rathbone, Emily A. (ed.), *Records of the Rathbone Family*
  (Liverpool, 1913).
Greg, Robert Hyde, *The Factory Question* (1837).
Greg, Samuel, *A Layman's Legacy* (including a preface by A. Stanley, Dean
  of Westminster) (London, 1877).
———, *Two Letters to Leonard Horner, Inspector of Factories* (1838 & 1840).
Greg, W. R., *An Enquiry into the State of the Manufacturing population and the
  Causes and Cures for the Evils existing therein* (Manchester, 1831).
———, 'England as it is', in *Essays in political and social science*, I (London, 1853).
———, *Enigmas of Life* (London, 1891).
———, 'Mary Barton', *Edinburgh Review* (1848).

Secondary sources

Aikin, John & Barbauld, Anna, *Evenings at Home; or, the juvenile budget
  opened. Consisting of a variety of miscellaneous pieces, for the instruction and
  amusement of young person* (London, 1792–96).
Aikin, John, *An address to the Dissidents of England on their late defeat*
  (London, 1790).
Anstey, Roger and Hair, P. E.H. (eds), 'Liverpool, the African slave trade
  and abolition,' *THSLC Occasional Series*, Vol. 2, 1976 (Chicago, 1992).
Axon, Ernest, *Memorials of the family of Nicholson* (Liverpool, 1928).

Bailey, William, *Liverpool Directory* (Liverpool, 1787).

Bickerton, T.H., *The medical history of Liverpool* (London, 1936).

Billson, C. J., *Leicester memoirs* (Leicester, 1924).

Boardman, J., *Liverpool Table Talk* (1856).

Bolam, C., Goring, J., Short, H.L. & Thomas, R., *The English Presbyterians* (London, 1968).

Brears, Peter, *Report on the historic development of Quarry Bank House* (NT, 2007).

Brewer, John, *The pleasures of the imagination* (London, 1997).

Brooke, R., *Liverpool as it was during the last quarter of the eighteenth century 1775–1800* (Liverpool, 1853).

Burton, F.A. (ed.), *Three Accounts of Peterloo* (1921).

Carpenter, Russell Lant, *Memoir of the Reverend Lant Carpenter LLD, edited by his son* (Bristol & London, 1842).

Clarkson, Thomas, *The history of the abolition of the African Slave Trade* (London, 1808).

Clayden, P.W., *The early life of Samuel Rogers* (London, 1887).

Collier, Frances, *Family economy of the Working Classes in the Cotton Industry* (Manchester, 1964).

Cookson, J. E., *The friends of peace: anti-war liberalism in England 1793–1815* (Cambridge, 1982).

Crawford, Patricia, 'Katharine and Philip Henry and their children: a case study in family ideology', *THSLC*, Vol. 134 (Liverpool, 1984).

Currie, William Wallace, *Memoir of James Currie of Liverpool* (London, 1831).

Curwen, Samuel, *Journal and letters of Samuel Curwen* (1842; reprinted 1959, Bedford Mass.).

Ditchfield, G.M., 'The campaign for the repeal of the Test and Corporation Acts in Lancashire and Cheshire 1787–90', *English Historical Review* lxxxix (1974).

Elder, Melinda, *The slave trade and the economic development of eighteenth-century Lancaster* (Halifax, 1992).

Engels, Friedrich, *The condition of the working class in England, 1844* (London 1969).

Fitton, R.S. and Wadsworth, A.P., *The Strutts and the Arkwrights 1758–1830* (Manchester, 1958).

Flavell, M. Kay, 'The enlightened reader and the new industrial towns, a study of the Liverpool Library 1758–1790', *The British Journal for Eighteenth-Century studies*, 8 (1985), 17–35.

Fletcher, Elizabeth, *Autobiography of Mrs. Fletcher: with letters and other family memorials, edited by the survivor of her family* (Edinburgh, 1875).

Freer, Beryl & Alan (eds), *The Travel Journals of Robert Greg* (Donington, 2007).

Fryer, Alfred, *Wilmslow Graves and Grave Thoughts from Wilmslow* (Stockport, 1886)

O'Gallchoir, Cliona, *Maria Edgeworth, women, enlightenment and nation* (Dublin, 2005).

Gattrell, V.A.C., 'Incorporation and the pursuit of Liberal hegemony in Manchester 1790–1839', in Derek Fraser (ed.), *Municipal reform and the industrial city* (Leicester, 1982).

Genlis, Mme de, *Adelaide & Theodore* (Paris, 1783 edition, translated and edited by Gillian Dow; London, 2007).

Gerard, Alexander, *An Essay on Taste* (London, 1759).

Gleadle, Kathryn, 'British Women and Radical Politics' in Amanda Vickery (ed.), *Women, Privilege and Power* (Stanford, 2001).

Goodwin, Albert, *The Friends of Liberty, the English democratic movement in the age of the French revolution* (London, 1979).

Gore, John, *Gore's Liverpool Directory* (Liverpool, 1766 and 1790).

Grey, Robert, *The factory question and industrial England 1830–1860* (Cambridge, 2002).

Haakonsen, Lisbeth, *Medicine and Morals in the Enlightenment* (Atlanta 1997).

Haakonssen, Knud (ed.), *Enlightenment and religion: rational dissent in eighteenth-century Britain* (Cambridge, 1996).

Harley, David, 'The Good Physician and the Godly Doctor', *The Seventeenth Century*, Vol. 9 (1974).

Heely, J., *Letters on the beauties of Hagley, Envil and the Leasowes* (London, 1777; reprinted New York, 1982).

Hewlett, Henry G. (ed.), *Autobiography, Memoir, and Letters of Henry F. Chorley* (London, 1873).

Holt, Anne, *Walking together, a study in Liverpool nonconformity 1688–1938* (London, 1938).

Honeyman, Katrina, *Child workers in England, 1780–1820: parish apprentices and the making of the early industrial workforce* (Aldershot, 2007).

Hope, Samuel, *A voice that is still Bristol* (1887).

Howe, Anthony, *The Cotton Masters 1830–1860* (Oxford, 1984).

Howman, Brian, 'Abolitionism in Liverpool', in Richardson, Schwarz and Tibbles (eds), *Liverpool and transatlantic slavery* (Liverpool, 2007).

———, *An analysis of Slave abolitionists in the North West of England* (PhD thesis, University of Warwick), 2006.

Hughes, J., *Liverpool banks and bankers 1760–1837* (Liverpool, 1906).

Huddleston, Jonathan, *And the children's teeth are set on edge: Adam Hodgson and the razing of Caton Chapel* (www.tioli.co.uk).

Hulme, A., *Missions at home* (London, 1850).

Hulton, Ann, *Letters of a loyalist lady* (Cambridge Mass, 1927; republished 1970).

Hunt, E.M., 'The anti–slave trade agitation in Manchester', *THSLC* (1977).

James, Felicity, and Inkster, Ian, *Religious dissent and the Aikin-Barbauld circle, 1740–1860* (Cambridge, 2012).

Janes, Michael, *From smuggling to cotton kings, the Greg story* (Cirencester, 2010).

Jebb, John, *The works theological, medical, political, and miscellaneous, of John Jebb, M.D. F.R.S. With memoirs of the life of the author; by John Disney* (London, 1787).

Kennedy, Catriona, 'Womanish Epistles? Martha McTier, Female Epistolarity and Late Eighteenth-Century Irish Radicalism', *Women's History Review*, Vol. 13, No. 4.

Kidson, Alex, *George Romney 1734–1802* (London, 2002).

Knight, F., *The strange case of Thomas Walker* (London, 1957).

Knox, Vicesimus, *Essays, moral and literary* (London, 1779).

———, *Liberal education: or, a practical treatise on the methods of acquiring useful and polite learning* (London, 1781).

Lascelles, David, *The story of the Rathbones* (London, 2008).

Lazenby, Walter, *Social and economic history of Styal, 1750–1850* (MA thesis, University of Manchester, 1949).

Leach, I., 'The Wavertree Enclosure Act 1768', *THSLC*, Vol. 83 (1931), 43–60.

Le Breton, Anna Letitia, *Memories of seventy years* (London, 1883).

Morley, John, *Critical Miscellanies III* (London, 1886).

Murphy, James, 'Robert Owen in Liverpool', *THSLC*, Vol. 112 (1960).

Navickas, Katrina, *Loyalism and Radicalism in Lancashire, 1798–1815* (Oxford, 2009).

Orchard, B.G., *Liverpool exchange portrait gallery* (Liverpool, 1884).

Ormerod, Sheila, *The Gregs of Westmill* (Buntingford, 1996).

Page, Anthony, 'No effort can be lost: the Unitarianism and republicanism of Ann Jebb' (1735–1812), in *Intellectual Exchanges, Women and Rational Dissent, Enlightenment & Dissent*, 26 (2010).

Patterson, Daniel (ed.), *John James Audubon's Journal of 1826, the voyage to the Birds of America* (Nebraska, 2011).

Peers Sarah, 'Negotiating Work, absenteeism at Quarry Bank Mill in 1790'. *THSLC*, Vol. 158 (2009).

(Peterloo): *Report of the proceedings on the trial in the Kings Bench between Thomas Redford and Hugh Birley* (Manchester, 1822).

Percival, E., *Memoirs of the life and writings of Thomas Percival MD* (London, 1807).

Percival, Thomas, *A father's instructions, Consisting of …A Socratic Discourse on Truth and Faithfulness* (Warrington and London, 1781).

Pickstone, J.V. & Butler, S.V.F., 'The politics of medicine in Manchester 1788–1792', *Medical History*, Vol. 28 (1984).

Pollard, Sidney, 'The Factory Village in the Industrial Revolution', in *English Historical Review*, Vol. 79 (1974).

Porter, Roy, *English Society in the eighteenth century* (London, 1982).

Prentice, Archibald, *Historical sketches and personal recollections* (Manchester, 1851).

Rathbone, Emily A. (ed.), *Records of the Rathbone Family* (Edinburgh, 1913).

Rathbone, William VI, *A sketch of family history* (Liverpool, 1894).

Rathbone, Herbert R. (ed.), *Memoir of Kitty Wilkinson 1786–1860* (Liverpool, 1927).

Rathbone, Winifred R., *The Life of Kitty Wilkinson* (Liverpool, 1910).

Redford, Arthur, *Manchester Merchants and foreign trade 1794–1858* (Manchester, 1968).

Reid, Thomas, *An Inquiry into the Human Mind, on the Principles of Common Sense* (1764; fourth ed., corrected: London, 1785).

Rendall, Jane, 'Women that would plague me with rational conversation: aspiring women and Scottish Whigs, *c.*1790–1830', in Sarah Knott and Barbara Taylor (eds.), *Women Gender and Enlightenment* (London, 2007).

Ritson, Joseph, *The Spartan Manual, being a genuine collection of the apothegms, maxims, and precepts of the philosophers, heroes, and other great and celebrated characters of antiquity … For the improvement of youth, and the promoting of wisdom and virtue* (London 1785).

Rivers, Isabel and Wykes, David L., *Joseph Priestley, Scientist, Philosopher, and Theologian* (Oxford 2009).

Robinson, Keith, *What became of the Quarry Bank Mill apprentices?* (Styal, 1996).
———, *Esther Price, The life story of an apprentice at Quarry Bank Mill* (Styal, 1994).

Robinson, Keith, and Rees, Rosemary, *Hetty: the slave* (Styal, n.d.).

Rose, Mary B., *The Gregs of Quarry Bank Mill* (Cambridge, 1986).
———, *The Gregs of Styal* (London, 1978).

Sanderson, F.E., 'The Liverpool delegates and Sir William Dolben's Bill', *THSLC*, Vol. 124 (Liverpool, 1973).

———, 'The Structure of politics of Liverpool, 1780–1807', *THSLC*, Vol. 111 (Liverpool, 1959).

———, 'The Liverpool abolitionists', in Anstey and Hair (eds), *Liverpool, the African Slave Trade and Abolition*.

Sanderson, M., 'Education in Industrial Lancashire 1780–1840', in *Economic History Review*, 20.2 (1967).

Saxton, Evelyn, 'The Binns family of Liverpool', *THSLC*, Vol. 111 (Liverpool, 1959), 167–80.

Scott, Diana E. & Lewis, Fiona, 'Motives to move: reconstructing individual migration histories in early eighteenth-century Liverpool', in Siddle, David J. (ed.), *Migration, mobility and modernisation* (Liverpool, 2000).

Seed, John, 'Unitarianism, political economy and the antinomies of liberal culture in Manchester 1830–1850', *Social History*, Vol. 7, No. 1 (1982).

Seed, John, 'A set of powerful men in many things', in Haakonssen, K. (ed.), *Enlightenment & Religion*, 167.

Sekers, David (ed.), *The Diary of Hannah Lightbody 1786-1790. Supplement to the Journal of Enlightenment & Dissent no 24, 2008*; also online at http://www.english.qmul.ac.uk/drwilliams/journal/issues/24(2008)Sup.pdf

Sellers Ian, 'William Roscoe, the Roscoe Circle and radical politics in Liverpool 1789–1807', *THSLC*, Vol. 120 (Liverpool, 1969).

Sharples, Joseph, *Liverpool* (London, 2004).

Shirren, Adam John, *The Chronicles of Fleetwood House* (London, 1951).

Simey, Margaret, *Charity Rediscovered* (Liverpool, 1992).

Spencer, Peter, *A portrait of Samuel Greg* (Styal, 1982).

Spencer, Peter, *A portrait of Hannah Greg* (Styal, 1982).

Sutton, Ian, 'The Extended Roscoe Circle: Art, Medicine and the Cultural Politics of Alienation in Liverpool 1762–1836', *British Journal for Eighteenth-Century Studies*, Vol. 30, No. 3 (2007).

Thom, J.H., *Letters embracing the life of J.J. Tayler* (London, 1872).

Thomson, W.H., *History of Manchester to 1852* (Altrincham, 1967).

Tomalin, Claire, *The life and death of Mary Wollstonecraft* (London, 1974).

Thornton, Robert Donald, *James Currie, the entire stranger and Robert Burns* (Edinburgh, 1963).

Troughton, Thomas, *The history of Liverpool* (Liverpool, 1810).

Truxes, Thomas, *Letterbook of Greg & Cunningham 1756–57* (Oxford, 2001).

Turley, David, *The culture of British antislavery* (Oxford, 1991).

Turner, M.J., *Reform and Respectability, The Making of a Middle-Class Liberalism in Early Nineteenth-Century Manchester* (Manchester, 1995).

Uglow, Jenny, *The Lunar Men* (London, 2002).

Walker, Gina Luria, 'Women's voices', in Clemit, Pamela (ed.), *Cambridge Companion to British Literature on the French Revolution* (Cambridge, 2010), 265–294.

Vickery, Amanda (ed.), *Women, privilege and power: British politics 1750 to the present* (Stanford, 2001).

Wallace, James, *General and descriptive history of Liverpool* (Liverpool, 1795).

Watts, Ruth, *Gender, power and the Unitarians in England 1760–1860* (London, 1998).

Yates, S.A.T., *Memorials of the family of the Rev John Yates* (London, 1890).

Index